# Webflow by E

Design, build, and publish modern websites
without writing code

**Ali Rushdan Tariq**

BIRMINGHAM—MUMBAI

# Webflow by Example

**Group Product Manager**: Pavan Ramchandani

**Publishing Product Manager**: Aaron Tanna

**Senior Editor**: Hayden Edwards

**Content Development Editor**: Abhishek Jadhav

**Technical Editor**: Saurabh Kadave

**Copy Editor**: Safis Editing

**Project Coordinator**: Rashika Ba

**Proofreader**: Safis Editing

**Indexer**: Pratik Shirodkar

**Production Designer**: Jyoti Chauhan

First published: November 2021

Production reference: 1261121

Published by Packt Publishing Ltd.
Livery Place
35 Livery Street
Birmingham
B3 2PB, UK.

ISBN 978-1-80107-539-8

www.packt.com

*To my father, for introducing me to the internet during my teens and encouraging me to kick off a love affair with designing and building for the Web.*

*And to my lovely wife, Sehrish, for always believing that I can accomplish way more than I believe I can.*

*Finally, to my son, Rayyan, for tolerating me writing this book over late nights while he was growing in his mum's belly.*

*– Ali Rushdan Tariq*

# Contributors

## About the author

**Ali Rushdan Tariq** is a product designer, strategist, and award-winning writer with more than 10 years of experience helping start-ups, scale-ups, and large corporations build simple solutions to complex problems while growing strong design teams. He is passionate about advocating user-centered design cultures in organizations and mentoring junior designers. At the time of writing, he is a Principal Designer and Associate Director of product design at Slalom Build, where he helps organizations design products that make a difference. When not designing, he enjoys traveling (in a non-pandemic-riddled world), photography, cooking, and the occasional video game. He is based in Kitchener, Canada, with his wife and son.

# About the reviewers

**Ethan Suero** is a freelance web designer and Webflow developer who has helped start-ups to build stunning brands and digital experiences. He has worked with agencies and clients alike from all over the world. Ethan is a gamer, as well as a vegan, traveler, and a Lakers fan.

**Andreu Pifarre** holds a master's degree (MSc) in computer science from the University of London and is a seasoned full-stack software engineer based in the UK. He has 20 years of industry experience working with global companies and clients to develop world-class software solutions, as well as web and mobile applications.

During his career, Andreu has served in numerous senior and lead roles in software engineering, product engineering, and web development with top-tier tech companies around the world.

Currently, Andreu works as a lead web engineer in London, United Kingdom. He provides consulting services to companies around the globe. In addition, he teaches computer science and software engineering online.

According to Andreu, Webflow promises a new era in web design and development. He is also an astronomy enthusiast.

Andreu can be reached at @andreupifarre on Twitter.

# Table of Contents

# 6
# Making It Responsive

# 7
# Introduction to Interactions and Animations

# 8
# Advanced Interactions

# Section 3: Building a Dynamic Website with Webflow CMS

## 9

## Getting Started with Webflow CMS

## 10

## Creating Your First CMS Project

## 11

## Creating Collection Pages

## 12

## Managing CMS Projects

# Section 4: Additional Topics

## 13

## Publishing Projects on the Web

## 14

## Using Webflow Editor to Update Websites

## Other Books You May Enjoy

## Index

# Preface

Webflow is a modern website builder that enables you to rapidly design and build production-scale responsive websites without code. This book, *Webflow by Example*, is a practical, project-based, and beginner-friendly guide to understanding and using Webflow to efficiently build and launch responsive websites from scratch.

The approach this book takes is to give you just enough foundational theory and principles before diving into actionable steps. In general, you'll be shown what you're going to build, why it's built that way, and then the actual steps showing how to do it.

You'll get to grips with modern responsive web development and understand how to take advantage of the power and flexibility of Webflow. The book will guide you through two projects that you'll be ready to publish to the world. The first will be a fully responsive landing page for a fictional mobile app. You will build a solid foundation for building modern websites, from the CSS box model to Flexbox and CSS Grid, including how to build slick custom animations and interactions and more, all within Webflow and without code.

The second project will be focused on building a dynamic website using Webflow CMS. We'll build our very own curation of some of the world's most interesting libraries. We'll learn all about content management in Webflow and how it makes building large websites easy and efficient.

Finally, the book covers important steps and best practices for making your website ready for production, including SEO optimization and how to publish and package a website.

By the end of this book, you will have gained the skills you need to build and launch modern responsive websites from scratch without any code in Webflow. The hope is that this will open up a new avenue for you and empower you to pursue crafting useful web experiences and exciting creative expressions!

## Who this book is for

If you've ever wanted to learn how to build websites but always found the prospect of learning to code off-putting, then learning Webflow is, arguably, the next best thing.

This book is aimed at anyone interested in building websites, regardless of their knowledge of web technologies. If you're a beginner, then you'll learn just enough about web design and development principles to understand how Webflow works. If you are familiar with some core concepts of web development, and maybe even specifically with Webflow, the book will help reinforce those fundamentals through repetition and practice.

# What this book covers

*Chapter 1, Why Webflow,* briefly introduces you to the main differentiating factors of Webflow and how it plays an increasingly trusted role in the growing no-code movement. You will learn when and why to use Webflow and how it can help make the web design/development process faster and more efficient than ever.

*Chapter 2, The Web in a Nutshell,* introduces you to some basic, but crucial, web design principles, specifically around how websites are structured. We'll take a closer look at the box model of web design and gain some basic understanding of how HTML and CSS work and how Webflow abstracts some of that away.

*Chapter 3, Setting Up Your First Project,* starts by taking a look at the finished website that you will build in Webflow. You will also be shown where to download some assets that will be used to build the website. Lastly, you will step through some basic website settings to make sure all the right fonts are installed, and that the images are uploaded to Webflow.

*Chapter 4, Building Above the Fold,* takes you through creating the navigation bar and the main Hero section from scratch. Throughout the process, you will be introduced to various foundational concepts of web development and specifically how Webflow can be used to quickly build different layouts and stylings. You will also be introduced to how Webflow can make responsive design efficient.

*Chapter 5, Building the Rest of the Body,* covers how, the rest of the sections of the website will be completed in Webflow. While many of the concepts will be repeated as good practice, there will be new concepts and best practices introduced, including how to use links, accessibility, grid layout, relative positioning, and more. This chapter will only cover the desktop layout of the web page.

*Chapter 6, Making It Responsive,* takes you through making the website fully responsive. You'll be shown how to think about responsiveness, adapting designs to various screen sizes (or breakpoints), and how to preview changes.

*Chapter 7, Introduction to Interactions and Animations*, introduces you to the basics of creating simple interactions and animations in Webflow and how they can be used strategically and intentionally to create a livelier experience on a website. This chapter will also help you understand how to create multiple states, and how to transition between them.

*Chapter 8, Advanced Interactions*, continues from the previous chapter by diving into creating modern and more complex interactions. These include parallax effects, scroll-triggered effects, and page-triggered ones. We'll see how easy it is to create custom-made interactions from scratch.

*Chapter 9, Getting Started with Webflow CMS*, introduces you to the basic concepts of content management systems, how Webflow CMS is different, and why and when to consider using Webflow CMS to create dynamic content. You will also make a start on the next project: a curated directory-listing website of some of the most interesting libraries from around the world.

*Chapter 10, Creating Your First CMS Project*, introduces you to Collections in Webflow and how to structure a Collection from scratch. You will create your first Collection, create fields, and populate them to create items. You will also learn how to import data directly into the Collection from an external file. Finally, you will learn how to display the Collection items dynamically on the home page of their website by binding web elements to CMS fields.

*Chapter 11, Creating Collection Pages*, continues to build out the libraries of the world project by creating a Collection Page. You will learn how to style a Collection Page such that each library gets its own unique detailed page. You will also learn how to use filters to dynamically structure Collection lists and learn how Webflow generates these pages automatically for all items in a Collection.

*Chapter 12, Managing CMS Projects*, explains the various ways to manage CMS pages, including how to optimize them for SEO and how to effectively edit the data and the data structure of CMS Collections.

*Chapter 13, Publishing Projects to the Web*, steps you through how to publish Webflow projects to the web for the world to see. You'll also see how to showcase a project for other Webflow developers to view and maybe even clone.

*Chapter 14, Using Webflow Editor to Update Websites*, will introduce you to the basics of using Webflow Editor to update live websites directly without having to know how Webflow works. This will be key to helping clients or other non-technical stakeholders manage their own content.

# To get the most out of this book

While having a basic understanding of HTML and CSS will only strengthen your ability to pick up Webflow, this book does not assume any prior knowledge of them. And since Webflow is entirely a cloud-based tool that auto-updates, you do not have to install any additional software to use it.

You should also have an internet connection and a desktop or laptop device with at least a 13-inch monitor. Furthermore, at the time of writing, Webflow is only supported in Chrome and Safari browsers.

| Software/hardware covered in the book | Operating system requirements |
| --- | --- |
| Webflow | Windows, macOS, or Linux |
| HTML/CSS | |

# Download the example code files

You can download the example code files for this book from GitHub at `https://github.com/PacktPublishing/Webflow-by-Example`. If there's an update to the code, it will be updated in the GitHub repository.

We also have other code bundles from our rich catalog of books and videos available at `https://github.com/PacktPublishing/`. Check them out!

# Download the color images

We also provide a PDF file that has color images of the screenshots and diagrams used in this book. You can download it here: `https://static.packt-cdn.com/downloads/9781801075398_ColorImages.pdf`.

# Conventions used

There are a number of text conventions used throughout this book.

`Code in text`: Indicates code words in the text, database table names, folder names, filenames, file extensions, pathnames, dummy URLs, user input, and Twitter handles. Here is an example: "Click the button and select the image called `AppStore.png`."

**Bold**: Indicates a new term, an important word, or words that you see on screen. For instance, words in menus or dialog boxes appear in **bold**. Here is an example: "Select the **Showcase Wrapper** element."

> **Tips or Important Notes**
> Appear like this.

# Get in touch

Feedback from our readers is always welcome.

**General feedback**: If you have questions about any aspect of this book, email us at customercare@packtpub.com and mention the book title in the subject of your message.

**Errata**: Although we have taken every care to ensure the accuracy of our content, mistakes do happen. If you have found a mistake in this book, we would be grateful if you would report this to us. Please visit www.packtpub.com/support/errata and fill in the form.

**Piracy**: If you come across any illegal copies of our works in any form on the internet, we would be grateful if you would provide us with the location address or website name. Please contact us at copyright@packt.com with a link to the material.

**If you are interested in becoming an author**: If there is a topic that you have expertise in and you are interested in either writing or contributing to a book, please visit authors.packtpub.com.

## Share Your Thoughts

Once you've read *Webflow by Example*, we'd love to hear your thoughts! Scan the QR code below to go straight to the Amazon review page for this book and share your feedback.

```
https://www.amazon.in/review/create-review/
        error?asin=%3C1801075395%3E
```

Your review is important to us and the tech community and will help us make sure we're delivering excellent quality content.

# Section 1: Getting Started with Webflow

In this section, you will learn about the rise of the no-code movement, what sets Webflow apart from other website builders, and how to get started with a Webflow project. We'll cover all the fundamentals that will help set us up for success with Webflow.

We will cover the following chapters in this section:

# 1
# Why Webflow

I designed and built my first website in 1998 as part of a self-chosen school project. Sitting in my high school's computer lab, I pored over lengthy, dry textbooks, learning about HTML and CSS (the building blocks and core technologies behind websites), constantly refreshing my internet browser to render my latest work. After months of toiling, I had proudly finished the project: a three-page website that marketed my very own school, complete with images, pricing tables, and even the obligatory rotating GIF of my school's logo. As tiresome as the process was, the World Wide Web promised many exciting things to come. The possibilities of creative expression in this new digital medium literally felt endless.

More than 20 years later (and well into a career in digital product design), website technologies have gone through major evolutions. While there are now many more resources and tools—many of which are free—than ever before to help you get up to speed in web design and development, the actual process is arguably more complex than ever, as well. In fact, so extensive are the technologies and skills required to design, develop, test, and deploy websites that you can quite safely build a flourishing career in any *one* of these areas.

And at a time in the mid-2000s when I was admittedly starting to get tech-fatigue, I happened to come across Webflow. It promised a whole new way to design, build, and deploy websites in a completely visual editor, all without code.

I should mention here that drag-and-drop website builders were not a new technology at this point. I had even used a number of them for various projects, with varying degrees of satisfaction. I still preferred opening up my favorite code editors and manually writing the code out as I felt this provided the most control and flexibility, rather than being constrained by a visual editor's limitations.

But Webflow, I was meant to believe, was supposed to be different.

And sure enough, after building my first few websites on Webflow, I was a believer. Unlike the many other web builders before it, Webflow's approach was built entirely on the foundations of the underlying web technologies that powered everything, only I didn't have to code any of it. Armed with a solid understanding of how websites are developed, and with a little patience, you could build and deploy a live website completely through Webflow in a fraction of the time (and skill) you would've needed if you were to do it by code. And as a cherry on top, Webflow generated cleaner, more efficient code than any of the other builders I had used before, all of which you could export if you wished.

For the first time since those months sitting in my computer lab in high school, I felt excited again for the future of the web. I felt my imagination fluttering again.

Indeed, one of the hallmarks of the Webflow phenomenon, you'll find, is the legion of fans who can't stop talking about it, and for good reason.

With this book, my aim is to provide you with what I wished I had when I first started with Webflow; a resource that I could go through at my own pace, which clearly laid out foundational principles of how web design/development all worked in the context of Webflow, and a variety of practical examples that put everything into practice.

This is not meant to be an exhaustive book on web design and development, nor an exhaustive manual on mastering Webflow. In this book, I will introduce you to *just enough* theory and principles in order to succeed with Webflow. In fact, I believe the main reason why a number of people fail to adopt Webflow in their process is that they are missing some of those foundational principles of modern web development.

In addition, I believe the majority of learning comes through doing. As such, in this book, we'll spend some time understanding theory and more time applying it to a variety of realistic projects. By the end, the hope is that you will have gone through numerous examples that will provide you with the knowledge and confidence to apply them in countless other ways that are only limited by your imagination.

In this chapter, we'll take a step back and examine the larger context that Webflow finds itself in today and, in particular, we'll take a look at the No-Code movement. We'll then address some common concerns that people have about Webflow and what makes it stand out from the crowd.

The topics we will cover more closely in this first chapter are as follows:

- The No-Code movement

- What sets Webflow apart

- Who will benefit from this book?

# The No-Code movement

Ever since software has been built, there has been continued effort to make it simpler. Coding languages are being written in more readable English-like syntax. Frameworks and libraries are available to provide almost plug-and-play functionality to websites with minimal extra code; website builders from WordPress to Squarespace now power a vast amount of the web.

To be sure, there is much to celebrate about this. The barriers of entry when it comes to creation on the web have been lowered, meaning more people are able to make their creations available to the masses. Side projects, blogs, and businesses are built every day online, making the world more connected.

In the spirit of this continued effort to make the web ever more accessible, the last few years have seen a growing trend toward what is being popularly called the **No-Code (or Low-Code) movement**. The main mission is straightforward: enable anybody to build functional, production-grade websites and apps with little to no coding.

And the appeal of this should be obvious: while knowing how to code has long been considered critical for building on the web, a growing number of entrepreneurs, builders, and enthusiasts have been challenging this concept in recent years. Not only can you now build fully functional websites without ever needing to write a line of code, but new technologies such as Zapier, Integromat, and Parabola unlock further power by allowing no-code developers to integrate their various tools and products, effectively creating fully automated systems of workflows.

What would have taken a team of developers a fairly hefty budget and a good amount of time to design, build, publish, and productionize a website now can take a single non-technical person a mere weekend to do at a fraction of the cost. Indeed, in a 2019 research report, Gartner estimated that low-code or no-code technologies will be powering nearly 65% of all app creations within the next few years.

> **Tip**
> If you want to read the 2019 Gartner report, you can find it here:
> `https://www.gartner.com/en/documents/3956079/`
> `magic-quadrant-for-enterprise-low-code-`
> `application-platf.`

We are at an inflection point in the advent of modern technology. With the internet at peak penetration, smartphones more readily available than ever, no-code apps and resources being made available at affordable prices, and a resurgence in the maker culture, I believe we are poised to see an explosion in websites and apps being built by previously underrepresented swathes of the population. We'll not only see more people delivering business value and solving important problems, but we'll see a rise in better self-expression and hear unique voices through imaginative and bold web design.

And it is against this exciting backdrop that I'd like you to view the place of Webflow. Not only has Webflow earned a reputation for being reliable and highly performant in the web-builder space, its continued support of integrations into the broader no-code ecosystem has also positioned it as one of the most important tools in the modern no-coder—and web design/development– tool chest.

Let's take a closer look at why that's the case.

# What sets Webflow apart?

As mentioned before, Webflow is not the only no-code web-builder available. Far from it. In fact, it appears that every month or so, a new no-code or low-code web-builder is announced. Such is the hype surrounding this era of democratized web design and development.

Squarespace and Wix remain major competitors, with the latter recently launching EditorX, a no-code web builder that was launched seemingly in direct response to Webflow. Furthermore, WordPress remains the most popular website builder and **Content Management System (CMS)**, reportedly powering a third of the internet.

So, why should you consider Webflow?

In this section, I will list out some common concerns I've heard about Webflow and will provide my views on why you should reconsider them. At best, I hope you will agree that these concerns actually put Webflow in a better light and help it stand out from the crowd. At the very least, I hope you do not let these concerns stop you from exploring the wonderful world of Webflow.

# Concern 1 – Is Webflow too difficult to learn?

Nearly everyone I know (including myself) who was first introduced to Webflow felt like the platform had too steep a learning curve. When you start a new project in Webflow, you are dropped directly into the builder interface, which may bear some resemblance to Photoshop. Faced with a number of options and selections, even those who may be familiar with the concepts of web design and development can feel a little overwhelmed, let alone those who are starting with no knowledge of the technologies. But stick with it, and you'll realize that the peculiar drag-and-drop nature of Webflow is inspired by web development best practices and will, in fact, give you an appreciation of how the underlying HTML and CSS technologies work. We'll dive more into this later.

Since its launch in 2013, Webflow has invested heavily in its educational resources; its Webflow University showcases a number of well-produced, step-by-step guides and lessons from the basics of web design through to using almost every feature of the builder.

But perhaps more importantly, over the years, a supportive community of Webflow users, designers, and developers have been sharing more and more material and how-tos, specifically targeted at newcomers to help them feel more at ease. In fact, this book is the product of my own enthusiasm for the tool motivating me to release it in the hope that it can help others climb over the initial ramp-up in learning how to build websites in Webflow. For some, the Webflow University courses can feel a little too quick, scattered, or tonally off. I hope this book fills the gap for you.

All that said, let it be clear that there is, indeed, a learning curve for Webflow. But like all things worth learning, I firmly believe that the learning curve is rewarding.

Crucially, take heart in knowing that a wonderful side effect of learning Webflow is that you will also learn the best practices of how modern websites are built. For me, this was a realization that took me by surprise. Even though I already had a fairly good grasp of the basics of HTML and CSS, there were a number of gaps in my knowledge of modern concepts around Flexbox, CSS Grid, layouts, interactions, and more. Webflow allowed me to put all this into practice and helped me address all these by applying them hands-on. As a professional UI/UX designer, I cannot overstate how tremendously this grew my overall confidence as a website builder. Moreover, it also fed back into my design process. And as any developer would attest, a designer who tempers their work in the realities of what is and isn't possible is a much stronger designer. It gave me the confidence and credibility to work more closely with developers and speak their language in my design practice, instilling much stronger collaboration.

Designer and Webflow developer Michael Riddering sums this up in his illuminating blog post when he says the following:

> *"With every website I create in Webflow I learn something new about HTML/CSS (and even JavaScript triggers to an extent). But the coolest part? I didn't even realize it most of the time! Because I was learning the Webflow editor, not how to actually write code or understand CSS syntax."*

> **Tip**
>
> You can read the rest of Michael Riddering's take on how Webflow changed his design and development process here: `https://www.michaelriddering.com/blog/the-tipping-point-in-my-career-as-a-product-designer`.

Part of the reason why this is possible is that Webflow's opinionated take on how to design and build websites is almost always an up-to-date reflection of the state of modern web development best practices. For the curious or more technically inclined, this is evident by the source code Webflow automatically generates for everything that is designed in its editor. The source code is popularly viewed as the cleanest, most bloat-free code by any web builder of its kind. In fact, you can even choose to export all its generated code, transfer it to any hosting provider of your choice, and publish it successfully with hardly any hitches.

As such, while it is indeed true that Webflow will likely take you longer to master, it is my belief that the rewards are far greater than using other web builders; you will not only build solid, professional, flexible, and exciting websites, but you will also gain a much deeper understanding of what it takes to build for the modern web.

## Concern 2 – Will Webflow scale well to larger projects?

This concern was more commonly raised during the early days of Webflow, and typically by those who were looking for web builders for more complex needs. Yes, it was positive and promising to see that the code it generated was remarkably readable and efficient, but could it support websites that needed tens, perhaps even hundreds, of pages?

Like any forward-thinking product, Webflow has put in significant effort to evolve with the times. The platform has matured and produced many success stories that demonstrate its capability of supporting large, moderately complex, production-grade websites. If you want to get an example of how large a website can get with Webflow, I invite you to visit its website, www.webflow.com. Nearly the entire site, including its **Community** pages and **Help** documentation, all of which contain likely hundreds of pages, is built in Webflow.

Furthermore, it is worth noting that if you're looking to build enterprise-grade websites that are fast, stable, secure, scalable, and supported by a rockstar team, Webflow offers a business plan that provides all that and more.

That said, in this book, we'll dive deep into some specific Webflow capabilities and features that will hopefully show you how practical and easy it can be to spin up and scale fully responsive and beautiful websites effortlessly with little to no code.

## Concern 3 – What kinds of websites can I build with Webflow?

Webflow is sometimes thought to be largely suited to single-page marketing landing pages. And while this is definitely a use case that Webflow excels at, it is by no means limited to it.

As mentioned previously, Webflow's capabilities afford it the ability to rapidly build out large and moderately complex systems, including multi-page sites, news publication-style blogs, curated directories, highly interactive multi-media showcases, dashboards, and more.

And while, at the time of writing, Webflow does not have any native support for advanced capabilities such as user profile registrations and account management, the industrious No-Code community has built various add-ons and third-party services that can be integrated into Webflow sites to address this. With the proper setup, Webflow sites have even been used in creating user-driven, dynamic websites that collect information, save information, and display information depending on who is accessing it.

And if you really want to get fancy, look no further than the works of prolific Webflow developer and builder, Sarkis Buniatyan. His concepts are full-blown recreations of highly complex interfaces, such as the strategy game Civilization, and even Playstation 4's UI.

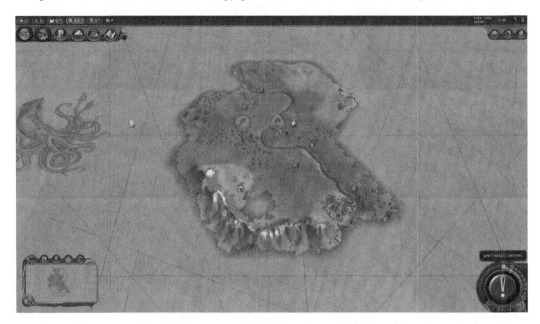

Figure 1.1 – Clone of Civilization VI by Sarkis Buniatyan

> **Tip**
> You can explore this project and many more by Buniatyan and his team on their *Webflow Showcase* page: `https://webflow.com/Protocore`.

If anything, this should excite you about the potential that Webflow has in your prototyping and development workflows. The limit really is your imagination!

While most of the preceding use cases are beyond the scope of this book, take heart in knowing that Webflow has been built for resilience and flexibility. The projects we will go through will arm you with enough about the fundamentals, some advanced concepts to get you up on steady and confident feet and will set you up to start taking Webflow in whichever direction you want.

# Concern 4 – Is Webflow too expensive?

This one is unfortunately more difficult to address. Webflow is offered in a number of differently featured tiers or plans. In fact, the sheer number of ways a Webflow setup can be priced can be dizzying! Depending on what you're looking to achieve with Webflow, you could find yourself using it without paying a dime all the way up to paying a fairly hefty amount in any given year. In *Chapter 3*, *Setting Up Your First Project*, we'll be covering the Webflow plans in more detail, but for now, rest easy knowing that you should be able to cover a fair bit of ground in your leveling up of Webflow skills on the free plan, which we'll be using for the majority of this book.

But what if you're considering whether it makes economic sense as a tool for your freelance work, maybe? Or your personal projects? Or your small business? Would it be prohibitively costly?

Unfortunately, there's no easy answer to this except for *it depends*. What features and capabilities of Webflow do you need? Will you be looking to use its CMS? Will you be looking to create an e-commerce store? Will you rely on Webflow to host your site, or do you have your own hosting domain? Are you just looking to use it to prototype your ideas?

Most of all, it will come down to knowing your alternatives. Will you be able to achieve your goals by using a free WordPress template and simply pay for your hosting costs? Will you need to outsource the work to a third party? Will you generate enough income from your website to pay for its costs? Does this matter?

Ultimately, you know your goals and limitations the best. By listing them and knowing what you're looking to get out of a web builder solution, you can begin to compare whether it would be worth it for you to go with Webflow versus choosing any of its alternatives.

# Deciding whether Webflow is right for you

So, now that we've covered some of the main questions and concerns about Webflow, how can you decide whether it is right for you? In general, if all the following criteria are important to you, Webflow is likely a great candidate to be your go-to web builder solution of choice:

- You want fully responsive websites that are interactive and feel custom-made.
- You want to minimize or eliminate coding.
- You want the flexibility to change and update not only the content of websites, but also their layout, structure, and overall look and feel.

- You want to create functional prototypes of web designs.

- You care about generating clean and efficient markup code that you can export or further customize.

- You care about learning the best practices of modern web development.

On the other hand, if the following criteria are important to you, then you may be better off exploring other platforms:

- You need only a single one-off website that likely won't need extensive custom styling. In this case, Webflow might be overkill and you may be better off considering a template from other web builders, such as Squarespace, Weebly, Wix, WordPress, or Carrd.

- You don't have the time or interest to customize web experiences.

- You want complex, scalable application capabilities such as Uber-like on-demand platforms, or video conferencing, or two-sided marketplaces. For these purposes, at the time of writing, you may want to consider other no-code builders such as Bubble or UI Bakery.

I will assume that by choosing to read further, you've expressed an interest to dive in and learn Webflow. Chances are also likely that you may have tried other resources. From its Webflow University to the many courses and videos that have been released by Webflow users around the world, there's no shortage of help!

So, where does this book fit in? Let's take a closer look.

# Who will benefit from this book?

If you are like me, then you may have found a number of the available resources did not match your preferred style of learning. Perhaps the videos or courses were too long or too fast. Perhaps the delivery of the topics was not to your liking. Some may even be too prohibitively costly.

I will admit that my journey of learning Webflow had many false starts. I would excitedly start a new tutorial, jump into the Webflow builder, and after following along for a few lessons, I'd inevitably stop understanding what it was I was doing, which would stunt my learning and motivation to continue.

Ultimately, I feel the underlying reason behind those moments was that I was missing a key point or concept, without which I was unable to understand how the platform was working. For me, this was the difference between simply following instructions blindly and truly learning the underlying principles. After many trials and errors, I managed to break through these impasses and unlock the power of Webflow, and I've not looked back.

And now I want to share my lessons with you, dear reader. This book is the resource I wish I had had when I first started my journey. It not only will help you build and publish a handful of useful websites that you can show off in a portfolio, but you will also understand *why* things are built that way. If you've ever been curious to understand modern web development concepts but were always too intimidated or overwhelmed by code, then this book will hopefully help bridge all those gaps together.

We'll start simple and slowly build layers of complexity on top. Like doing reps in the gym, we'll repeat a number of the concepts so they are reinforced, and your web design/development muscles are growing. Everything will be practical and rooted in real examples. Where appropriate, we'll introduce relevant web development concepts that will help you understand the magic behind how Webflow is working.

If you're a designer, it will make you think like a web developer. If you're already a web developer, it can help you experiment with designs in a quick and visual manner. And if you're neither, Webflow will at best introduce you to the possibility of being a professional designer/developer and, at the very least, provide you with enviable skills in creating customized websites for your personal needs.

And not only will we build functional websites, but we'll also put the *fun* back into *functional* as well.

## Summary

In this chapter, we took a high-level look at what Webflow is as a technology and the larger context in which it finds itself. Specifically, we took a brief look at the history of web design and development, leading up to today's No-Code movement.

We then explored and addressed some of the most common concerns about Webflow. Through this, we peeled back some of the layers of the capabilities and limitations of Webflow, and hopefully made a strong case for how and why Webflow can factor into your modern web design and development process.

We also broke down how you can decide whether Webflow is right for you. You know your goals the best, but if designing and building performant websites efficiently is on your agenda, then Webflow should be a serious consideration!

And finally, we looked at how this book is positioned to help you on your journey to learning and putting Webflow to use. Through practical examples, supported by just enough theory that shines a light on key web development principles, you'll develop the appreciation and confidence that Webflow can bring into your workflow.

In the next chapter, we will be spending a little time developing some foundational knowledge that is crucial to succeeding in Webflow. Specifically, we will take a concise, no-nonsense look at some core concepts that govern the entire web—the box model and HTML/CSS. And in the book's intended fashion, these concepts will be repeated and reinforced throughout the book.

And even if you're familiar with these concepts, scanning through the next chapter can act like a good refresher that level-sets us before we dive into the nitty-gritty of Webflow. I hope you're as excited as I am to dive in!

# 2
# The Web in a Nutshell

Unlike many other website builders, learning to design and develop websites in Webflow efficiently and with confidence requires a good understanding of how modern websites are structured. In fact, it may even be argued that it is a prerequisite to learning Webflow. Spending some time grasping these foundational concepts will help you unlock the true power and unique value of Webflow.

In this chapter, we'll take a closer look at two of these foundational concepts. First, we'll explore the **CSS box model**, a set of rules and constructs that govern how websites are structured. Understanding the box model will give you an appreciation for how websites are laid out and why, all of which will directly help you in understanding how Webflow works.

With some basic understanding of the box model in place, we'll then take a closer look at two of the main technologies that underpin the entire visual web: **Hypertext Markup Language** (**HTML**) and **Cascading Stylesheets** (**CSS**). We'll cover how HTML is used as the actual building blocks of websites and how CSS is used to stylize them.

If a website were a wall, HTML would represent the actual bricks that construct it, CSS would govern the aesthetic look and feel of the individual bricks, and the CSS box model would be the set of rules that bind it all together.

If you're an absolute beginner in these topics, please note that this chapter is not an exhaustive overview of HTML and CSS, nor is it meant to be. We'll be covering the bare essentials that will set you up for success in Webflow. If you're already very comfortable with HTML and CSS, you may choose to skip straight to the next chapter.

Specifically, in this chapter, we'll cover the following topics:

- The box model
- The basics of HTML and CSS

# The box model

Before beginning to build websites in Webflow, it is crucial to get some basic understanding of the box model. Indeed, it is a concept that underpins how all websites are structured, and in my experience, has been the main point of friction for people who were looking to get started with Webflow without prior web development experience.

The basic implications of the box model (also referred to as the CSS box model) can be summarized in the following simple directives:

- Web pages are made out of boxes of content.
- Each box consists of a variety of different pieces that make up the box. We will look at this in more detail in *The anatomy of a box* section later in this chapter.
- Some boxes can have other boxes inside of them, though it's not necessary.
- Boxes can be stacked on top of each other, vertically above or horizontally next to each other.
- Boxes also generally understand their placement in relation to the boxes around them, so changing one box's placement or inner dimensions may affect other boxes.
- Boxes have implicit names but can also be named explicitly in order to aid in identifying individual boxes.

And that's it.

There's obviously a lot more nuance to these rules, but that's essentially the high-level breakdown. Now let's examine how these boxes play out in practice.

# Boxes in boxes

Take a look at the following screenshot from www.cnn.com. Do you notice any logical groupings of content into boxes? Take a minute or two to identify as many as you can.

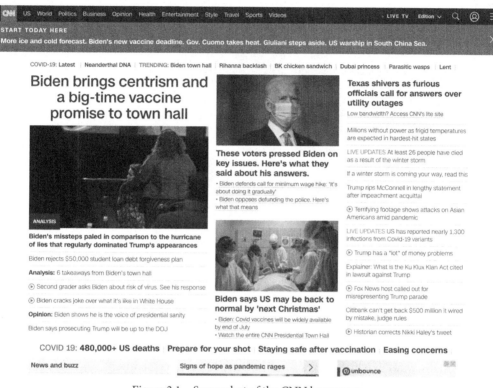

Figure 2.1 – Screenshot of the CNN home page

I've included my take on it in *Figure 2.2*:

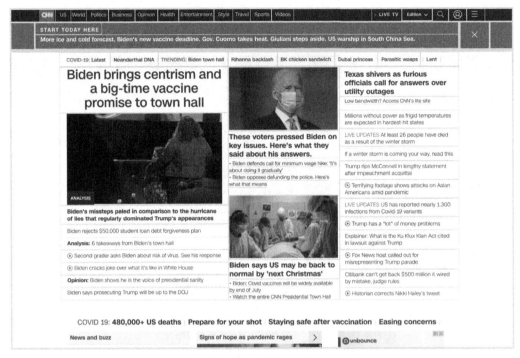

Figure 2.2 – The boxes of the CNN home page

Did this surprise you?

There are many ways in which boxes can be arranged to lay out content, and my attempt is only my best guess as to how the developers at CNN went about it. For instance, if you were to take a look at the navigation menu at the top of the page, the entire menu is a single rectangular box. Inside of it, the logo and the individual page links make up other boxes that are laid out side by side. At the far-right end of the menu are some utility links, including the **Profile**, **Search**, and **Language** options. These are inside their own boxes. Together, these utility links could make up a collective box of their own.

The rest of the page itself is then broken up into roughly three columns of content, each column representing its own box. Together, the three columns find themselves in a larger box. The content itself is also built up with images and text, again (you guessed it) bounded in their own boxes.

In fairness, a page like the CNN website may be an easy one to demonstrate boxes of content; its visual appearance immediately conveys a structured and rigid feel.

Let's take a look at another example: `https://www.meta-craft.com/`. At first glance, this example may look less boxy.

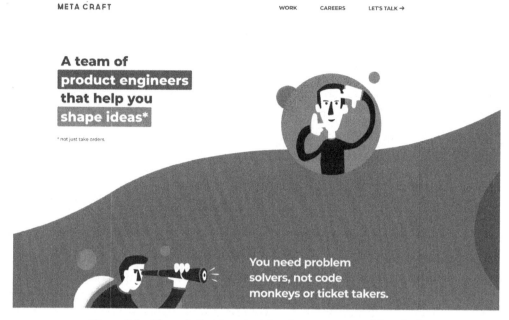

Figure 2.3 – The website of product development agency Meta Craft

Take a minute or two to slice this section of the web page up into smaller boxes. How difficult was it?

I've included my take on this in *Figure 2.4*:

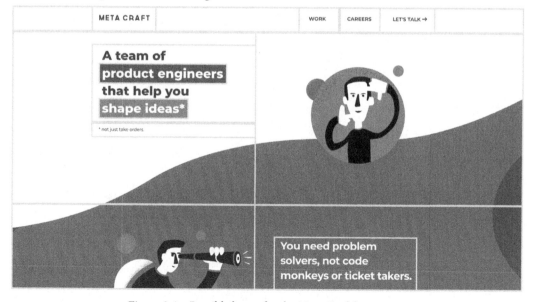

Figure 2.4 – Possible boxes for the Meta Craft home page

And, again, the actual separation of the content into boxes may differ, but the central point is the same: websites are made up of many boxes of content, no matter how non-box-like they may appear.

But how does all this play out in practice and what does it mean for you?

## Implications for designers

If you're a web designer and this is your first time hearing about the box model, then what you've read so far may have caused you to reflect on your own design process. If not, consider the following few points.

At the time of writing, the most common user interface design tools include the likes of Figma, Sketch, and Adobe XD. If you're at all involved in website or mobile app design, it's very likely that you're using these tools in your daily work.

The main commonality between all these tools (and many other similar ones) is their infinite canvas on which you can add objects to your heart's desire, with hardly any constraints. Even though modern features such as Smart Layout in Sketch or Auto-Layout in Figma introduce helpful constraints that have been welcomed by designers, they still are not a true reflection of the box model, nor are they intended to be.

For example, in *Figure 2.5*, we see a glimpse of Figma's infinite canvas, which allows the designer to create or add a large number of assets and screens with hardly any restrictions on orientation or layout:

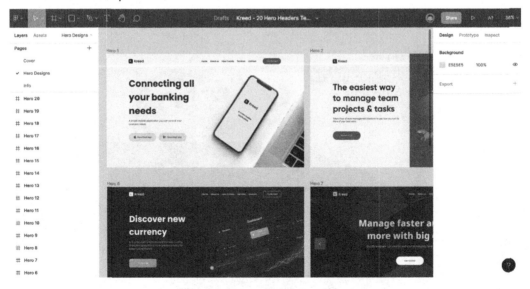

Figure 2.5 – Figma's infinite canvas

In fact, so far, the tools are largely agnostic to any specific rules, leaving it to the designer to decide what is necessary based on the needs at hand.

And this is why, I believe, designers can have a tough time switching to a tool like Webflow. Whereas Figma, Sketch, and Adobe XD allow freeform design, Webflow, on the other hand, rigidly sticks to the box model. It's a shift in paradigm that's crucial to make in order to be successful in Webflow.

But this is also where Webflow shines and why it can be such a powerful addition to your design and development process. Specifically, designing in Webflow will help you learn the language of how websites are built, which in turn, will flow back into your design process. Going forward, any designs you create in your favorite UI design tools can then be tempered by the constraints that the box model sets. In effect, you'll start thinking like a developer. And if you're ever collaborating with other developers, you'll be able to articulate your design decisions using language that they are familiar with.

Crucially, Webflow is not just another design tool. With it, you are in fact building the actual web page in a visual way. Furthermore, unlike most design software such as Sketch and Figma, any designs you create on a page in Webflow affect all screen sizes simultaneously, making it a powerful way to build websites responsively.

## The anatomy of a box

We've talked a lot about boxes and how they make up the overall look and feel of a website. But now let's take a single box and examine it up close, X-ray style.

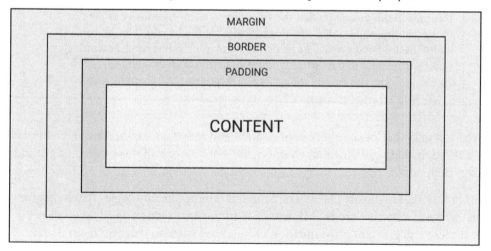

Figure 2.6 – The anatomy of a box as per the standard CSS box model

Let's break the box down into its individual parts:

- **Content**: This constitutes the actual content that is meant to be displayed on the website and can take the form of multiple types, including text, images, videos, embedded media, and so on.

- **Padding**: This refers to the space between the content and any border around it. Padding can be defined on all four sides of the content – left, top, right, and bottom.

- **Border**: This wraps around the content and the padding. If defined, the border can have a number of different styling attributes applied to it, including how wide it is, what color, whether it is a solid line or dashed, and more.

- **Margin**: This refers to the outer space between the box and the rest of the content on the web page. Like padding, margins can be defined on all four sides of the box.

When content is added to a page, unless widths and heights are explicitly stated, the content will try to fill any provided space. Furthermore, according to the standard CSS box model rules, any padding, borders, and margins added to the content are then added to the size of the content in order to calculate the total size of the entire box that it represents.

> **Important Note**
>
> If you're thinking that the standard CSS box model rule of making padding, border, and margin sizes additive to the size of the content makes things a little odd, you're not alone. The alternate CSS box model was created in response to this and states that the size of the content is *inclusive* of the size of the padding and border. Margins will still need to be added to the content width. In this book, we will be using the standard CSS box model exclusively, but if you're interested in learning more about the alternate model, read this: `https://developer.mozilla.org/en-US/docs/Learn/CSS/Building_blocks/The_box_model`.

We've been talking a lot about boxes of content and how they can be placed, positioned, and stylized, including their inner components, but how are all these different attributes actually defined?

Turns out, boxes are mostly just abstract models. The real technologies that help give them form and structure are HTML and CSS. In the next section, we'll take a closer look at these and give a basic foundation of how they work so that you're set up for success in Webflow.

# The basics of HTML and CSS

At their core, HTML and CSS are the main technologies and building blocks of websites. Whereas HTML is a markup language used to define what specific content types are being displayed, called **elements**, CSS is the language that then defines what shape or form, called **attributes**, that content appears in on the page.

If you were to describe a face in HTML and CSS, the former would enumerate elements such as eyes, nose, and lips, and the latter would list out attributes such as blue, pointed, and thin.

One of the challenges for newcomers to HTML and CSS is simply knowing what types of elements can be defined and what attributes can be applied to them. Indeed, over the years, the lists of both have only grown.

While doing an exhaustive overview of all that HTML and CSS have to offer is far beyond the scope of this book, in this section, we'll cover some basic rules, elements, and attributes that will hopefully help you to grasp how websites are generally built. The hope, then, is that this will help demystify how Webflow allows you to control these items.

## HTML

If you ever look at a page of HTML, you'll find it is made up of a series of elements that come together to define the content that appears on a web page. As such, it is often referred to as a markup language, that is, it's used to lay out and format elements on the page. In the context of websites, these elements can include paragraphs, links, headings, images, and more.

In Webflow, all HTML elements will be visible in the Navigator panel on the left side of the screen, which we'll see more of in *Chapter 3*, *Setting Up Your First Project*.

In addition, HTML also uses special elements that define whether a group of elements belong together in a defined section of the page. For instance, a group of paragraphs and images can come together to form the BODY of the page. Likewise, a group of links and text can form the FOOTER of the page, too.

All elements, whether grouped or not, are defined by **tags**. Most tags have opening <TAG NAME> and closing </TAG NAME> brackets around the element that they are defining. Here is a simple example:

```
<p>The quick brown fox jumped over the lazy dog</p>
```

This piece of HTML is defining a paragraph element by wrapping a piece of text in between an opening `<p>` tag and a closing `</p>` tag. This paragraph element, then, is essentially a box of content. By default, it will have no border, no padding, and no margins defined.

By default, most elements are displayed as what are called block-level elements while some others are displayed as inline-block elements. It is worth knowing the difference between them.

Block-level elements occupy a block of space of their own that is not shared with any other blocks. When added to a page, they automatically start on a new line and try to fill up the entire horizontal space available while pushing other surrounding content underneath. Block-level elements are usually also given dimensions for their widths and heights. In addition, they can have top and bottom margins defined.

Here are some of the common block-level elements that you will likely become familiar with when building websites:

- `h1, h2, h3, h4, h5`: These define the main header sizes that will be found on the web page, from largest to smallest.

- `body`: This constitutes the main area of the web page wherein most of the visible content will be located. This is where most styling properties are also defined such that they get passed down to any children elements, that is, any elements that are nested inside the body.

- `p`: These represent paragraph elements, which are effectively the main pieces of text on the page. As we've already seen, anything in between an opening `<p>` tag and closing `</p>` tag is considered a single paragraph element. So, if you wanted to create a second paragraph of text, you would have to start a new paragraph element.

- `div`: Beginners usually stumble over this element. A `div` element is essentially an empty container that is used to group together any number of other elements. For example, if you wanted to group an `<h1>` heading, three `<p>` paragraphs, along with an `<img>` image, then you could wrap them all up in between an opening `<div>` tag and a closing `</div>` tag. You would then be able to manipulate the `div` element to affect how the grouped elements work together.

We could keep going but, again, the intent here isn't to be exhaustive. Rather, for now, it's good enough to understand the general gist of how block-level elements work.

In contrast, inline-block elements behave differently. These constitute elements that do not start on a new line. Furthermore, they take up only as much space as they need and generally do not have top and bottom margins defined.

Common examples of inline-block elements include the following:

- Hyperlinks, defined by the `<a>` and `</a>` opening and closing tags, respectively.

- `<span>` elements, which are groups of text that are isolated usually for the purpose of adding special styling or effects.

- `img` elements, which can be placed almost anywhere on the page and allow text to flow around them.

One last thing to note is that HTML allows you to forcibly make block-level elements behave like inline elements and vice versa. Don't let this confuse you too much. Once we start developing your first website in Webflow in *Chapter 4, Building Above the Fold*, you'll see how easy and useful that functionality will be.

So, putting a number of these elements together, here's what a simple HTML snippet could look like:

```html
<html>
    <body>
        <h1>Welcome to my Awesome Site!</h1>
        <div>
            <h2>A collection of links and quotes that inspire me
                </h2>
            <img src="welcome_image.png" />
            <p>Take a look around and I hope you see something
                that inspires you too.
            </p>
        </div>
    </body>
</html>
```

All HTML documents are required to open with the `<html>` tag and close with the `</html>` tag. These tags essentially let the web browser know that everything enclosed between the tags is meant to be interpreted as HTML.

Inside, we see a `<body>` section that contains an `<h1>` header, followed by a `<div>` section, which encloses more content inside of it. Note that almost every tag that is opened is eventually closed off.

Don't worry if all this still feels a bit tricky to grasp. Indeed, there are many more nuances we haven't covered yet.

> **Tip**
>
> If you're still curious about how HTML looks, there are two ways you can quickly explore this.
>
> The easiest way is to open a website in the Chrome web browser. Then, right-click anywhere on the page and select the option called **Inspect**. This will reveal the underlying HTML code that marks up the page. You can do this in other browsers too, but the steps are a little more involved. We'll leave it to you to look up resources on how to achieve it.
>
> Secondly, you can open up a new blank document in Notepad on Windows or an editor such as TextEdit on Mac. Type anything in, such as, `Hello world!`. Then save the file in the format `filename.html`. Next, open up the file with your favorite browser. You should notice it appear. You can now inspect the HTML code of this page as you did in the previous paragraph.

Building in Webflow circumvents the need to code any HTML by hand as it will generate all the required code behind the scenes for you. As we dive deeper into practical examples over the next chapters, you'll be introduced to more characteristics of HTML and how Webflow can be used to quickly and visually manipulate them all.

And now that we've taken a brief look at how HTML dictates what content elements are included in a page, it's time to examine how these content elements can be stylized.

# CSS

Like HTML, CSS is a language that has a strict syntax that governs how websites appear. It defines a set of parameters for the HTML elements. So, while HTML defines the content on the page, CSS dresses it up. And while they work together to shape a web page, they are typically saved in separate files and can exist independently of each other.

In Webflow, all CSS properties are visible and configurable on the right side of the screen in the Style panel. We'll be exploring this in more detail in *Chapter 3*, *Setting Up Your First Project*, as well.

The main advantage of separating content from style is to increase the efficiency of building and updating websites. Various HTML web pages can all refer to the same CSS rules. If the look and feel of a button, for example, needs to change, then all you need to do is update its styling attribute in one CSS file rather than having to individually change all the web pages that contain the button. As you can imagine, this is a major time-saver.

So how do you define these styling rules in CSS?

It turns out that most HTML elements have associated styling attributes. These attributes can be manipulated directly in the HTML file; however, for the reasons of efficiency we have mentioned, the more recommended approach is to list the attributes out with their appropriate settings in a separate CSS file.

As long as the HTML file references the CSS file, the browser will reconcile the HTML and CSS attributes, and render the web page accordingly.

For a successful reconciliation to happen, a few conditions need to be met:

- The CSS file that the HTML is referencing needs to identify a specific HTML element by type or name.

- Once the element is identified, the CSS file needs to specify which attributes of the HTML element it is looking to change.

- The CSS file then sets the values of the attributes.

*Figure 2.7* shows a very simple example of how this can happen:

home.html

```html
<html>
  <head>
    <link rel="stylesheet"
href="home.css">
  </head>
  <body>

    <div>
        <h1>Welcome back,
John!</h1>
    </div>

  </body>
</html>
```

home.css

```css
.body {
    font-family: 'Work
Sans', sans-serif;
}

.div {
    padding-top: 20px;
    padding-bottom: 20px;
    padding-left: 10px;
    background-color: aqua;
}

.h1 {
    color: #727272;
    font-size: 24px;
    font-weight: 600;
}
```

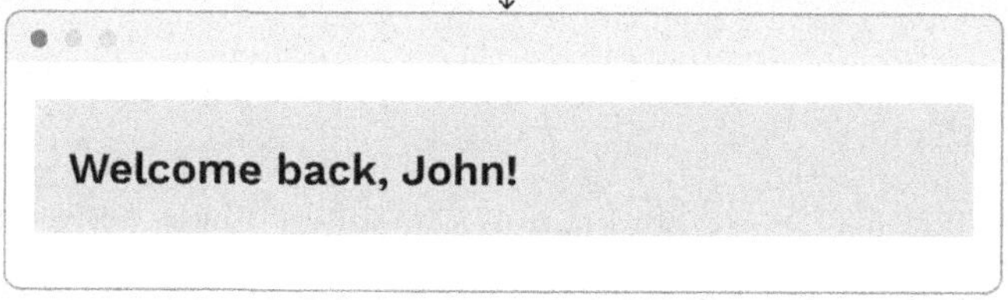

**Welcome back, John!**

Figure 2.7 – HTML and CSS working in tandem to help render a web page in the web browser

In the example, the HTML page has listed out three elements: a `body`, a `div` block, and an `h1` block inside of it.

On the CSS page, the body tag is referenced by using the body { } notation. Inside it, the Work Sans font is selected by using the font-family attribute. This is telling the browser that all text that is enclosed in the BODY element of the page should be displayed in the Work Sans font. Note that this also trickles down to any other HTML elements that are enclosed in the body tag (that is, to the children elements of body).

The div block is one such child element. It is referenced by pointing directly to the div tag using the div notation. Under it, a number of attributes are listed, including padding (which are set here using pixels) and the HEX code of the background color of the div block itself.

Next, the h1 element is directly referenced by using the .h1 notation. Then, under this, the font color and size are directly being manipulated. Notice how we don't specify the font name again here? This is because the h1 element is a child of the div element that was a child element of body. By default, children will look to inherit values of their parents unless the child explicitly sets the attribute and overrides it. Since no override values are set here, h1 inherits the last font name that was specified on a parent element. In this case, it happens to be Work Sans, which was specified in body.

The end result is a marriage of the HTML and CSS instructions, revealing a large heading that says, Welcome back, John! in the Work Sans font, written against an aqua-colored background. Since the h1 element is block-level, and no explicit sizing was defined, it takes up the entire width of the screen. It also respects the padding amounts that were set.

At its core, CSS is simple in that it is just a list of attributes and settings. However, one of the things beginners struggle with is knowing exactly which attributes are available to manipulate for each HTML element. And generally, practice and repetition are the best teachers for this.

But the beauty of using Webflow to build websites is that nearly every CSS attribute you'd need to stylize pages is visually available for you to manipulate to your heart's desire with immediate visual feedback. No more digging around references and no tedious refreshing of pages.

In effect, the learning curve then shifts more to how to understand and take full advantage of the attributes at hand.

At this point, you may also be wondering how CSS differentiates between multiple HTML elements of the same type; for example, if there were multiple div blocks, headings, and paragraphs, how would CSS be able to pinpoint which ones need specific styling?

This is where the concept of **classes** comes in. All elements can be classified by identifiers called class names. Elements that are similar to each other can then be given the same class name; any styling properties we apply to an element with a class name will then get passed to all other elements that share the same class name. In Webflow, we'll be using a lot of class names to identify and organize our content.

But rather than spending more time here going through the various nuances of CSS rules and attributes, we'll leave it to the following chapters to gradually reveal increasingly more powerful and complex capabilities where you'll have the opportunity to learn them while putting them into practice.

# Summary

We started this chapter by examining the CSS box model and its implications for web development. We learned to dissect websites as groupings of boxes of content, all of which can be manipulated in various ways. We also discussed why thinking about the box model can help improve one's design process as it more accurately reflects the way websites are actually developed. More relevantly, we learned that in order to be successful in Webflow, you have to shift your thought process away from the free-form nature of modern user interface tools and think more along the lines of the box model.

We then took a high-level overview of two of the most fundamental technologies of web development: HTML and CSS. We saw that HTML is a language that defines the content elements that make up a web page. We took a look at some basic HTML elements and how they can be structured together with some very basic examples. We then looked at how CSS complements HTML by marking up the styling and presentation of the HTML elements. We saw some basic examples of styling attributes that CSS can manipulate and how it all comes together to render a web page.

In the next chapter, we will begin our dive into Webflow. We'll get introduced to the very first project that we'll be building out and then spend some time quickly setting up our first Webflow project. Things are going to start getting real!

# 3
# Setting Up Your First Project

Now that we've covered some foundational principles, it's time to step into Webflow.

In this chapter, we'll take a look at the first project you'll be building in Webflow: a landing page for a fictitious food delivery app. After signing up for a free plan on Webflow, we'll do a quick tour of the Webflow interface and have you set up and ready to start building.

As such, we'll cover the following topics in this chapter:

- Landing page project overview
- Understanding the Webflow plans and signing up
- Downloading the required assets for the first project
- Quick orientation tour of the Webflow interface

Since every journey worth taking starts with vision setting, let's start at the end, taking a look at what you'll have proudly built by the end of your first project.

# Technical requirements

As part of the setup of our first Webflow project, we'll need to upload a number of assets, including some images and iconography. You can get all of these from the following link: https://github.com/PacktPublishing/Webflow-by-Example/tree/main/Chapter03/Assets.

# Project overview

One of the most common types of websites available is the marketing landing page. Landing pages are critical in that they usually give viewers their first (and often instant) impression of the subject at hand. The subject can be anything, including a specific person, company, product, or service.

For our first project, we'll be creating one such landing page from scratch. It will be for a fictitious food delivery service and app called **SecondPlate**. It will showcase the main features of the app and how it provides value to the user. Its primary purpose will be to drive visitors to download the app. This is a modified version of a landing page design that was initially created by Nigerian designer Marvis Dosa.

We'll be referring to a Figma design file to help us define the specifics around the dimensions and properties of the various elements of the page. But note that once we begin building it out in Webflow, we may find ourselves further tweaking the design and straying a little from the mockups. This is usually on par with typical design and development workflows; the more real a design becomes, the more opportunities we'll uncover to refine and polish the design.

Let's take a closer look at how we'll break out the individual sections of the landing page.

The first section we'll be focusing on is the top portion of the landing page, often called the **Hero section** or the portion of the website that is **Above the Fold**. As shown in *Figure 3.1*, this section will include a navigation menu along the top of the page, followed by a large banner image, a headline, and some buttons that a visitor can click to download the app. Finally, it will include some showcase images of the app itself:

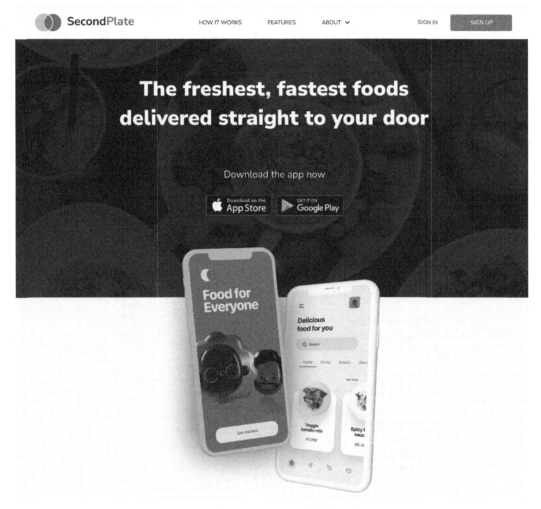

Figure 3.1 – The Hero section of the landing page

Next, we'll build out a section that showcases how the app works. We'll do this by showing a series of screenshots of the app accompanied by some concise descriptions of specific app features. *Figure 3.2* shows what this will look like:

Figure 3.2 – The How it works section of the landing page

The next section will list the main features and capabilities of the app. These will be presented on content cards that will be laid out in a grid format, as shown in *Figure 3.3*:

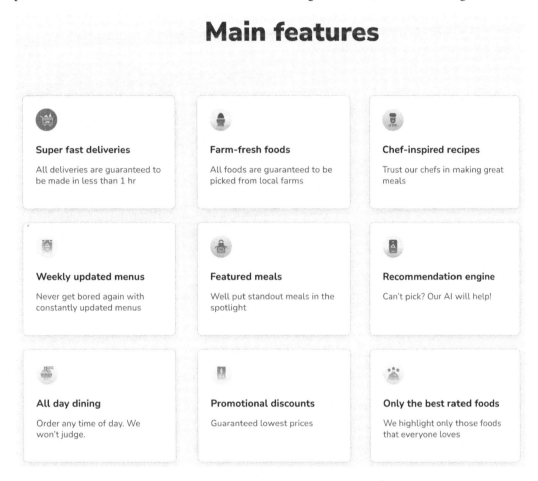

Figure 3.3 – The Main features section of the landing page

The final portion of the page contains two sections. First, we'll have a **call-to-action** section that is meant to be our final attempt to drive visitors to download the app. This section will feature an image and some call-to-action buttons. Finally, we'll have a simple footer that will include some social links if the user wants to explore further. *Figure 3.4* shows how these will come together:

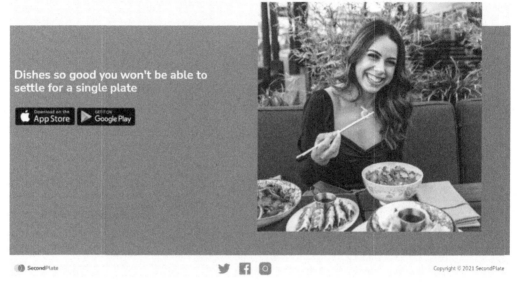

Figure 3.4 – The final call-to-action section and the footer of the landing page

By the end of the project, we will have picked up the following skills:

- Building an attractive and clear Hero section

- Working with various positioning and layout configurations with modern tools such as Flexbox and CSS Grid to create websites with visual interest and depth

- Learning how to structure a website in Webflow with proper naming conventions

- Working with various commonly used web components and elements, including images, icons, buttons, dropdowns, lists, and menus

- Making a web page fully responsive across multiple screen sizes from phones to widescreen TVs

- Adding animations and interactions to bring a page to life

There's a lot of ground to cover but what you'll quickly learn is that most of these concepts are repeated frequently. Once you become comfortable building a single web page out, you'll be able to apply the same concepts elsewhere. The key is to practice with as many different variations as possible. This project will be a gentle introduction to many of these commonly used elements.

But we still have some setting up to do before we can start building, so let's start with signing up!

# Getting set up in Webflow

Over the next few steps, we'll walk through how to sign up for a free plan on Webflow. Note that while Webflow's free plan is indeed free forever, it limits you to only two projects. This will be sufficient to follow along for all of this book except our final project, which will involve building an e-commerce store—a feature that requires a paid upgrade. Also note that in the free plan, websites have a limit of two pages. Again, this should be fine for our purposes.

If you plan on making Webflow an important part of your toolset, it is worth spending some time understanding the different pricing plans that Webflow offers.

## Understanding Webflow's priced plans

Since Webflow provides so much flexibility in how it can be used, an unfortunate side effect of this is its complicated pricing plans and schemes. We'll break it down as follows.

Webflow's priced plans fall into two categories: **account plans** and **site plans**. Let's break these down a bit.

### Account plans

You need to sign up for an account plan if you want to use Webflow. Account plans fall into two categories:

- **Individual plans**: You must choose any one of the three available plan types, which include the free **starter** plan, the **lite** plan, and the **pro** plan. The starter plan is ideal for those who are looking to try out Webflow before committing to purchasing it; however, it limits you to two projects. While the lite plan bumps this limit up to 10 projects for 16 USD/month on an annual plan, the pro plan has no limit at all to the number of websites you can build. At the time of writing, the pro plan comes in at 35 USD/month on an annual plan.

- **Team plans**: For those who are part of a team of Webflow developers, a team plan may be more appropriate. It is similar to the individual pro plan in all features and comes with additional features that make team collaboration a little easier.

## Site plans

Unlike account plans, site plans are optional. Without a site plan, however, any websites you publish will be done so on a *webflow.io* subdomain. If you need to publish Webflow sites onto your own custom domain, you will need to sign up for one of the site plans. Note also that each website you are looking to host will need its own site plan. These come in the following flavors:

- **The basic plan**: At 12 USD/month, this is the most cost-effective plan. It allows up to 100 pages per website but does not support any **Content Management System (CMS)** capabilities. As such, the basic plan is usually best suited for static websites and landing pages.

- **The CMS plan**: If you're looking to build a blog or website that will support dynamically entered content, you may want to consider this plan. It allows up to 2,000 CMS items.

- **The business plan**: This plan is best suited for websites and projects that will expect to receive large amounts of viewers and content. At 36 USD/month, this plan expands the limit of CMS items to 10,000.

- **The enterprise plan**: Webflow offers this plan for any large-scale projects that don't fit the preceding offerings with pricing that is made custom to your needs.

- **Ecommerce plans**: Lastly, if you expect to build and host an online store or marketplace through Webflow on a custom domain, you will need an ecommerce plan. These also come in multiple flavors: **standard** (best for small stores with sales up to 50,000 USD), **plus** (medium-sized stores with sales up to 200,000 USD), and **advanced** (no sale limits).

It's worth mentioning that at the time of writing, all site plans are limited to 100 pages per project. This means if you're expecting to work on very large-scale sites that will have more than 100 pages, Webflow might not yet be best suited for your needs. That said, there are signals that the team appears to be working on expanding this limit in the near future.

> Tip
>
> If you are already paying for a hosting plan elsewhere and wish to use it to host your site, you can choose to export all your Webflow code and transfer it to your preferred hosting provider. For this, you will need at least the lite account plan, as the starter account does not allow for code exports. At the time of writing, the lite account plan goes for 16 USD per month with an annual payment. Note that if you want to take advantage of Webflow's CMS capabilities, you will need at least the CMS site plan, which at the time of writing is charged at 16 USD per month.

If you don't need to publish any Webflow project to a custom domain anytime soon, and you don't need e-commerce features, you don't need to sign up for any site plan.

> **Important Note**
>
> Webflow's pricing schemes and plans are admittedly complex. For more detailed explanations of what each plan offers and the most up-to-date information regarding pricing, refer to Webflow's pricing page, located at `https://webflow.com/pricing`.

All that said, in order to follow along with this project, all we need is the free starter account plan. So, let's go ahead and sign up for one!

## Signing up for Webflow

To sign up to Webflow, follow these steps:

1.  Navigate to Webflow's website at `https://webflow.com/`:

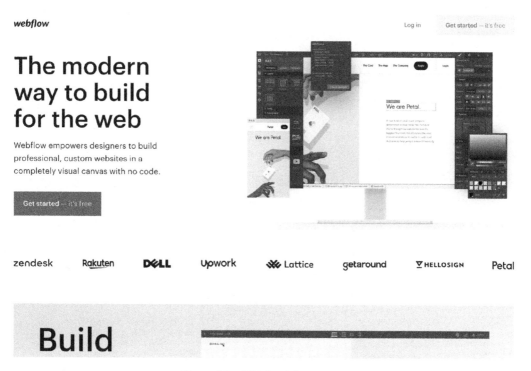

Figure 3.5 – Webflow's home page

2.  Go ahead and click the **Get started—it's free** button.

3.  Next, select your preferred method of sign up, whether it's by signing in with your Google account or by entering your email address.

4.  Over the next few steps, you will be onboarded into Webflow by answering a few personal questions. After the onboarding, you will be asked whether you want to start a tutorial. For our purposes, you can skip this for now.

5.  After you've successfully created and onboarded onto your new account, you will be greeted with your main dashboard page, as shown in *Figure 3.6*. Click on the blue **New Project** button on the top right of the screen:

Figure 3.6 – Your dashboard page

6.  You will now see a screen from which you can start a project using a multitude of templates, as shown in *Figure 3.7*. Templates are provided by Webflow itself or are submitted by the community. They range from simple and free blog templates to complex business websites and dashboards that need to be purchased. Since we'll be building our website from scratch, go ahead and select **Blank Site**:

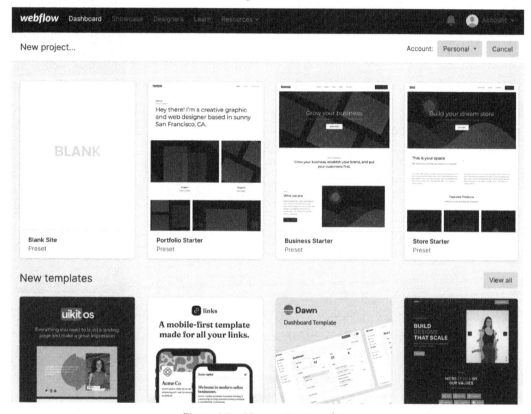

Figure 3.7 – New project templates

7.  You will be asked to name your project. Webflow goes ahead and suggests a random name for you. Erase this and call it SecondPlate Landing Page.

You will now land directly into the Webflow Designer, which is where you will be spending the vast majority of your time building websites. As you can see in *Figure 3.8*, the Designer is currently a blank canvas:

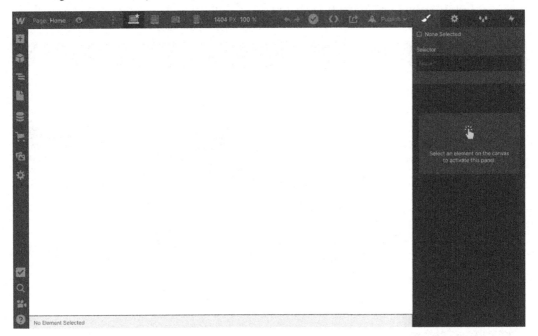

Figure 3.8 – The Webflow Designer

For many beginners, this presents the first big hurdle of the Webflow journey— where do you start?

But before we take a tour of the Designer interface and get oriented with it, let's take a couple of minutes to set up the files for our first project.

## Setting up your project

In order to set up your first project, follow these steps:

1.  Click on the Webflow logo at the top left of your screen.

2.  In the drop-down menu that appears, click on **Project Settings**, as shown in *Figure 3.9*:

Figure 3.9 – Project Settings menu item

3.  You should now land on the **General** tab of the **Project Settings** page, as shown in *Figure 3.10*. We can see by default that the project has been assigned the name **SecondPlate Landing Page**. Once you publish the project, it will be hosted on the `http://secondplate-landing-page.webflow.io` subdomain. You can change this to anything you want at any time. For now, let's keep it as is:

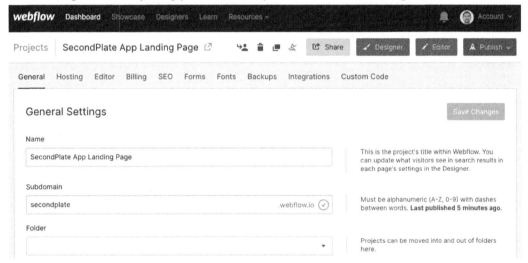

Figure 3.10 – Project General Settings page

4.  Since we'll be using custom fonts for this project, click on the **Fonts** tab.

5.  Under the **Google Fonts** section, select the dropdown that says **Select Google Font…**:

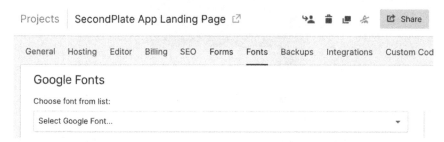

Figure 3.11 – Selecting a Google font

6.  Scroll through the fonts in the dropdown and select **Nunito Sans**. Since we don't need all the font weights, select only **Regular**, **700**, and **900**.

7.  Hit the **Add Font** button once you're done, as shown in *Figure 3.12*:

Figure 3.12 – Adding the Nunito Sans font weights

> **Important Note**
>
> While it may be tempting to add multiple fonts to a project, keep in mind that every additional font weight and family you add will increase the loading time of your website since it has to do more work to find and fetch the fonts in question. So, if you want fast websites that load quickly, it is good practice to only add the specific font weights and families that you need and no more.

8.  Now that we've successfully added our fonts, click on the purple **Designer** button at the top of the page to go back to the Webflow Designer.

9.  Once you're in the Webflow Designer, click on the icon of photos in the left-side menu, as shown in *Figure 3.13*. This will take you to the **Assets** section of the Designer:

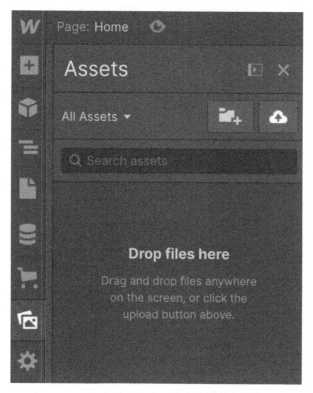

Figure 3.13 – The project Assets area

10. Add all the project assets to this **Assets** area by either selecting them manually through the file picker or dragging and dropping them into the provided area. You can find all project files and assets directly from this location: `https://github.com/PacktPublishing/Webflow-by-Example/tree/main/Chapter03/Assets`.

Once you've successfully added all the assets to the **Assets** section, you should be able to view their individual thumbnails, as shown in *Figure 3.14*:

Figure 3.14 – Successfully uploaded assets

> **Important**
>
> By default, all images you add will not contain any alt text properties. Adding alt text properties to your images is considered an important step to making them accessible to viewers who may be using screen readers to browse your website as the screen reader will be reading out any alt text you provide, thus ensuring that even if the viewer is unable to physically see the image, they're at least able to hear a short description of it. In general, making sure your designs are accessible to people regardless of their mental and physical capabilities is a critical part of the modern web design and development process.

To add alt text properties to your images, simply select any of the images from the **Assets** section and type a short but clear description of the image in the text box under the **Descriptive** tab, as shown in *Figure 3.15*:

Figure 3.15 – Adding descriptive alt text to an image

Also note that not all images will need an alt text entry. Some images, such as icons and background patterns, are simply used as decoration and don't need alt text. Images that form an important part of the page's content, however, will require good alt text descriptions.

Great! We've now completed setting up our first project! It's time to move on to the final part of this chapter: getting oriented with the most important parts of the Webflow Designer.

# Orienting yourself to the Webflow Designer UI

At first look, the Webflow Designer seems to be mostly taken up by a blank canvas with few obviously noticeable capabilities. However, once you start clicking around in the different sections of the Designer, you will start uncovering more subsections and details. Newcomers might find the menu choices and properties to be overwhelming or intimidatingly technical. Don't worry—over the course of the book, we'll peel back the layers slowly and get progressively more exposed and trained on how the individual parts work.

For now, let's take a whirlwind tour of the most important parts of the Designer and how it's laid out.

Taking up the most space, as we've mentioned, is the center panel. This is a blank canvas where you will be adding your HTML elements and building them visually. What you see here will be a fairly good, yet not absolutely accurate, representation of what you can expect to see if you were to publish your website. We'll see what we mean by this once we start building the site in *Chapter 4, Building Above the Fold*.

On the left-hand side of the Designer, you have a side menu that reveals more options. You've already interacted with this menu when you accessed the **Assets** section in the previous section of this chapter. Let's now turn our attention to the topmost item in the side menu, represented by a plus icon. Click this to reveal the **Add | Elements** section of the Designer. As shown in *Figure 3.16*, this is where you will find a host of various HTML elements that you can add directly to your website by either clicking them or dragging and dropping them directly to the canvas:

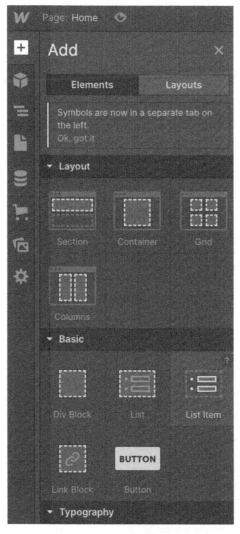

Figure 3.16 – The Add | Elements menu

The elements are divided into categories of similar items for easy scanning, including **Layout**, **Basic**, and **Typography** elements. You'll notice elements such as **Button**, **Columns**, and **Images**, as well as a number of other ones that may not yet be as obvious. We won't be using all these elements exhaustively, but we'll be covering a fair bit of them in future chapters.

Note, also, that at the top of the **Add** section, there is a second tab called **Layouts**, under which you'll be able to access a variety of premade templates of layouts. While we will be building all our layouts from scratch in this book, these prebuilt layouts can come in handy down the road.

To the far right of the Designer is a collection of sections that will allow you to style your website. However, since you haven't selected anything on the canvas yet, you shouldn't be seeing any styling properties either.

Go ahead and select the blank canvas if you haven't already done so.

Immediately, you should notice a few new things. First, the canvas should now be highlighted to show your selection. Specifically, the **Body** element should be shown in blue both on the canvas and in a new side panel called **Navigator**. **Navigator** is where you will see a hierarchical breakdown of all the elements on your canvas. In this case, only **Body** is shown, as in *Figure 3.17*, since it is the only element that currently exists on the page:

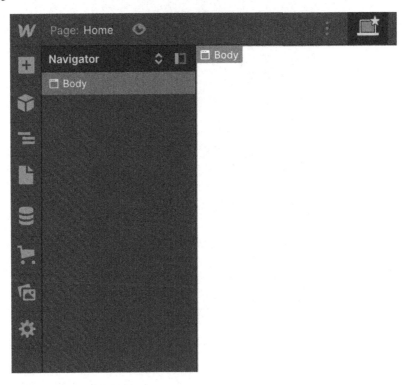

Figure 3.17 – Navigator

In addition, you should also now see a host of new styling properties appear on the far right of your screen, as seen in *Figure 3.18*:

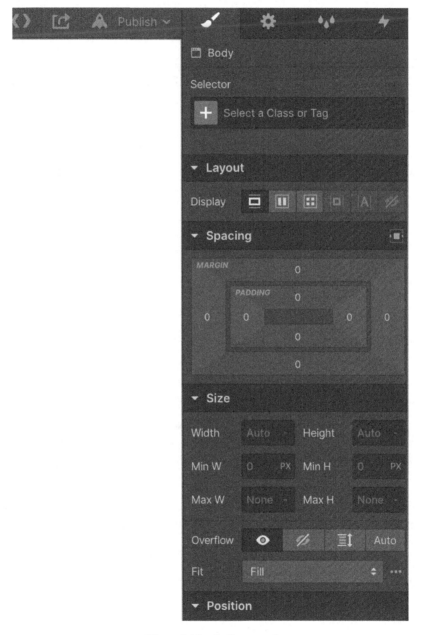

Figure 3.18 – Styling panel

Almost every element you add to the canvas will have its accompanying styling properties that you can manipulate and immediately visualize on the canvas. Essentially, these properties all map back to CSS attributes, from font size to padding and margin values, background colors, and much more. While these properties may feel overwhelming right now, we'll cover a good deal of them over the course of the book.

To demonstrate how these properties work, while you've got **Body** selected in the canvas, scroll down in the **Style** panel to the section titled **Backgrounds**.

Click on the **Color** attribute. This will reveal a color picker popup. You'll notice here that as you move the picker across the colors, the background color of the canvas (that is, the body) immediately changes as well.

As you gain more exposure and experience with the various styling settings, you'll come to appreciate the power of this capability to see your changes in real time.

> **Tip**
> Webflow comes packed with its own set of keyboard shortcuts to further speed up the design and development process. These include common ones you may already be familiar with, including copying (*Ctrl + C* on Windows or *Command + C* on Mac), pasting (*Ctrl + V* or *Command + V*), and undoing (*Ctrl + Z* or *Command + Z*). We'll cover other useful keyboard shortcuts throughout the book.

The final part of the Designer you should turn your attention to is toward the top center of the screen, where you'll see icons of various devices, including a laptop, tablet, and mobile, as shown in *Figure 3.19*:

Figure 3.19 – Previewing designs responsively across device sizes

These will come in handy once we start making our website responsive across multiple devices and we're looking to preview how they would appear on different screen sizes. We'll cover this in more detail in the section titled *Making it responsive* in *Chapter 4, Building Above the Fold*.

While there are plenty more sections and subsections of the Designer to cover, we've now covered some of the main ones that you'll be using frequently. As we progress through the projects in this book, we'll be revisiting these features and properties in addition to seeing new ones.

# Summary

We covered a lot of the preliminary steps in getting started with Webflow in this chapter.

We started off by taking a look at the end of our project. We took a high-level overview of the landing page that we will be building as part of our first Webflow project, providing us with a vision of what we'll be working toward.

Then, we jumped into how to get started with Webflow. We took a look at the different types of accounts and plans you can sign up for on Webflow, and then went through signing up for a free personal plan.

Once signed in, we then took some necessary steps to set up our first project. We did this by starting a new project from a blank template, adding some custom Google fonts, and uploading all necessary project assets.

Finally, we took a quick tour of some of the most important parts of the Webflow Designer so that we have our bearings with the interface and to start demystifying how it all comes together. Specifically, we quickly saw how to add new elements to the canvas and how stylistic properties can be applied to them, and with all that completed, we're now ready to jump straight into the nitty-gritty of building our first website.

In the next chapter, we'll be spending all of our time in the trenches of designing and developing with Webflow. By the end of the next chapter, you'll have the top portion of the website completely built and made mobile-responsive.

Let's get building!

# Section 2: Building a Mobile Responsive Landing Page with Webflow

In this section, we take a deep dive into building a full-page website in Webflow. We'll cover core web design principles and move into more modern concepts, all the while building a fully responsive page without any code.

We will cover the following chapters in this section:

# 4
# Building Above the Fold

Now that you've learned some basics about getting started with Webflow, it's time to get our hands dirty!

In this chapter, we'll dive straight into building out our first project, a landing page for a fictitious food delivery app called SecondPlate. We'll spend the whole chapter focused on the section of the page that is commonly referred to as being **Above the Fold**. In essence, this refers to the area of the page that can be immediately seen without having to scroll down the page.

Specifically, we'll cover the following in this chapter:

- Building the main **Hero** section of the page, complete with a cover image and product screenshots
- Adding a navigation menu along the top of the page and customizing it
- The differences between static, absolute, and relative positioning
- How to use flexbox to align content
- How to develop responsively across multiple screen sizes

Along the way, we'll uncover lots more little details that will become key in building websites in Webflow. Let's get started.

> **Tip**
>
> The phrase *Above the Fold* comes from print design. If you picture a folded
> newspaper, the content that viewers could read on the top without needing to
> unfold the newspaper was considered prime real estate, as it would stand to
> catch the most attention. In digital design, the term feels like an anachronism
> but it has stuck. C'est la vie!

# Technical requirements

If you haven't yet uploaded any of the required assets to your project yet, now is the time
to do so. You can get all of these from the following link:

`https://github.com/PacktPublishing/Webflow-by-Example/tree/`
`main/Chapter03/Assets.`

For details on how to upload the assets into the project, please refer back to *Chapter 3,
Setting Up Your First Project.*

Luckily, you can also refer to the live version of this website and open it in Webflow to see
the exact property values that were used to create it. You can find it here:

`https://webflow.com/website/App-Landing-Page-CLONE-READY-or-`
`SIGN-UP-LINK-INSIDE.`

And once you're ready, let's jump into setting up the body of our page.

# Setting up the Body

Starting with the body of a web page is usually a good idea because the changes will
govern how some properties across the entire page will look, saving you time in
the process.

Firstly, always make sure you start every project on the base breakpoint. This is the default
view and screen size that you will be targeting. The most common base breakpoint size is
`1440px`, so I will assume for this project that you are on it as well.

To ensure you're on the base breakpoint, click the icon on the top of your page that
shows a laptop with a star on it, as shown in *Figure 4.1*. And if the dimension is not set to
`1440px`, manually change it now:

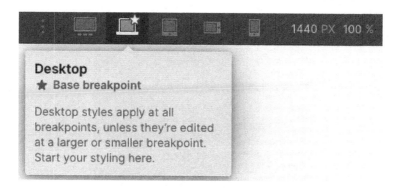

Figure 4.1 – The base breakpoint of 1440px

Any changes you make to the page on the base breakpoint will cascade down to all device sizes smaller than it. Later in this chapter, we will then change breakpoints sizes to ensure that the page looks great on other device sizes too.

Now, let's set up some properties on the **Body** element. Since **Body** is the parent of all other elements, the properties we set here will be inherited by all other elements by default. As such, when setting **Body** properties, it's good practice to think of them as properties you want to make available across your entire website.

Here's what we'll do:

1. In **Navigator**, select the **Body** element.

2. In the **Style** properties, under the **Typography** section, change the **Font** property to Nunito Sans. This will ensure that all text on the website will default to Nunito Sans.

3. Set the **Size** property to 24px and the **Height** property to 1.4 -. This will ensure that the line heights of any **Body** text will be 140% of the font size. Generally, it is good practice to set line heights to anywhere between 120% and 150% for optimal legibility, but the actual value can always be tweaked and overridden based on the context.

4. Under the **Backgrounds** section, change the **Color** property to #fafafa. This will give the background of the website a light gray color.

The properties should now resemble *Figure 4.2*:

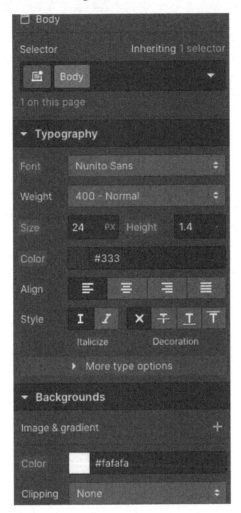

Figure 4.2 – Body property settings

Now that the **Body** properties are set, we can turn our attention to the **Hero** section of the page.

In broad terms, the section of the website that is Above the Fold is split up into two parts, the top navigation menu and the **Hero** section, as shown in *Figure 4.3*:

Figure 4.3 – The navigation menu and the Hero section of the page

Let's tackle the **Hero** section first.

# Building the Hero section

In order to get started, let's quickly map out the content boxes we anticipate building based on the designs. *Figure 4.4* shows one way we can do this. You'll notice that the background image is in its own box, as are the headings, buttons, and screenshot images. Altogether, they form bigger boxes that make up the full **Hero** section:

Figure 4.4 – The content boxes of the Hero section

Taking the time to plan out the course of action this way – especially if you're brand new at web design and development – is a good practice that can help you plan ahead. With enough repetition, this will become second nature, and you'll be able to do much of it in your head.

Now that we have an idea of how the content in the **Hero** section can be split up, let's start building it out. We'll tackle the **Hero** section by breaking it down into smaller bits. First, let's tackle the background image.

## Adding the background image

To add a background image to the **Hero** section, we first need to create the container within which it will exist. Then, we can specify its background properties. Let's go ahead and do this:

1.  From the **Add** section on the left-hand side, under the **Layout** section, select the **Section** element. This will add a **Section** element onto the page, and it will be nested under the **Body** element:

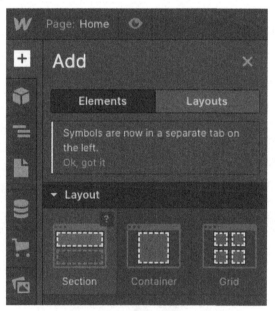

Figure 4.5 – Add the Section element

2.  In the **Style** panel, you'll notice that the **Section** element has a `Section` class assigned to it in the **Selector** field. Change this to say `Hero` instead, as shown in *Figure 4.6*:

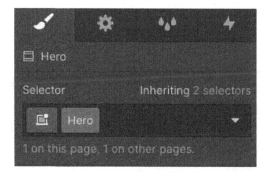

Figure 4.6 – Changing the class name of the Section element

3.  Next, let's add a background image to **Hero**. In the **Backgrounds** section, next to **Image & gradient**, click the + icon. Now, click the **Choose image** button, as shown in *Figure 4.7*. This will open up the **Assets** panel on the left-hand side of your screen. Select the image called `Hero-Banner.jpg`:

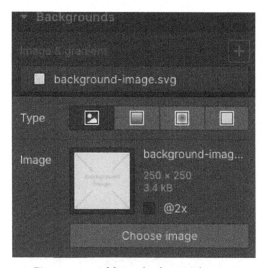

Figure 4.7 – Adding a background image

Note that even though you've now selected your image, you may not be seeing it on the page. This is because by default any element that has a background image needs to have an explicit size set in order to view the image. To demonstrate this, try changing the **Height** property of **Hero** to any size, say, 400px. You should now see the background image.

4. Change the **Height** property of **Hero** to 75vh. This ensures that the **Hero** section is always 75% of the vertical height of the page. Your page should now resemble *Figure 4.8*:

Figure 4.8 – Setting the vertical height of the Hero section

5. Click on the Hero-Banner.jpg image again under the **Backgrounds** section. In the **Size** field, click on **Cover**.

6. Under the **Position** section, make sure that you select the center dot and remove the **Tile** property. *Figure 4.9* shows what the properties should resemble:

Figure 4.9 – Background image settings

The background image should now cover the entire width of the **Hero** section, be centered, and not appear in a tile format.

7.  Lastly, let's add a dark overlay on top of the image so that when we eventually add text onto the page, we'll be able to read it comfortably against the background. In the **Image & gradient** section again, click the + icon. Click the **Color** overlay option. You should now see a dark overlay on top of the image. Click on the color thumbnail and increase the alpha value to 75 in order to add some transparency to the overlay. This will help the background image appear through the overlay while still providing enough contrast between any text we eventually put on top.

Figure 4.10 – Adjusting the overlay color

And with that, we've now added our **Hero** section element and given it an appropriate background image! Now, it's time to move on to adding the copy text.

## Adding the copy text

Without copy and good typography, a website becomes almost unusable. How else would a visitor know what the website is about if not for the words that are on the page? As such, let's now look at how we can add copy and configure the typography with a proper visual hierarchy, that is, to arrange the text by priority on the page:

1.  First, with the **Hero** section selected, go into the **Add** panel and select the element called **Container**. A **Container** element is essentially a **div** element (or you can think of it as a box) whose purpose is to simply collect other elements inside of it so that they can be laid out in the center of the page.

> **Tip**
> To save yourself time, you can access the **Add** panel quickly by either hitting the *A* key on your keyboard or hitting *Ctrl + E* and then typing the name of the element you'd like to add.

2.  In the **Style** panel, in the **Selector** input box, give **Container** the class name of Container if it doesn't already have one.

3.  By default, the **Container** element has a size of 940px. Since this will be too narrow for our project, change the width to 1200px in the **Max W** field. This will ensure that, by default, all of our containers will not exceed a width of 1200px, no matter how large the screen size gets.

4.  Next, with the **Container** element selected, give it **Left** and **Right** padding values of 40px. This will ensure that no matter what the size of the page is, there will always be 40px of whitespace on either side of the **Container** element, ensuring that the page doesn't feel cramped.

5.  Now, with the **Container** element still selected, hit the *A* key on your keyboard to access the **Add** panel and select the **Heading** element. This will add a heading to the **Container** element and by default set it to **H1**, the largest text heading available.

6.  Give the **H1** heading a class of H1. Now set the following properties:

    **Max W**: 780px

    **Size**: 52px

    **Color**: White

    **Align**: Center

7.  Now replace the placeholder text in the **H1** heading to the text that is written in the original designs, The freshest, fastest foods delivered straight to your door. The header should now resemble *Figure 4.11*:

Figure 4.11 – The H1 header

8.  Let's center-align the header properly on the page. To do this, change both the left and right margins of the **H1** header to **Auto**. This ensures that whatever the size of the screen, the browser will automatically calculate the left and right margins depending on the size of the text, which defaults to equal margins on either side. This results in the header getting centered on the page.

Another quick way to center-align an element on the page is to select the element, and in the **Style** panel, in the **Spacing** section, click on the tiny square icon on the right side of the page, as shown in *Figure 4.12*. This will automatically assign auto-margins on both sides of the selected element:

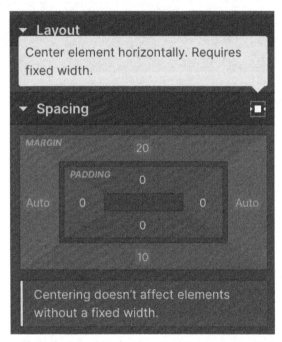

Figure 4.12 – Setting auto-margins

9.  Let's continue adding some copy text. Select the **Container** element in **Navigator**. Hit the *A* key on your keyboard to go back to the **Add** panel, and now select the **Text Block** element. This will add a new block of text on the page, right underneath the **H1** header. Give the new **Text Block** element a class name of Body Text (or anything else you want to call it). Now give it the following properties:

**Top Margin**: 64px

**Color**: White

**Align**: Center

Your page should now resemble *Figure 4.13*:

Figure 4.13 – Body Text added to the page

10. Change the text in the **Body Text** element to match what it says in the design, `Download the app now`.

With that, we've seen the basics of adding **Heading** and text elements and configuring some of their typographic properties. Since type will factor a lot into the website design, we'll keep uncovering more ways to stylize copy throughout the project.

For now, let's continue building out the **Hero** section.

## Adding Call to Action buttons

Another crucial part of effective websites is creating clear **Call to Actions** (**CTAs**). That is to say, once the visitor understands what the website is about, we want to direct them to take an action. In our case, these will be in the form of buttons that the visitor can click on to download the app.

Typically, when adding buttons in Webflow, we should be using the special button element. In this case, though, we'll be using images as buttons instead. This is because we'll be using special App Store and Google Play buttons, as required by both Apple and Google respectively.

Also, note from the landing page designs that the buttons will be sitting next to each other. When you anticipate similar objects in close proximity to each other such as these two download buttons, there's usually a good chance that they can be grouped together into a box. In this case, we'll create that box by using a **Div** element. Let's begin:

1. With the **Container** element selected, hit the *A* key on your keyboard and select the **Div** element. Rename the class of this **Div** element to `CTA Wrapper` or anything else you want.

> Tip
>
> **Div** elements that are used primarily to group other elements together are typically referred to as **wrappers**. Note that there is no such HTML element explicitly and officially called a wrapper, so you can call them whatever you want. This book will be referring to them as such though.

2. With the **CTA Wrapper** element selected, give it the **Top Margin** property of `32px`.

3. With the **CTA Wrapper** element still selected, hit *A* on your keyboard and select the **Link Block** element. **Link Block** elements are essentially boxes that can be clickable. In this case, select the **Link Block** element, hit *A*, and select the **Image** element.

4. With the **Link Block** element selected, click the **Choose Image** button and select the image called `AppStore.png`.

5. Now, let's repeat this step for the Google Play button. In order to save some steps, select the **Link Block** element in **Navigator**, and hit *Ctrl + C* if you're on a PC or *Cmd + C* if you're on a Macintosh in order to copy the element. Now, hit *Ctrl + V* or *Cmd + V* to paste it. *Figure 4.14* shows what you should be seeing at this moment:

Figure 4.14 – Added CTA buttons

6.  Now, click the image in the second **Link Block** element. Click the little cog icon to access **Image Settings**. Click on the **Replace Image** button and select the image called GooglePlay.png, as shown in *Figure 4.15*:

Figure 4.15 – Google Play Image Settings

The buttons are now added but they appear quite large. Let's resize them.

7.  Select the first **Link Block** element. Give it a class name of CTA Button.

8.  Do the same for the second **Link Block** element.

9.  Now, select any of the **Link Block** elements and give it a **Max W** size of 200px.

You should have noticed that changing the size of one of the **Link Block** elements affected both of them automatically. This is the power of classes. By giving similar elements the same class name, you can affect changes across multiple copies or instances of that element by changing it only in one place. This is why it is also a good idea to give your elements good class names.

> **Tip**
>
> The official documentation of Webflow advises the following naming conventions for class names:
>
> *"Classes should be Title Case and not abbreviated. Do not use dashes or other traditional CSS conventions (for example camelCase). Class names should follow correct spelling."*
>
> Keep in mind that this is a guideline and that you may encounter other ways to write class names. In this book, we'll be following what Webflow recommends.
>
> For more information on this topic, read the section titled *Naming Conventions* at the following page: `https://webflow.com/templates/submission-guidelines`.

We're making good progress! We've now added the copy text and the CTA download buttons onto the **Hero** section. Let's finish off this section by adding some showcase images of the app itself.

## Adding showcase images

Now that visitors understand what the website is about and have buttons to click on in order to download the SecondPlate app, it's a good idea to actually give them a glimpse of what the app looks like. In this section, we'll do just that and add two images that will showcase the mobile app:

1.  Select the **Container** element from **Navigator**. Hit *A* on your keyboard and add a **Div Block** element. Change its class name to `Showcase Wrapper`.

2.  With the **Showcase Wrapper** element still selected, hit *A* on your keyboard and select the **Image** element. Click the **Choose Image** button and select the image that is named `Hero-Phone1.png`.

3. The image that is added might be looking quite large. In the **Image Settings** window that you should be seeing now, change the **Height** field from Auto to 456px, as shown in *Figure 4.16*:

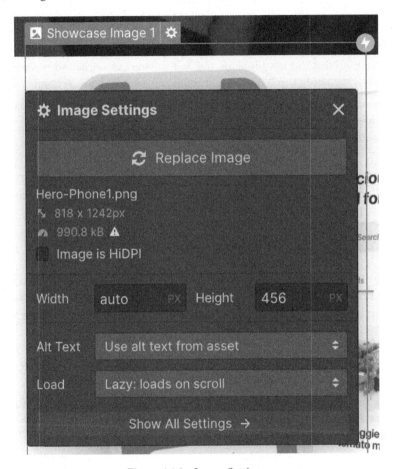

Figure 4.16 – Image Settings

4. Select the **Image** block in the **Navigator** section. Copy and paste it so that you now have a duplicate. Select the second **Image** element and hit the small **Settings** cog icon to reveal its **Image Settings** section. Hit the **Replace Image** button and select the image called Hero-Phone2.png, giving it a **Height** property of 500px.

5. Now, select the **Showcase Wrapper** element and, in the **Align** property, center it. The device images should now be centered on the page, as shown in *Figure 4.17*:

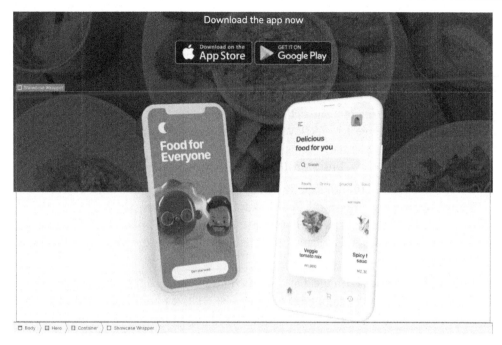

Figure 4.17 – Added device mockups

But we want these device mockup images to overlap each other in a way that gives an interesting visual depth to the page. Let's accomplish this:

6.  First, select the **Showcase Wrapper** element and set its **Max W** property to 50%. This will ensure that the **Showcase Wrapper** element never exceeds 50% of the page width.

7.  Next, with the **Showcase Wrapper** element selected, go to the **Style** panel, and down under the **Position** section, change the **Position** property from Static to Relative. This will allow us to control any of its children elements' positions relative to itself. We'll see what this means shortly.

8.  Next, select the first **Image Block** element and give it a class name of Showcase Image 1. Then, select the second **Image Block** element and give it a class name of Showcase Image 2.

9.  Select the **Showcase Image 1** element. Next, in the **Position** section of the **Style** panel, change the **Position** property from Static to Absolute. This will allow us to have full flexibility of the layout and position of this element with respect to its closest parent item that is of **Position** type Relative. In this case, that parent is **Showcase Wrapper**.

10. Next, select **Showcase Image 2** and change its **Position** property to Absolute as well.

11. The images should now be overlayed on top of each other. This is the general effect we want, but we need to ensure that **Showcase Image 1** is overlayed on top of **Showcase Image 2**. So, select **Showcase Image 1**, and under the **Position** section in the **Style** panel, change the **z-index** property to anything larger than 1 – say, 5. We'll explain what this means in the next step.

12. Select **Showcase Image 2** and set its **z-index** property to 1. We should now notice that **Showcase Image 1** is overlayed on top of **Showcase Image 2**, as desired. So, the **z-index** property essentially helps us layer images on the page in relation to each other. The higher the **z-index** property, the higher the image is being layered.

13. But the images are still not exactly where they should be on the page. Select **Showcase Image 1**, and in the **Position** section in the **Style** panel, set the left position to 5%. This means that **Showcase Image 1** will be placed 5% away from the left edge of its closest relative parent, which in this case is the **Showcase Wrapper** element.

14. Now, select **Showcase Image 2** and set its right position to 5%. This will position the image 5% from the right edge of its closest relative parent, again the **Showcase Wrapper** element. Ultimately, the properties for the showcase images should resemble *Figure 4.18*:

Figure 4.18 – Settings for the showcase images

Good job! You've now put together your first **Hero** section! In the top left of the screen, hit the icon in the shape of an eye to preview what your page will look like. It should be looking similar to *Figure 4.19*:

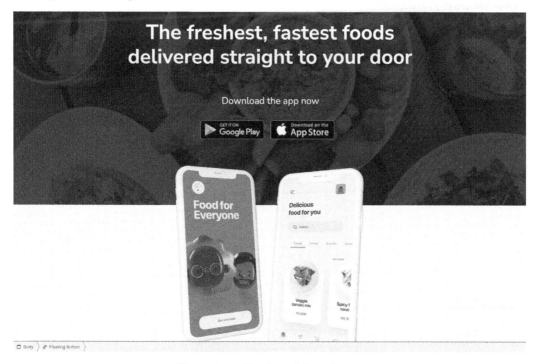

Figure 4.19 – Preview of the web page

It's looking much better!

> **Tip**
>
> You will notice that a portion of these showcase images now extends *below* the fold, that is, you have to scroll to see them in full. I thought we were only designing Above the Fold, you might ask. It turns out that a good thing to think about whenever you're designing web pages is the principle of **continuity**. In other words, how can you tease the user to continue scrolling down the page without explicitly telling them to do so? One way is by doing what we've done here: use large imagery that extends out of view, inviting the user to scroll to view it in full. Subtle but effective!

Before moving on, let's do a quick visual recap of what we just did with the **Position** properties, as shown in *Figure 4.20*:

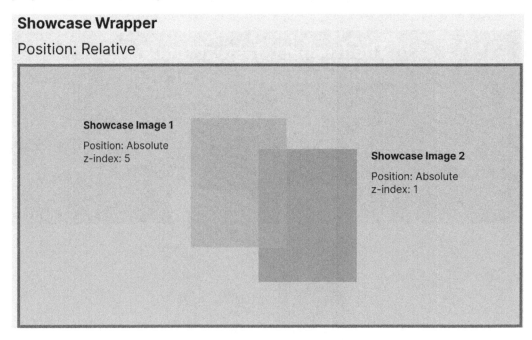

**Showcase Wrapper**

Position: Relative

**Showcase Image 1**

Position: Absolute
z-index: 5

**Showcase Image 2**

Position: Absolute
z-index: 1

Figure 4.20 – Relative and absolute positioning

15. First, we created a **Div Block** element, renamed it Showcase Wrapper, and gave it a **Position** property of Relative. Whenever you know you need to have elements that are positioned as Absolute, it's more likely than not you will need a parent element that is set to Relative. But how can you tell you'll need Absolute positioning? If you know you're going to have elements on the page that overlap one another as we do on our page, that's a telltale sign you're looking at an element that will need Absolute positioning, because it will give you the most flexibility when laying out elements on the page.

16. Next, we added one image and called it Showcase Image 1. We set its **Position** property to Absolute, which essentially told it to *"look for the closest parent that has Position of Relative and use that as a reference point for positioning."* If none of its parents had a position of Relative, then it would've set its positioning relative to the entire page.

17. We then positioned `Showcase Image 1` a certain distance away from the left edge of **Showcase Wrapper**. Next, we changed its **z-index** value to 5. This essentially elevates the element off the page. If you had a stack of papers, for example, then a sheet of paper that has a **z-index** value of `100` will have 99 sheets of paper underneath it. The only difference on a web page is that, unlike a stack of physical paper, you can have multiple elements co-existing on the same z-index layer.

18. Then, we added `Showcase Image 2` and also set its positioning to `Absolute`. This time, we gave this image a **z-index** value of 1. This ensured that it was layered below `Showcase Image 2`. We ended by adjusting its left and top positioning relative to `Showcase Wrapper`.

Note that this view is on the base breakpoint of `1440px`. You can also use the device icons on the top of the page to switch between how the page will be viewed on other breakpoints and screen sizes. If you do so, you'll notice that the page doesn't look as great on other screen sizes as it does on our base breakpoint. We'll take care of this once we start designing for responsiveness soon!

For now, we're not quite done yet. We still have the top navigation menu to add. Let's do that now.

# Adding the navigation menu

As with the **Hero** section, let's start by planning how we can break down the navigation menu into smaller boxes of content. *Figure 4.21* shows one such way we may be able to do it:

Figure 4.21 – The boxes of the top navigation menu

In essence, the navigation menu is one entire box that can be further split up into three smaller boxes: one for the logo, another for the navigation links, and the last one for the **Sign In** and **Sign Up** buttons. Each of these boxes will then have smaller boxes of content inside them.

The following steps will show you how you can achieve this:

1. Select the **Body** element in **Navigator**.

2. Hit the *A* key on your keyboard and select the **Navbar** element in the **Components** section.

3.  The **Navbar** element will be added to the bottom of the page by default. Select it in **Navigator** and drag it right underneath **Body**, as in *Figure 4.22*:

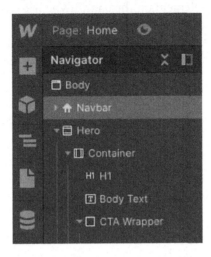

Figure 4.22 – Adding the Navbar element into Body

4.  The **Navbar** element should now be at the top of the page. Select the **Brand** element in the **Navbar**. Hit *A* on your keyboard and select the **Image** element.

5.  Click the **Choose Image** button and select the image called logo.png.

6.  The logo will be inserted at its original size, which is looking quite large at the moment. With the **Image Settings** popup still visible, change the **Height** property to 40px. Your **Navbar** element should now resemble *Figure 4.23*:

Figure 4.23 – Navbar in progress

7.  The logo is aligned to the top whereas we want it aligned with the navigation links. In order to accomplish this, we can use the power of **flexbox**, a modern web capability that provides flexibility in page layouts. To do this, expand the **Navbar** element in **Navigator** and select the **Container** element that is nested in it. We are selecting **Container** because it is the immediate parent or box that contains all the content we're looking to align together. With **Container** selected, over in the **Style** panel, under the **Layout** section, select **Flexbox**.

8.  Next, for the **Align** property, set it to Center. Your menu and properties should resemble *Figure 4.24*:

Figure 4.24 – Setting Flexbox on the Navbar Container element

9.  It's looking better! But there's more we can do. First, notice that the **Container** class name has been automatically changed to Container 2. This is because Webflow is differentiating between this **Container** element and the **Container** element we had created in the **Hero** section. Let's go ahead and give it a better class name. Click the dropdown on the class and rename it to Nav Container, as shown in *Figure 4.25* (though, as always, you can name it anything you want):

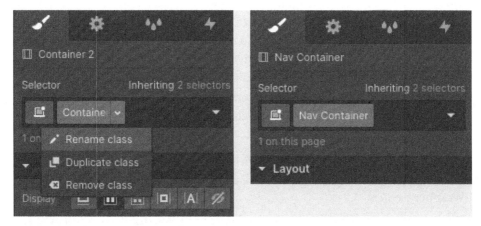

Figure 4.25 – Renaming the class as Nav Container

10. Next, select the first **Nav Link** element that has the **Home** link in it. Give it a class name of Nav Link. Change its font size from its current 24px to 14px.

11. Give the **Nav Link** element that says **About** a class name of Nav Link as well.

12. Delete the third **Nav Link** element, which says **Contact**, since we won't be needing it.

13. As per the original designs, rewrite the **Home** text to say How it works. Similarly, rewrite the **About** text to say Features.

14. Now, select the **Nav Menu** element in **Navigator**. Hit the *A* key on your keyboard and select the **Dropdown** element. Give this element a class name of Nav Dropdown. Change its font size to 14px. The **Navbar** element should now resemble *Figure 4.26*:

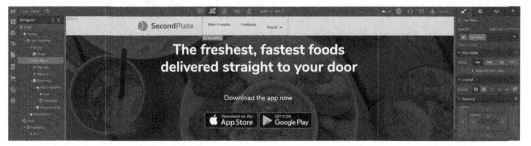

Figure 4.26 – The updated Navbar element

15. The links don't look aligned anymore. Just as before, however, we can fix this by setting a **Flexbox** property on the links. Select the **Nav Menu** element again, since this is the parent of the links we want to affect. Now, change its **Display** layout property to **Flexbox** and **Align** to **Center**. The links should now be all vertically centered in the **Navbar** element.

16. We still have the **Sign In** and **Sign Up** buttons to add. First, let's add the **Div** element that they will be grouped in. Select the **Nav Menu** element in **Navigator**. Next, hit *A* on your keyboard and select the **Div Block** element.

17. Give the new **Div Block** element a class name of Buttons Wrapper.

18. Now, copy one of the existing **Nav Link** elements and paste it into the **Buttons Wrapper** element.

19. While you have the **Buttons Wrapper** element selected, hit *A* on your keyboard and add the **Button** element. Give this new **Button** element a class name of Sign Up Button.

20. Give the **Sign Up Button** element **Left** and **Right** padding of 32px and **Top** and **Bottom** padding of 12px. Then, change its **Size** property to 14px. The properties should resemble *Figure 4.27*:

Figure 4.27 – Properties of the Sign Up Button element

21. Finally, let's give the button a gradient color to match the original design. With the **Sign Up Button** element selected, go to the **Backgrounds** section and click on the **Image & gradient** property.

22. Select the left handle on the color picker and give it a **HEX** value of #f3bc68.

23. Select the right handle on the color picker and give it a **HEX** value of #dd1e6d.

24. Change the **Angle** property of the color gradient to 130 DEG. The color properties should now resemble *Figure 4.28*:

Figure 4.28 – Color gradient properties for Sign Up Button element

25. In order to make sure these new links are center-aligned, select the **Buttons Wrapper** element and change its **Display** property to Flexbox. Then, change the **Align** property to Center.

26. The navigation menu is looking good, but the three sections of the menu (that is, the logo, the links, and the buttons) appear too closely packed to each other, as in *Figure 4.29*:

Figure 4.29 – The updated Navbar element

27. Select the **Nav Container** element. Give it a **Max Width** property of 1200px. Set its **Display** property to Flexbox.

28. Change its **Align** property to Center. Next, change its **Justify** property to Space Between. This will ensure all the elements are evenly spaced with relation to each other in their parent element.

29. The **Nav Links** and **Buttons Wrapper** elements are still too close together. Click the **Buttons Wrapper** element and give it a **Left Margin** property of 64px.

30. Now, select the **Navbar** element. Under the **Background** section in the **Style** panel, change its background color to **White**.

31. Next, under the **Typography** section, click on **More type options** and select the **Capitalize** text effect. This will ensure that all text in the **Navbar** element will be capitalized as in the original designs. See *Figure 4.30* for the updated **Typography** properties for the **Navbar** element:

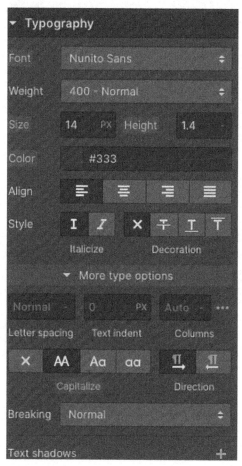

Figure 4.30 – Typography properties

32. The last thing we need to do in the **Navbar** element is to finish the **About Dropdown** element. Select it now. Then, in the right-hand panel, select the **Element Settings** tab. You can also select it by hitting the *D* key on your keyboard.

33. In the **Dropdown Settings** section, click on the **Open Menu** button. This will open up a dropdown on the page, revealing three links, as shown in *Figure 4.31*:

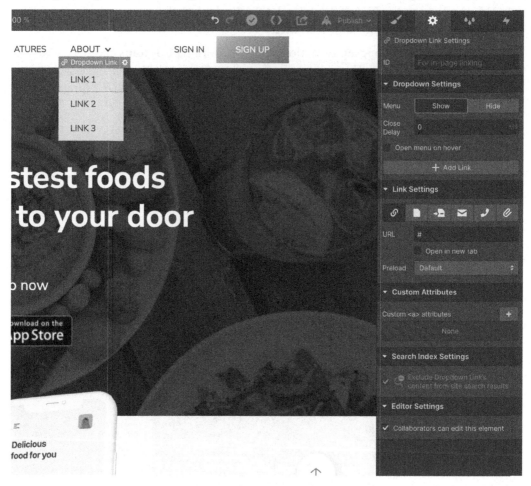

Figure 4.31 – Opening the drop-down menu

34. In the opened drop-down menu, change **LINK 1** to Our Story, **LINK 2** to FAQs, and **LINK 3** to Careers.

35. Click the **Open Menu** button again to close the **Dropdown** element.

Your navigation menu is now complete! It should look very similar to *Figure 4.32*. Give yourself a good pat on the back, as we've covered a lot of concepts:

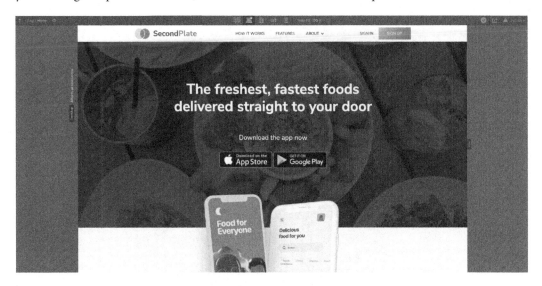

Figure 4.32 – The finished Navbar

But one thing that stands out is that the header in the **Hero** section now looks too close to the navigation menu. We can quickly fix this.

Select the **Hero** element. Give it a **Top Padding** property of 120px.

Preview your page now by clicking the little eye icon in the top left of your screen. It should resemble *Figure 4.33*. You can even click on the **About** dropdown to preview how the drop-down menu behaves:

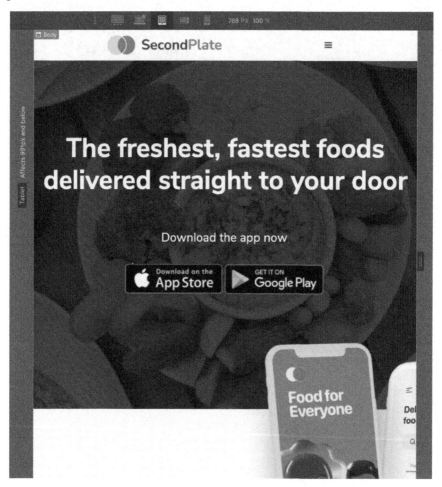

Figure 4.33 – How everything looks Above the Fold

Now, try viewing the page on other breakpoints by clicking the tablet or phone icons at the top of the page. As you can see, the page doesn't look great in other device sizes!

Let's finally turn our attention to addressing this and making the page fully responsive.

# Making it responsive

Making pages responsive in Webflow is easier than it sounds, but it does require being thoughtful and deliberate.

One of the main ideas, as explained before, is to always start from the base breakpoint. In this case, our base breakpoint started at `1440px`, which is the typical size of many non-retina laptop screens.

Any styles set on this breakpoint will cascade down to smaller screen sizes. This is why when you switch to tablet or mobile breakpoints, the layouts of the page look wrong; they are blindly applying the same layouts of the base breakpoint to the smaller screens.

In order to ensure the page is fully responsive, we'll adjust the layouts on each breakpoint, starting with the tablet.

## Tablet breakpoint

When you switch to the tablet screen, you'll see something resembling *Figure 4.34*:

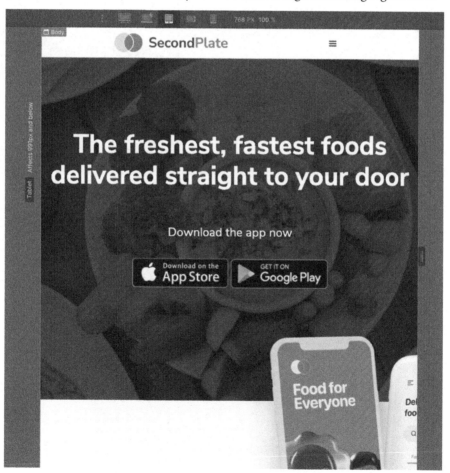

Figure 4.34 – Tablet breakpoint

For the most part, it doesn't look too bad. Webflow even does some of the work for you and conveniently collapses the menu links into a hamburger menu. However, if you open the menu up, you'll notice some of the elements are misaligned and could use some cleaning up. Besides the menu, we'll also need to make the heading a little smaller and realign the showcase images.

So, let's switch out of the preview mode and jump right in:

1.  Click the **H1 Heading** element in the **Hero** section. Click on **Size** to reduce the font to 48px.

2.  Next, select the **Showcase Wrapper** element. Change its **Max W** property to 75%.

3.  Next, select the **Menu Button** element. In order to view it in an open state, click on the **Element Settings** tab or hit the *D* key on your keyboard. Click the **Open Menu** button. The navigation menu should resemble *Figure 4.35*:

Figure 4.35 – The tablet navigation menu

Select the **Buttons Wrapper** element. Switch back to the **Settings** tab. Notice that the **Left Margin** property is set to 64px. This value is being inherited from the base breakpoint. Set this value to 0:

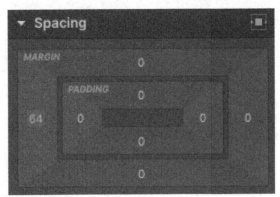

Figure 4.36 – Inherited Left Margin property of 64px

4.  Now, select the **Sign Up Button** element. Change its **Width** property to 250px and give it a **Left Margin** property of 20px.

5.  Next, select the **Buttons Wrapper** element again and give it a **Bottom Padding** of 24px.

6.  Finally, select the **Nav Menu** element and change its **Background Color** property to the #e9e9e9 **HEX** code. Before closing the color picker window, click the + icon. This will add the **HEX** code as a new color swatch that you can reuse later in this project. Webflow will intelligently give it a color name, but you can name it whatever you want. In my case, Webflow named it White Smoke, which I'm going to keep:

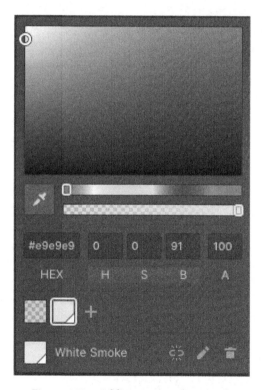

Figure 4.37 – Adding a new color swatch

And that's it! Now, when you preview the Tablet breakpoint, it should look better, as shown in *Figure 4.38*:

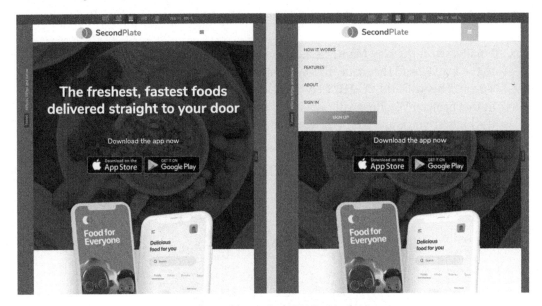

Figure 4.38 – The updated Tablet breakpoint

---

**Tip**

You likely would've noticed by now that some property values are highlighted in an amber color while others are highlighted in blue. Properties in amber are those that have been inherited from another source, usually a parent element or a higher breakpoint. If you click on any amber property, Webflow will inform you from where that value is being inherited.

Blue properties, on the other hand, are values that have been explicitly set on the current element in the current breakpoint you're viewing. These values override any existing inherited values.

---

## Mobile Landscape breakpoint

When you switch to the next breakpoint, the Mobile Landscape, you'll notice it doesn't look so bad. Even when you open up the menu, there doesn't seem to be much work to do. That's because it's using the values from its next highest breakpoint, that is, the tablet breakpoint, which we had just completed. Those values seem to be working well for this breakpoint as well.

The only thing that could use a little tweaking is the showcase images. Let's get to them now:

1.  Select the **Showcase Image 1** element. In the **Size** section of the **Style** panel, change the **Height** property to 380px.

2.  Now, select the **Showcase Image 2** element and, just as before, change its **Height** value, this time to 380px.

And since everything else on the page looks good, that takes care of the Mobile Landscape breakpoint!

## Mobile Portrait breakpoint

Once you switch to the narrowest breakpoint, the Mobile Portrait, you'll notice there are a lot more things that need attention, as is often the case with small screen sizes.

So, let's get right into it!

1.  Select the **H1 Header** element in the **Hero** section. Set its font **Size** property to 30px.

2.  Next, select the **Body Text** element and set its font **Size** property to 20px.

3.  Select the **Hero** element. Change its **Top Padding** property to 64px.

4.  Next, select the **Showcase Wrapper** element and change its **Max W** property to 100%.

5.  Now, select **Showcase Image 1**. Change its **Height** value to 300px.

6.  Change the **Left** position to 0.

7.  Next, select **Showcase Image 2**. Change its **Height** value to 300px.

8.  Change its positioning to the right side so that it's positioned at 0 from the right edge.

Following these steps, the properties of the showcase images should resemble *Figure 4.39*:

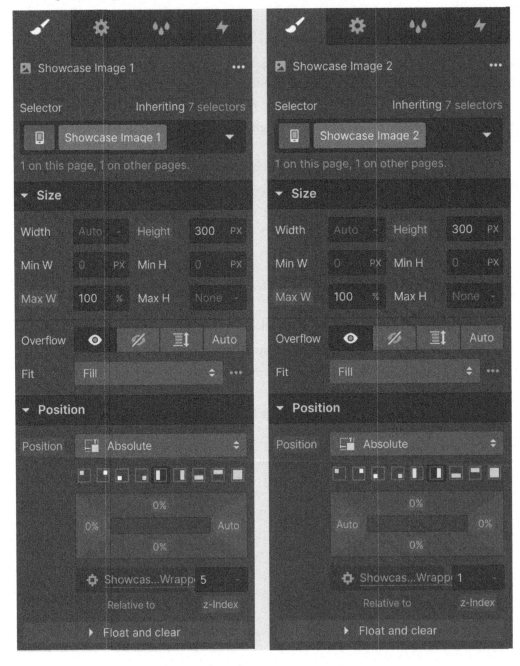

Figure 4.39 – The Mobile Portrait properties of the showcase image elements

And now, when you preview the Mobile Portrait breakpoint, it should look good, as shown in *Figure 4.40*:

Figure 4.40 – Preview of the Mobile Portrait breakpoint

While it may seem we've covered all the breakpoints, there is in fact one more that is worth considering. With modern retina screens and large monitors, the screen width of `1920px` is becoming more and more commonplace. And in order to make sure our designs look good on those larger screens, it is worth adding that extra breakpoint. Let's take a closer look at how to design responsively for larger screens.

> **Important Note**
>
> Remember that any changes you create on a breakpoint will get cascaded down to smaller breakpoints. That is why it's also important to make sure you always start designing and building on the base breakpoint, as it will save you a lot of time when designing responsively at smaller breakpoints. Moreover, if you then make adjustments on smaller breakpoints, the larger ones will not be affected by them, as changes do not cascade up.
>
> And so, when you add a breakpoint that is *larger* than the base breakpoint, the changes you have on the base breakpoint will not apply to the larger one. That's why you need to explicitly design for larger breakpoints and not depend on values from smaller breakpoints to cascade upwards.

## Large screen size breakpoint

Let's go ahead and set up a large breakpoint and then adapt our design to it:

1.  On the top of your screen, click on the ellipses menu to the left of the **Base breakpoint** icon. This will reveal a popup, as shown in *Figure 4.41*. Choose the breakpoint at 1920px:

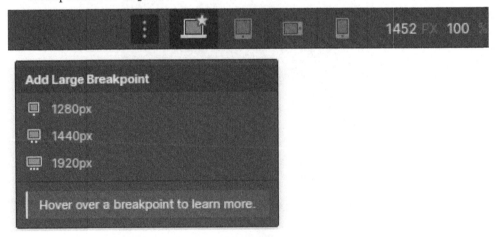

Figure 4.41 – Adding a large breakpoint

2.  Select the **Showcase Image 1** element. Change its **Height** value to 640px and its **Left Position** value to 0.

3.  Next, select the **Showcase Image 2** element. Change its **Height** value to 640px and its **Right Position** value to 0.

And with that, your new large-screen breakpoint has been set up, and the design works just as well on it too! It should look similar to *Figure 4.42*:

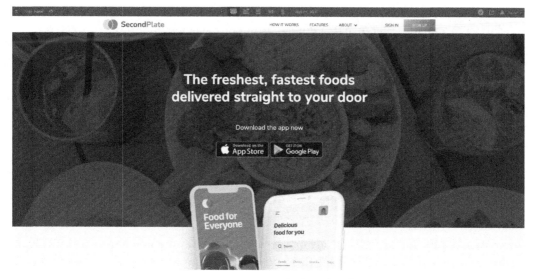

Figure 4.42 – Previewing the large breakpoint

> **Important Note**
>
> While we covered the main breakpoints, in actuality, screens today come in a plethora of sizes. In Webflow, while you're in the **Design** view, you can drag the sides of your page window up and down to reveal a slider that shows the various screen sizes and breakpoints, including all the way down to a Nintendo handheld gaming system. Designing responsively for all of them is a skill set that takes time, practice, and continuous improvement. And while there are advanced ways to design and develop responsively to take into account this complexity, they are beyond the scope of this book. That said, don't be worried that you haven't accounted for all screen sizes. In practice, you should be ensuring first and foremost the screen sizes that your primary audience will be using and making sure that your designs look great on them. You are encouraged to explore some other breakpoints and how you can update your page to work responsively on them.

Congratulations! You've completed developing the portion of your first website that is Above the Fold. It's time to take a breather. You've earned it!

# Summary

In this chapter, we developed the portion of a website that is commonly known as *Above the Fold*, which is the portion that is visible before you scroll the page. We used our design mockups as a valuable reference that guided us in our development. In the process, we covered a lot of important concepts, some of which may have been completely new to you.

We took a look at how we can plan our development by thinking about how to break up our preexisting designs (if available) into boxes of content. Then, we split up the page into two main sections, the navigation menu and the **Hero** section, starting with the latter.

We explored how to add elements from containers to background images and links. We learned how to style them, add classes to them, and how to lay them out.

We saw the difference between static positioning, relative positioning, and absolute positioning. We then turned our attention to the navigation menu, starting with our breakdown of how to lay out the content boxes inside of it.

In building out the menu, we took advantage of flexbox to lay out and align the individual elements. We got introduced to using drop-down elements and buttons. Next, we spent some time making our page responsive across various screen sizes. We looked at the need to start everything from the base breakpoint and how to take advantage of the fact that changes cascade down from larger breakpoints to smaller ones.

Finally, after making the pages responsive on tablet and mobile screens, we added a large breakpoint to account for modern high-resolution screens. Believe it or not, this chapter introduced you to a large chunk of everything you need to know in order to create great websites in Webflow. From here on, it's a matter of repeating a number of steps and adapting to new contexts and needs.

In the next chapter, we'll finish building the rest of the website on the base breakpoint. We'll go faster than we did in this chapter, as a lot of it is a repetition of concepts. But again, just like getting your reps in at the gym, it's important to go through the motions. And even though we'll be applying the same concepts, we'll uncover new layouts and be introduced to some new elements along the way.

After you've taken a much-deserved break, let's hop on to *Chapter 5, Building the Rest of the Body*!

# 5
# Building the Rest of the Body

In the previous chapter, you successfully built out the **Hero** section (or everything **Above the Fold**) and made it responsive across tablet and mobile screens. In that section alone, we learned about a lot of the main features and capabilities of Webflow.

In this chapter, we'll continue building the rest of the SecondPlate landing page. By the end of this chapter, you'll have practiced some more of the basic Webflow skills and built upon them as we dive deeper into a range of concepts.

We'll only be focused on the base breakpoint, however. In the next chapter, we'll focus exclusively on making it responsive.

The topics we'll cover in this chapter include the following:

- Building a **How it Works** section that showcases product mockups and descriptions, all while utilizing the power of flexbox
- Using the grid layout to build a collection of cards that explains the main features of the app

- Building the main **Call to Action** (**CTA**) section, which will showcase how to use gradient backgrounds and relative positioning, among other skills
- Building the footer of the page, which will give us more opportunity to explore the additional features of flexbox
- How to develop responsively across multiple screen sizes

As mentioned before, a lot of the steps will feel repeated, but reps are the best way to build your Webflow muscles. Along the way, you'll see the same techniques being used in new ways, and we'll introduce brand-new capabilities as well.

Let's jump in!

# Technical requirements

As before, you can access all the required assets for this project from the following link:

`https://github.com/PacktPublishing/Webflow-by-Example/tree/main/Chapter03/Assets`

For details on how to upload the assets into the project, please refer back to *Chapter 3, Setting Up Your First Project*.

If you've already set up, move on to the next step.

# Adding the How it Works section

The first section that we'll be starting with is titled *How it Works*. Many landing pages feature this as a showcase of the main steps a user takes to get the value of a product. In our case, we'll be showcasing three separate features of the SecondPlate app, each feature showing a product mockup and some supportive text. We'll see how to use layout features and how to reuse content.

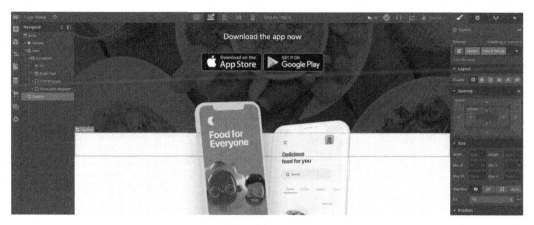

Figure 5.1 – Adding a new section

Execute the following steps to add the section:

1. As shown in *Figure 5.1*, select the **Body** element and add a new **Section** element. While having this new **Section** selected, go to the **Style** pane on the right and select the **Selector** text box. Inside it, type **Section** to give the **Section** element a class name of `Section`. Next, let's add a second class by typing `How it Works`. This creates what's called a **combo class**. We'll dive deeper into what combo classes are later, but for now, suffice it to say that a combo class serves to uniquely identify elements.

2. With the **Section** element selected, add a **Container** element. Give it a class name of `Container`.

3.  Select the **Container** element and add a **Heading** element; set it to **H2**. Give it a class name of `Header`. Give it a font size of `36px` and rewrite it as `How it Works`:

Figure 5.2 – Adding the How it Works header

4.  Center-align the **Header** element and give it a **Top Margin** property of `140px` and **Bottom Margin** property of `96px`.

5.  Add a **Div Block** element inside the `Container` element. Give **Div Block** a class of `Step Row`.

6.  Inside **Step Row**, add another **Div Block** element and give it a class name of `Step Image`.

7.  Select the **Step Image** element and add an **Image Block** element inside of it. Add the image called `iPhone-1.png`. Change its class name to `Step Image 1`.

8.  Inside **Step Row**, add another **Div Block** element and give it a class name of `Step Description`.

9.  Inside **Step Description**, add **Text Block** and give it a class name of `Step Caption`. Double-click the text inside of **Text Block** and replace it with `Create an account`.

10. Give it a **Font size** property of 14px.

11. Change its color to match the color in the design: #fa4f0c.

In *Figure 5.3*, you'll note how the color we just chose shows a **Fail** message. This is an example of a feature built into Webflow that makes it easier to choose colors that pass accessibility requirements. In this case, Webflow is essentially telling us that the red color we chose is not contrasted well enough against the background color, making it tough to see, especially for people with visibility impairments. We need to darken the red so that it is better contrasted against the white background:

Figure 5.3 – Color contrast tool for accessibility tests

12. You can either choose any darker red color in the color selector until the **Contrast ratio** value is high enough that it passes the accessibility requirement, or you can just go ahead and change the **HEX** code to #ce3f07. Note that it now passes the accessibility requirement.

> **Important Note**
>
> **Accessibility** is an important and large topic. The general principle is that everything we design and build should be usable by anyone, regardless of their capabilities. In fact, it turns out that when you design websites and apps while keeping in mind the accessibility needs of people, everyone benefits.
>
> Common accessibility concerns include color contrasts, text legibility, alternative text entries for images, and keyboard usability. While we won't be devoting specific sections to these concepts, for the most part, we will try to ensure that our designs are accessible. It is generally a good habit to cultivate.
>
> Today, the main international standards for accessibility for the web are published under the **Web Content Accessibility Guidelines (WCAG)**. Webflow's color contrast tool that we just saw complies with WCAG 2.0 AA standards. Under these standards, body text, for example, needs to have a color **Contrast ratio** property of 4 . 5 for it to pass.
>
> You can read more about WCAG standards at this URL: `https://www.w3.org/WAI/standards-guidelines/wcag/`.

13. Now that we've found an accessible color, add it as a new swatch, as shown in *Figure 5.4*. This will become the red color that we can reuse throughout the page:

Figure 5.4 – Adding a new accessible color swatch

14. Note that the text that says **Create an account** is now sitting below the image, as shown in *Figure 5.5*:

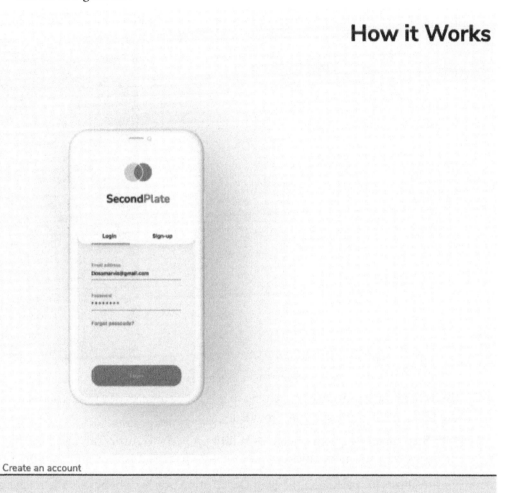

Figure 5.5 – Content by default gets stacked on top of each other

This is because it's behaving like a block item, which means it's going to start stacking on top of other content. Let's fix this so that it's aligned side by side with the image.

15. Select **Step Row**. Select its **Layout** property to be **Flexbox**.

Now they should be side by side. But you may notice that **Create an account** is now positioned all the way to the right edge of the **Step Row** block, as shown in *Figure 5.6*:

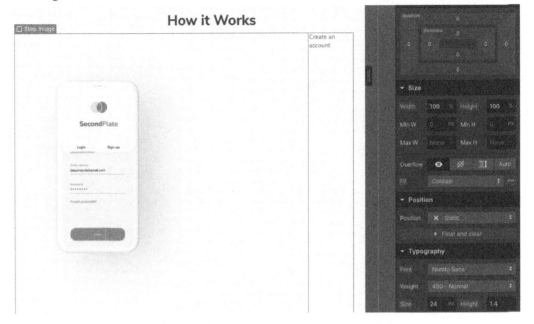

Figure 5.6 – Flexbox content tries to spread out by default

This is because **Step Image** is likely set to a **Width** property of 100%. This is telling it to fill as much of the space as provided.

16. With **Step Image** selected, change its **Width** property to **Auto**. This specifies that the image will only automatically take as much space as it is wide and no more.

Now it adjusts properly, and the **Step Description** box is right next to the image, as shown in *Figure 5.7*:

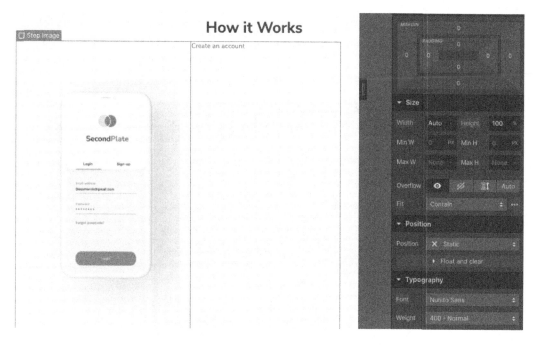

Figure 5.7 – Setting width to Auto

17. As you can see, though, the image is still rather big. This is because the original size of the image we're using was big to begin with. Let's override this. Select the **Step Image 1** element and access the **Image Settings** by clicking on the cog icon next to the element's name. Then, set its **Width** property to 600px. This should adjust the size of the image appropriately.

18. Next, select the **Step Description** element, add a **Heading** element, and set it to **H3**. Rename the class for the **Heading** element to **Step Heading**. Give it a font size of 32px. Rewrite it to say Create/login to an existing account to get started.

19. Inside of the **Step Direction** element, add a **Text Block** element. Give it a class name of Body Text and a combo class of Dark.

20. With the `Body Text` element selected, give it a color with #727272 as the **HEX** code. As before, note that it is accessible and passes the **AAA** standard, the highest rating we can get. Great! Add it as a new swatch and call it `Text Grey`, as shown in *Figure 5.8*:

Figure 5.8 – Adding Text Grey as a new color swatch

21. Note that the text doesn't line up well. This is because it is inheriting the properties of **Body Text**.

    Remove the top margin and left align it. Note it doesn't affect the white **Body Text** element at the top of the page. Thanks to the `Dark` combo class that we added to this **Body Text** element, any changes we make to it only apply to this specific element and not all the other **Body Text** elements:

# How it Works

Create an account

## Create/login to an existing account to get started

▣ Body Text

An account is created with your email and desired password.

Figure 5.9 – Using combo classes to affect specific instances of an element

But now the content on the right is not aligned with the phone mockup image. Let's fix that.

22. Select **Step Description** and set its **Display** property to **Flex**. Align it vertically and click on **Justify** to move it to the center, as shown in *Figure 5.10*:

Figure 5.10 – Vertically aligning content with flexbox

The text is looking a little too wide in comparison to the image. Fix this by giving **Step Description** left and right padding values of 80px. It should resemble *Figure 5.11*:

Figure 5.11 – Adding padding to the content

23. We've now completed a single row in this section. But we'll need two more. Luckily, Webflow allows us to duplicate content easily. Select the **Step Row** block and hit *Ctrl + C* and *Ctrl + V* to copy and paste a duplicate of it (or *Cmd + C* and *Cmd + V* if you're on a Mac).

    Note that a second instance of **Step Row** is created with the exact items in it. But we need to switch the orientation of the image and text in this second instance so that it matches the original designs.

24. Select the second **Step Row** block from **Navigator** and open it. Select the **Step Image** block inside of it and, while having it selected, drag it below the **Step Description** block. That's it! You now have a second instance of **Step Row**, only this one has a swapped orientation, as shown in *Figure 5.12*:

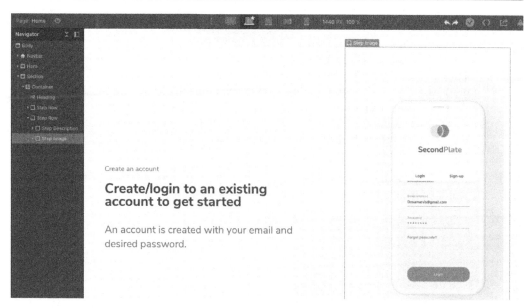

Figure 5.12 – Duplicating content and swapping its orientation

Now, let's update the content in this second **Step Row** block.

25. Select the **Step Image 1** element. In the **Style** panel, select the `Step Image 1` class name and select **Duplicate Class**. Give it a class name of `Step Image 2`, as shown in *Figure 5.13*:

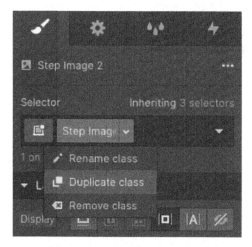

Figure 5.13 – Duplicating a class

> **Important Note**
>
> When working with multiple instances of the same element, make sure to use the **Duplicate class** selection and *not* the **Rename class** selection on class names. Renaming the class will change all the other elements that have the same class name – something you may not be intending to do. Duplicating it essentially creates a brand-new instance and allows you to set a new class name for only the new instance. This then allows you to make changes to only this single instance, rather than all elements with the class.

26. With the **Step Image 2** element selected, click the cog icon on the element and hit the **Replace Image** button, as shown in *Figure 5.14*:

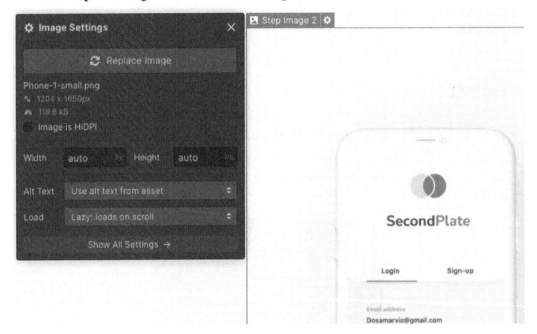

Figure 5.14 – Replacing an image

27. Select Phone-2.png. The image is now appropriately updated.

28. Select the **Step Caption** element and rewrite the text in it to Explore varieties so that it matches the original design.

29. Proceed to update the text in **Step Heading** and **Body Text** accordingly so that it matches *Figure 5.15*:

Figure 5.15 – Varieties section

Now, let's repeat these steps one more time for the third and last row.

30. Select the first **Step Row** block in **Navigator** and duplicate it again by hitting the *Ctrl + C* and *Ctrl + V* keys to copy and paste it (or *Cmd + C* and *Cmd + V* if you're on a Macintosh).

31. Make sure that you move the new **Step Row** block to the bottom of **Navigator**.

32. Select **Step Image 1**, duplicate it, and change its class name to `Step Image 3`.

33. Click the cog icon on **Step Image 3** and replace the image with Phone-3.png.

34. Update the **Step Caption**, **Step Heading**, and **Body Text** elements to match the designs.

The last **Step Row** block should now resemble *Figure 5.16*:

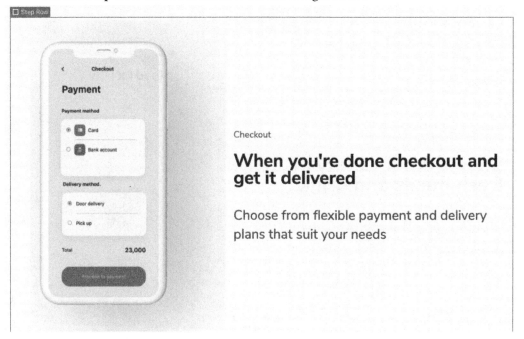

Figure 5.16 – The Checkout section

And we're done with this section!

In building out the **How it Works** section of the landing page, we learned a number of key concepts. We learned about accessibility and how to choose colors with good color contrasts using Webflow's built-in color contrast checker. We also got more hands-on practice with using flexbox and especially saw how it can help to lay out content along a single plane, horizontally or vertically. We also used combo classes to ensure our changes are made to specific instances of elements, rather than across all of them. We saw how to work with images and lay them out nicely alongside text-based content.

We'll continue to see these concepts being reused, so don't worry if some of that felt uncomfortable. We'll be strengthening our understanding of these concepts throughout this chapter.

Now, before we move on to building the next section, now's a good time to preview our work. Go ahead and select the **Preview** button at the top left of the Webflow window. Make sure you're at the base breakpoint. Looking good so far!

In the next section, we'll build the **Main features** section, where we'll specifically get practice using grids. Let's jump in!

# The Main features section

Before we dive headfirst into this section, let's begin by taking a bird's eye view of what it is we'll be building.

The **Main features** section consists of nine content blocks, commonly referred to as cards, arranged in a grid consisting of three columns and three rows. *Figure 5.17* shows what this looks like from the original designs:

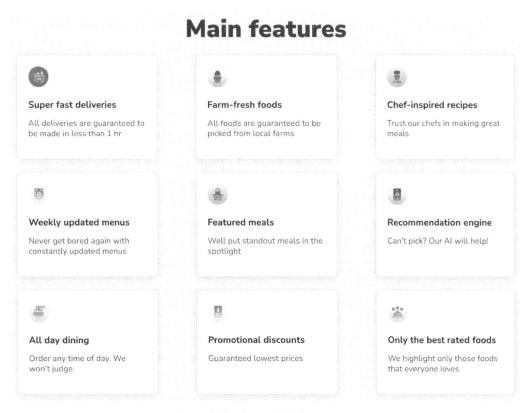

Figure 5.17 – 3x3 grid of feature cards

Each card consists of one icon, one headline, and a short paragraph of text, as shown in *Figure 5.18*:

**Super fast deliveries**

All deliveries are guaranteed to
be made in less than 1 hr

Figure 5.18 – A single content card

As such, this entire section is essentially a content box that contains a 3x3 grid of more content boxes, each of which is a content box of its own.

So, with that, let's start by building the larger grid!

## Creating the grid

As always, make sure you're in the base breakpoint before you start.

1.  Let's start by creating a new section. Select the **Body** element from the **Navigator**. Add a new **Section** element and give it a class of `Section`. Then, give it a second class (or combo class) called `Features`.

2.  With the **Section** element selected, add a **Container** element and give it a class of `Container`.

3.  Select the **Container** element. Add a **Heading** element to it and turn it into an **H2** heading. Rewrite it as `Main Features`.

4.  With the **Container** element selected, add a new **Grid** element inside it. By default, this will create a 2x2 grid. Note that each column has a header that says **1FR**. This refers to what fraction of the total grid space a single column is taking. In this case, the grid is being divided into each of the columns equally with one fraction a piece, as shown in *Figure 5.19*:

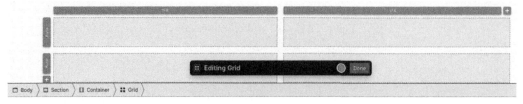

Figure 5.19 – Adding a grid

5.  We need a 3x3 grid based on our initial designs. So, first, click on the red plus icon on the far right of the grid. This will automatically add a new column. Next, click on the red plus icon at the bottom left of the grid. This will add a new row.

6.  Next, select the gap between any of the columns and, while selecting it, drag it so that the space is increased to 72px. Note that as you change one of the gaps, it affects the gaps between all the columns.

7.  Similarly, select a gap between one of the rows and drag it so that it is set to 24px.

> **Tip**
> Note that while you have a grid selected, you can also manipulate the number of columns and rows, including the gaps between them from the side panel, as shown in *Figure 5.20*. Either method works; however, the side panel is typically easier if you know exactly what numbers you want:

Figure 5.20 – Grid properties panel

8.    Click on the blue **Done** button to save your changes to the grid.

We've now created the skeleton of our grid! Let's move on to populating it with content.

## Adding elements to the grid

Now that we've created the grid itself, it's time to start populating it with the individual card items. Each of these cards will be highlighting a specific feature of the SecondPlate app.

1.    With the **Grid** element selected, add a new **Div Block** element and give it a new class name of `Feature Card`.

2.    Select the newly created **Feature Card** element. Give it a background of **White** or `#FFFFFF`. Give it a border radius of `8px`.

3.    With the **Feature Card** element selected, add an **Image** element to it. Select the image called `Serving Cart Icon`. Give it a **Width** property of `40px` and a **Height** property of `40px`.

4.    Select the **Feature Card** element again and, this time, add a **Heading** element. Change it to **H4**. Give this a **Font Size** property of `18px`.

5.    Next, select the **Feature Card** element again and add a **Paragraph** element. Change its **Font Size** property to `16px`. Change its **Font Color** property to `#727272` or, if you had already saved the color swatch from before, you can select that too. Your **Feature Card** element should now be resembling *Figure 5.21*:

Figure 5.21 – Feature Card

6.  It's looking good, but it could use some more padding to give the text some room to breathe. Select the **Feature Card** element and change its **Top**, **Right**, **Bottom**, and **Left Padding** values to 24px. You can change each of them manually or drag one of the values while holding the *Shift* key down.

7.  Let's give the card a drop shadow to give it some depth. Select the **Feature Card** element and, in the **Style** panel, go under the **Effects** section and select **Box shadows**. Give it a **Blur** property of 20px. Select the default **Black** color and bring its opacity down to 8%. The card should now be resembling *Figure 5.22*:

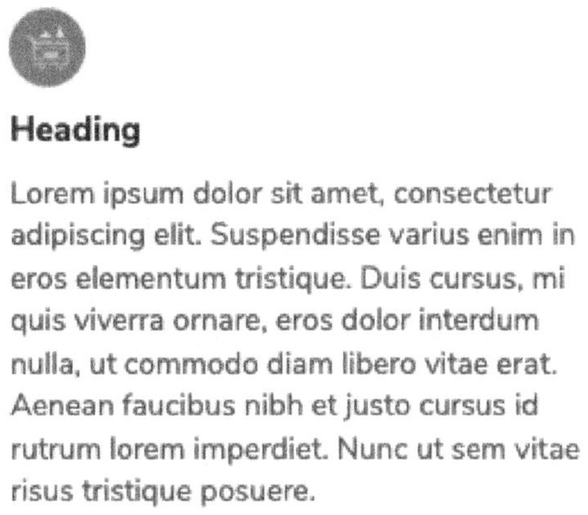

### Heading

Lorem ipsum dolor sit amet, consectetur adipiscing elit. Suspendisse varius enim in eros elementum tristique. Duis cursus, mi quis viverra ornare, eros dolor interdum nulla, ut commodo diam libero vitae erat. Aenean faucibus nibh et justo cursus id rutrum lorem imperdiet. Nunc ut sem vitae risus tristique posuere.

Figure 5.22 – Adding some padding to the Feature Card element

8.  Since we're going to be reusing this card across the rest of the grid, we need to give each card a specific identifier so that we can tell them apart. As such, give the **Feature Card** element a combo class and call it 1 (or anything you want).

9.  Now, select the **Feature Card** element, and copy it by hitting *Ctrl + C* if you're on a PC or *Cmd + C* if you're on a Macintosh. Then, hit *Ctrl + V* or *Cmd + V* to paste it. Paste it eight times in total. Note that as you paste it, each new copy is being automatically pasted into its proper location in the grid. It should resemble *Figure 5.23* when you're done:

Figure 5.23 – The full grid of feature cards

10. Keep in mind that each of these **Feature Card** elements has a combo class of 1. As we've seen before, what this means is that if you change any one card, the change will be replicated across all the cards. We don't want this. Select the second **Feature Card** element, select the dropdown next to its combo class, select **Duplicate Class** as shown in *Figure 5.24*, and rename the duplicated class to 2:

Figure 5.24 – Duplicating the combo class

11. Repeat this for all the cards, making sure that you're renaming the combo classes from 2 to 9 for all nine **Feature Card** copies. Now, when you change each card, the changes will only be made to that specific card.

12. Go ahead and update each of the icons and text labels in each of the cards to match the initial design. When you're done, it should resemble *Figure 5.25*:

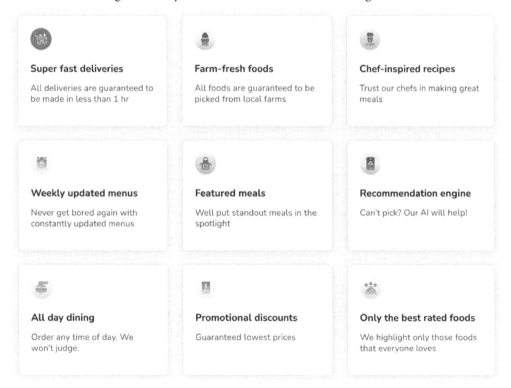

Figure 5.25 – The completed grid of feature cards

Good job! **Features Grid** is done! You've learned how to set up a grid, customize it, and create content inside of it.

We've now covered how to use both flex and grid layouts to organize content on a page. But how do you know when to use flex and when to use grid?

As a guiding principle, you can think of the following, as shown in *Figure 5.26*:

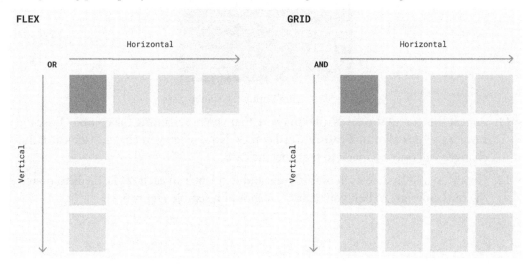

Figure 5.26 – Flex versus grid

Whenever you need to layout content along a single dimension, whether horizontally or vertically, flex is the way to go. Whenever you need to layout content along both dimensions, horizontally and vertically, a grid layout would serve you best.

Note that you probably could use multiple flex implementations to achieve the effect of a grid, and you could use a simple grid to lay out content across a single row or column, but either of these options would be overkill. It's best to use the layout type that is most appropriate for the context you're faced with.

Now, let's move on to the second-last section of the page, the CTA section.

# Adding the final CTA section

This section will be the site's final attempt at convincing the user to download the app. It features bold colors, an image, and some buttons that will allow the user to download the app. When finished, the section will resemble *Figure 5.27*:

Figure 5.27 – The CTA section

As always, let's quickly take a look at how we can break this down into its parts, as shown in *Figure 5.28*:

Figure 5.28 – The content boxes of the CTA section

First, we'll split the content into two general areas, the left and the right. On the left, we'll further split the content into the text and the CTA buttons. On the right, we'll have the image. Note also that the image overlaps the background a little. We've already covered how we can achieve this effect in *Chapter 4, Building Above the Fold*, when we were doing the *Above the Fold* section. We'll cover it again here to reinforce some key concepts.

Okay, now that we've covered the general action plan, let's begin!

1.  As usual, select the **Body** element and add a new **Section** element. Give it a class name of `Section`. Give it a combo class of `Final CTA` as well. Give it a **Top Margin** property of `224px`.

2.  Let's give the **Section** element a gradient background color. Select the **Section** element; in the **Style** panel, in the **Backgrounds** section, select the **Image & gradient** option and select the **Linear gradient** type, as shown in *Figure 5.29*:

Figure 5.29 – Adding a linear gradient background

3.  For one end of the color gradient, select a **Color** property of `#fc7743`. For the opposite end of the spectrum, select a **Color** property of `#f31e77`.

4.  Give the gradient an angle of `132` degrees. The settings should resemble *Figure 5.30*:

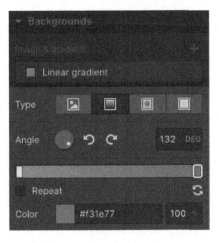

Figure 5.30 – Adding a color spectrum

5. Next, select the **Section** element and add a **Container** element to it. Give the **Container** element a class of `Container`.

6. Select the **Container** element and add a **Heading** element. Make it an **H2** heading. Rewrite it as `Dishes so good you won't be able to settle for a single plate`. Give it a font color of **White**. The section should now resemble *Figure 5.31*:

Figure 5.31 – The section with the gradient background added

7. It's looking a little cramped, but before we address that, let's add the **Download** buttons. Recall that we've already done this before in the **Hero** section of our page. Go back up to the **Hero** section and select the **CTA Wrapper** element, as shown in *Figure 5.32*:

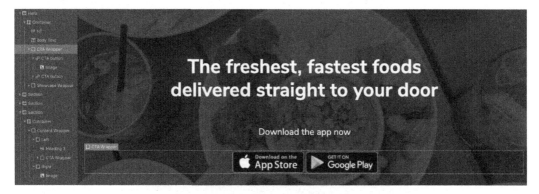

Figure 5.32 – The CTA buttons in the Hero section

8.  Copy and paste the **CTA Wrapper** element right under the **H2 Heading** element you had created in *step 6*.

9.  The buttons are looking big and centered, so we'll need to change that. However, because we want the change to only affect this instance of **CTA Wrapper** and not the one in the **Hero** section, we're going to have to add a combo class to this. Go ahead and create a combo class called `mini`, as shown in *Figure 5:33*:

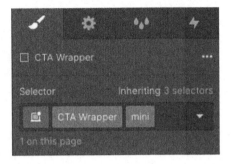

Figure 5.33 – Adding a new combo class

10. Now, while this new instance of the **CTA Wrapper** element is selected, change its alignment to **Left** and use the cog icons on each of the **Image** elements to change the button heights to `54px`, as shown in *Figure 5:34*:

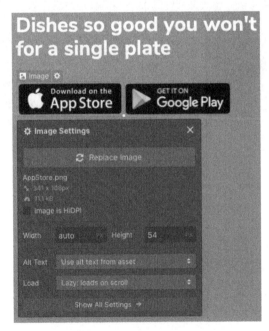

Figure 5.34 – Adding the CTA buttons

11. Now that we've got the left side of this section's content done, let's wrap it together in a self-contained box of its own. Select the **Container** element. Now add a new **Div block** element and give it a class name of `Left`. Drag the **H2** element and the **CTA Wrapper** element under the left **Div block** element so that they are now children of **Left**.

12. Let's now go ahead and add a wrapper for the right side, which is where the image will go. Select the **Container** element again and add a new **Div block** element to it. Give it a class name of `Right`.

13. Select the right **Div block** element and add an **Image** element to it. Select the image labeled `girl-dining.png`. Your section should now resemble *Figure 5:35*:

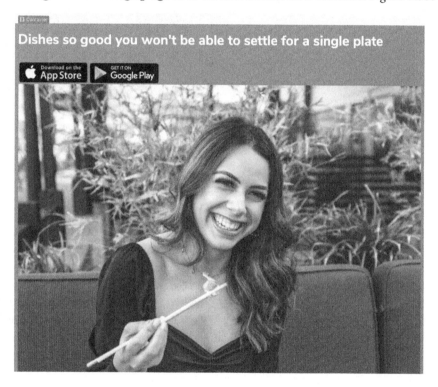

Figure 5.35 – Adding the image to the section

14. These items are getting stacked on top of each other, which is not what we want. To fix that, let's first wrap up the left and right **Div block** elements so that we can contain them together. First, select the **Container** element again and create a new **Div block** element. Give it a class name of `Content Wrapper`. Drag the left and right **Div block** elements under the **Content Wrapper** element.

15. Select the **Content Wrapper** element and change its **Display** property to **Flex**. You'll suddenly notice that the content elements are now laid out side by side, as shown in *Figure 5.36*:

Figure 5.36 – Changing the Content Wrapper element to flex display

16. Note, however, that in the original design, the image overlaps the section background a little bit, which provides an attractive feeling of depth. Let's achieve this effect. Select the **Right** element. Change its **Position** property to **Relative**. Note that the element is now considered to be relative to itself. This means that we now have the ability to manipulate its placement relative to where it would be placed by default, which is what you see now. As such, go ahead and change its **Bottom** positioning property to 64px. This pushes the 64px element up from where it would have been placed by default, as shown in *Figure 5.37*:

Figure 5.37 – Manipulating the image with relative positioning

17. This is looking great! Let's give this element a little more breathing room. Select the **Right** element again and give it **Left** and **Right** padding properties of 64px. Much better.

18. Now, the content in the **Left** element is looking a little too close to the top. Select the **Left** element and give it a **Top padding** property of 96px.

19. Let's also give it some additional padding on the right so that the text looks more balanced. Select the **Left** element and give it a **Right padding** property of 48px.

Well done! If you preview your page at your base breakpoint, your entire section should now resemble *Figure 5.38*:

Figure 5.38 – The completed CTA section

Although this section did not contain too many items, we learned and reinforced some key concepts. We used flex to lay out content, created color gradients, and dove deeper into how to use relative positioning to manipulate the positioning of content in interesting ways.

We're now left with the last section of SecondPlate's web page, the footer. Let's continue.

# Adding the footer section

The last section of this page is a simple footer. Footers are on almost every website, and although they may seem like an afterthought, well-designed footers provide shortcuts to key pages that visitors may find useful. In this case, SecondPlate's footer will simply contain links to its social media accounts. We'll see how we can achieve this.

Again, as always, let's begin by drafting out a plan of action for how we'll break up the content. As seen in *Figure 5.39*, we can break the footer up into these sections:

- The outer section
- The footer container
- The logo on the left

- The social media icons in the center

- The copyright text on the right

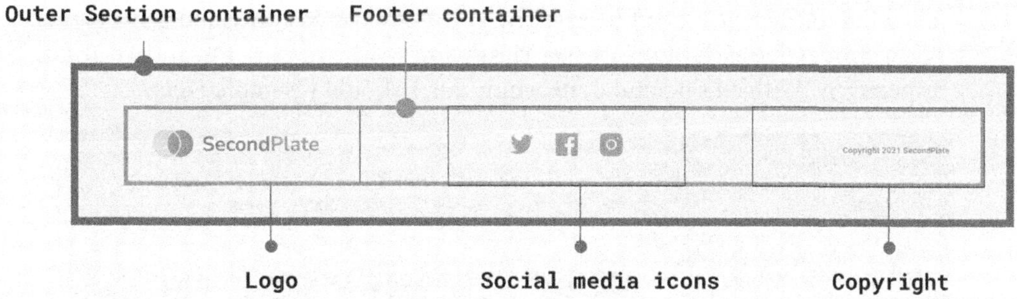

Figure 5.39 – The content boxes of the footer section

Also, note the layout of the content; we'll be putting these elements in a straight line along a single row.

Pop quiz: what layout positioning do you think we'll use to lay these out? Static, flex, or grid? Give it a thought before moving on.

And now, let's jump into building it out!

1.  Select the **Body** element. Add a new **Section** element. Give it a class name of Section and a combo class of Footer.

2.  Select the **Footer** section and add a **Container** element. Give it a class name of Container.

3.  With the **Container** element selected, add a new **Div Block** element. Give this a class name of Footer Wrapper. We'll be using this **Div Block** element to contain all the content elements that will make up our footer.

4.  Select the **Footer Wrapper** element. Add an **Image** element and give it a class name of Footer Logo.

5.  For this image, select the file called logo.png in **Image Settings** and change its **Width** property to 240px.

6.  Select the **Footer Wrapper** element again and, this time, add a new **Div Block** element to it. Give it a class name of `Social Icons`.

7.  Select the **Social Icons** element. Add three new **Image** elements to it and add the following image icons: `twitter-icon.png`, `fb-icon.png`, and `instagram-icon.png`. Give each of the images class names of `Twitter`, `FB`, and `Instagram` respectively. With all said and done, your footer should resemble *Figure 5.40*:

Figure 5.40 – The Footer Wrapper looking stacked with content

8.  The icons don't have links associated with them yet. Let's do that now. Select the **Social Icons** element. Inside, add a **Link Block** element and give it a class name of `Social Link`. Make two more copies of the **Link Block** element so that you have three in total. Now, drag each of the social icons into a **Social Link** element so that all three of your **Social Link** elements have a different icon.

9.  Let's add a little bit of space between the icons. Select any **Social Link** element. Change its right-margin property to `16px`. All the **Social Link** elements should now be updated.

10. To add a URL to your icons, select any **Social Link** element and click the cog icon to open the **Link Settings** pop-up window. Here, you can enter your link in the **URL** field. Make sure to select the **Open in new tab** checkbox to ensure that whenever the user clicks on the link, it will not lose the current page. The pop-up window should resemble *Figure 5.41*. Repeat the step for any other links you want to set:

Figure 5.41 – Adding a link

11. Now, let's add the third and last part of the footer in the **Footer Wrapper** element, the copyright text. Select the **Footer Wrapper** element and add a new **Div Block** element. Give it a class name of Copyright.

12. Select the **Copyright** element and add a new **Text Block** element to it. Inside the **Text Block** element, write Copyright © 2021 SecondPlate. If you're on a PC, you can create the © symbol by pressing *Ctrl + Alt + C*, and if you're on a Macintosh, you can insert it by pressing *Option + G*.

13. Select the **Copyright** element and change the **Font size** property to 14px.

14. The content elements are still stacked on top of each other. How can we change this so that they are aligned horizontally? If you guessed flexbox, then you're right! Select the **Footer Wrapper** element and change its **Layout Display** type to **Flex**. They should all now be horizontally aligned and resemble *Figure 5.42*:

Figure 5.42 – Applying flexbox to the Footer Wrapper element

15. With the **Footer Wrapper** element selected, change the **Align** property to *center alignment*.

16. Next, change the **Justify** property to *space between*. This will push the elements out to the ends, leaving equal space between them. All told, the flexbox properties should resemble *Figure 5.43*:

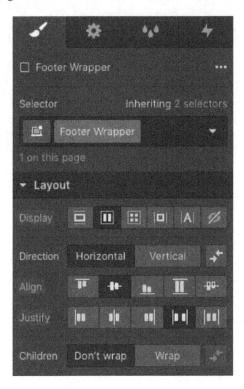

Figure 5.43 – The Footer Wrapper flexbox properties

17. The footer looks much better but could use some padding. Select the **Section** element and change its **Top** and **Bottom** paddings to 56px.

It should now resemble *Figure 5.44*:

Figure 5.44 – The completed footer section

Big congratulations – you've now completed the footer section of this page, which you can preview on the base breakpoint!

In this section, we got more practice using flex and saw how it can be used to align content in one box that is, in turn, wrapped within other flex elements. We also saw how to add links and configure them.

# Summary

In this chapter, we picked up from where we left off when we completed the **Hero** section in *Chapter 4, Building Above the Fold*. The rest of the SecondPlate landing page had us completing the **How it Works** section, a features section, a CTA section, and lastly, the footer section.

In doing so, we continued practicing Webflow basics, from adding elements to adding images and customizing styles.

Moreover, we had the opportunity to get a lot more practice with flex and grid display layouts. Specifically, we learned that flex is best used when we're looking to align elements along a single dimension, vertically or horizontally, such as elements in a card or a row of items. On the other hand, grids are best reserved for elements that need to be laid out vertically as well as horizontally, such as the cards in our features section.

In the CTA section, we also got a chance to further explore the concept of positioning. We learned that by using relative positioning, an element can be moved around relative to its expected default position without affecting anything else around it. This is useful when we're looking to make small and interesting positioning adjustments with little effort.

Beyond those concepts, we also picked up a number of other useful concepts and tools. We saw how to create accessible color palettes using Webflow's color contrast tool. We learned how to use combo classes to uniquely identify specific elements. We saw how and when to duplicate and rename class names in order to efficiently reuse styles. We created color gradients and saved color swatches for reuse as well, and we also learned how to add and configure links.

We have yet to make these new sections on this landing page responsive on tablet and mobile screens. We'll be tackling that in the next chapter. Rather than spending time creating new things, we'll be focusing on adjusting what we already have for other screen sizes.

For now, pat yourself on the back for a job well done. See you in the next chapter!

# 6
# Making It Responsive

In the previous chapter, we finished building the landing page for SecondPlate, however, we had focused only on its base breakpoint of 1440px. In other words, if you preview the SecondPlate landing page on other screen sizes, such as a tablet or a mobile, the page will likely not look very good. And in an age where people can access websites from a variety of devices and screen sizes, this isn't ideal.

So, in this chapter, we'll focus our efforts on making the SecondPlate landing page responsive across multiple screen sizes. In particular, we'll make it responsive on a tablet and mobile, as well as very large screens.

Specifically, we'll tackle the following:

- Adjusting the flex layouts in the **How it Works** section properly for the various screen sizes

- Dealing with large grids on multiple screen sizes

- Setting different layout and positioning settings on different screen sizes

- How to efficiently make adjustments so that changes cascade properly across all relevant screen sizes

Over the course of the chapter, we'll understand how changes we make on one screen size may affect others. As such, we'll learn how to use this to our advantage to save us time. In essence, we'll be learning how to be efficient responsive web builders.

> **Tip**
>
> In this book, we've been tackling responsive design as a mostly linear process where we tackle one screen size before another. This is well and good, however, in actuality, responsive design can be an iterative and organic process, where you're testing sections of your page on the most important breakpoints for your project as often as possible. There's no right or wrong way to do it. The goal here is for you to understand the overall principles and processes so that you may then find the best workflow that works for you.

# Making the How it Works section responsive

In the previous chapter, we built the **How it Works** section to be a collection of rows that showcased a screenshot and a description of a key part of the SecondPlate app experience. On our base breakpoint of 1440px, the preview resembles *Figure 6.1*, where the image and text alternate their positions from the left to the right and then back to the left again:

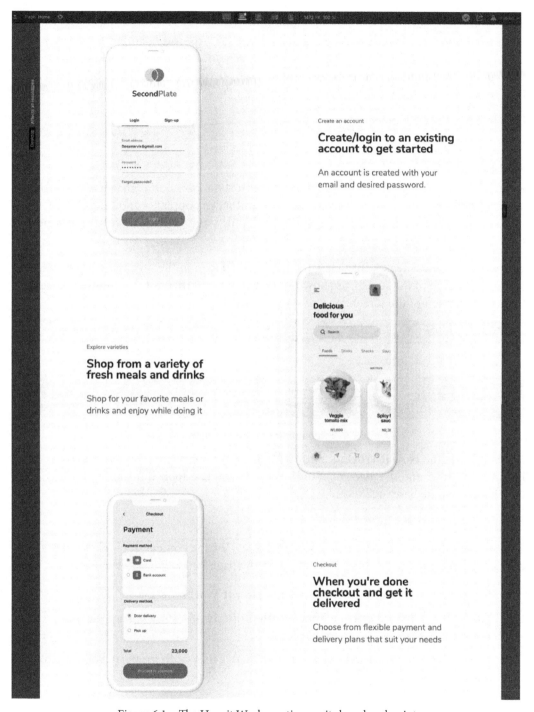

Figure 6.1 – The How it Works section on its base breakpoint

We're going to ensure that this section looks good on three other important breakpoints: large screens (1920px wide and up), tablet screens (768px wide), and mobile screens (320px wide). Since there are in fact many other screen sizes in between these main breakpoints that audiences may be viewing the website on, we'll also take a brief look at how to account for them (including even Nintendo DS screens).

Let's begin with large screens.

## Large screen sizes

Recall that our base breakpoint was originally set to 1440px. But in an age where retina screens and large monitors are becoming more and more popular, a good number of our audience may be viewing the SecondPlate landing page on screens with a resolution higher than 1440px.

To switch to higher breakpoints, click the large screen icon in the breakpoint shortcut section at the top of the screen, as shown in *Figure 6.2*, and then hit the **Toggle Preview** icon at the top left of the screen.

Figure 6.2 – Switching the Large Screen breakpoint

At first glance, the **How it Works** section actually looks pretty good on large screens! The layout of the rows and the placement of the images and text look almost identical to how they looked on the base breakpoint.

But we can improve it a little.

Since on larger screen sizes we have more real estate for the content, let's take advantage of it and increase the width that the content on the page takes:

1. Select the **Container** element under the **How it Works** section.

2. Notice that it has inherited a **Max Width** property of 1200px from the base breakpoint. Change this to 1440px.

3. Next, select the **Step Image** element and change its **Width** property from **Auto** to 1000px.

That's it!

All inherited values are represented by properties that are highlighted in an amber color. Clicking directly on the property label reveals where the value is being inherited from. For example, if you click on the **Max W** property of the **Container** element, you'll see that the value of 1200px was inherited from the **Container** element on the base breakpoint, as shown in *Figure 6.3*:

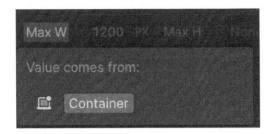

Figure 6.3 – Viewing where a value is inherited from

Anytime you override the value with a new one, the property label gets highlighted with a blue color.

You'll notice a few things have happened:

- The **How it Works** section has grown to 1440px, which has allowed the app screenshots to also grow automatically. This happens because the **Width** property on the image elements was set to **Auto** and the **Height** property to 100%. In other words, we've set them so that they fill in the space available. When we updated the **Width** property of the **Step Image** element to 1000px, we basically explicitly said we always want the image on large screen sizes to be set to 1000px.

- Since the **Container** element is actually used throughout the landing page, our change to this **Container** element has propagated across all the sections on the page, not just the **How it Works** section. This is very helpful, since it lends consistency across the page and makes our lives easier down the road.

But we can make a few more changes to make the best use of the larger screen size. If people are viewing this page on a kiosk or TV screen, it makes sense to increase the font sizes for better legibility. Let's do that now:

1.  Select the **Step Caption** element in the first **Step Row** element of the **How it Works** section, as shown in *Figure 6.4*:

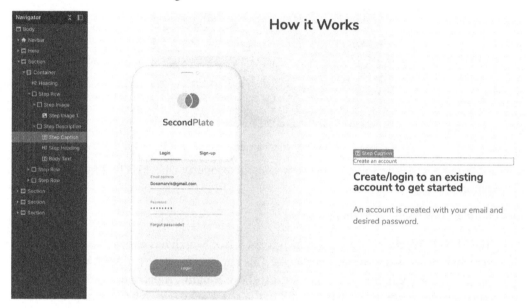

Figure 6.4 – The Step Caption element in the first row

2.  Change its **Size** property to 21px.

3.  Next, select the **Step Heading** element and change its size from 32px to 40px.

4.  The text looks bigger now, but it's also looking a bit squished. We need to adjust its line height to let it breathe a little. Change its **Height** property from 40px to 1.2 – (don't forget to include the dash). Essentially, this is a shorthand that tells the browser to make the spacing between the lines 1.4 times the size of its font. This way, whatever size we give the text, the line height will scale proportionately.

5.  Now, select the **Body Text** element and change its **Size** property to 32px.

    *Figure 6.5* shows what a single row in the **How it Works** section should now resemble:

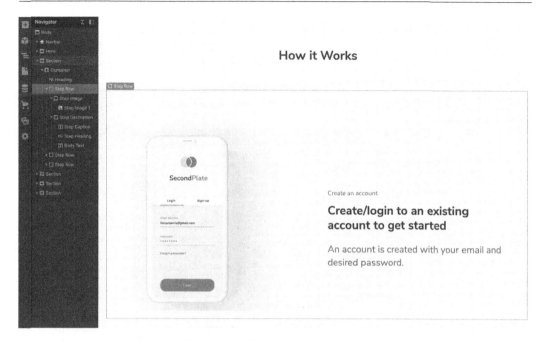

Figure 6.5 – The completed row item

This completes our adjustments of the **How it Works** section to large screens! We've taken advantage of the larger screen real estate to increase the size of the content container, including the image sizes and the font sizes. These tweaks are small, but they will make for a better viewing experience on larger screens.

Now, let's turn to tablet screens.

# Tablet screens

Select the **Tablet Portrait** icon in the breakpoint shortcut menu, as shown in *Figure 6.6*:

Figure 6.6 – Switching tablet portrait mode

In Webflow, tablet screen sizes start from an assumed screen size of 991px and scale down to 768px. Notice that the default screen size in tablet view is set to 768px. To extend this to the largest tablet size, drag the handle on the side of the screen up to 991px, as shown in *Figure 6.7*:

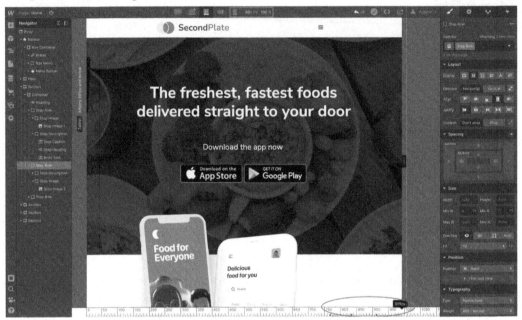

Figure 6.7 – Changing the tablet breakpoint size to 991px

When you scroll down to the **How it Works** section, the page should resemble *Figure 6.8*:

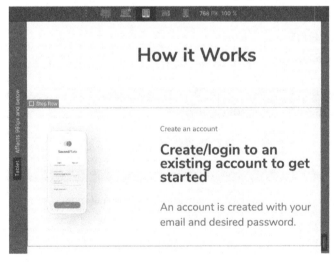

Figure 6.8 – The How it Works section in the tablet breakpoint

Let's go ahead and make some adjustments to this:

1.  Under the **How it Works** section element, select the **Container** element.
2.  Give it left and right padding properties of 40px. This ensures that the page has some breathing room on either side of the screen.
3.  Next, select the **Step Row** element. Change its left and padding properties to 48px.
4.  Select the **Step Heading** element. Change its font size to 28px.
5.  Select the **Body Text** element. Change its font size to 20px.

After these steps, a single row in the **How it Works** section should now resemble *Figure 6.9*:

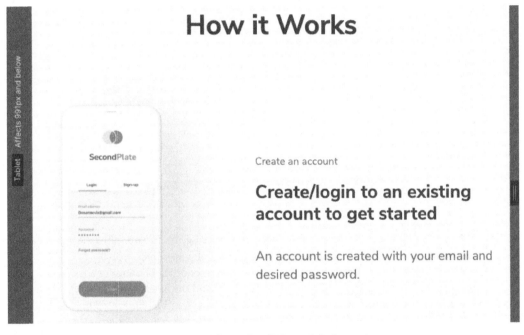

Figure 6.9 – The updated How it Works section

You can even try reducing the size of the screen viewport down to 768px (which, if you remember, is the lowest end of the tablet breakpoint). It should still look good with the above changes we made.

And with that, we've seen how to make the **How it Works** section responsive over a range of tablet screen sizes.

Let's now turn our attention to mobile screens.

# Mobile screens

In Webflow, anything under a screen size of 768px is technically considered as being in the mobile device category of breakpoints. In general, they are split into two categories, landscape mode and portrait mode.

## Mobile Landscape mode

If you switch to Mobile Landscape mode in the breakpoint shortcut menu, it will default you at the 568px breakpoint, as shown in *Figure 6.10*:

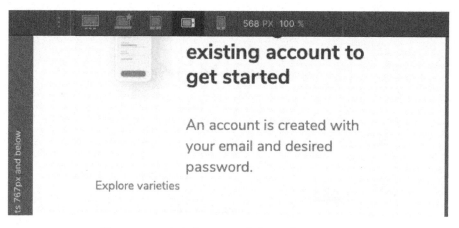

Figure 6.10 – Switching to Mobile Landscape mode

> **Tip**
>
> When you drag the right edge of the screen and increase the size up to the maximum value of 767px, in the lower right hand of your screen, you'll notice that Webflow identifies a number of devices as good candidates for this breakpoint. These include devices like the iPad Pro and the Microsoft Surface. We generally recognize these devices as tablets; however, in Webflow, we'll be designing for them as mobile devices. Either way, it doesn't really matter in the grand scheme of things.

Let's begin designing responsively for mobile landscape views:

1. Make sure you're at the largest mobile landscape screen size of 767px. Just as before, you can do this either by dragging your screen until it is at 767px or you can simply type it into the breakpoint size input at the top of your screen.

2. For this screen size, since we want to make more efficient use of smaller screen real estate, let's reduce the padding of the content. Select the **Step Row** element and change its left and right padding values to 0px.

3. Next, select the **Step Heading** element. Change its font size to 24px.

With those changes, the rows look a lot better now and make better use of the screen size.

Now, drag the screen down over the other Mobile Landscape breakpoint sizes to see it adapt to screens smaller than 767px. Once you hit the 600px breakpoint, you'll notice the design starts to look a little cramped, as seen in *Figure 6.11*:

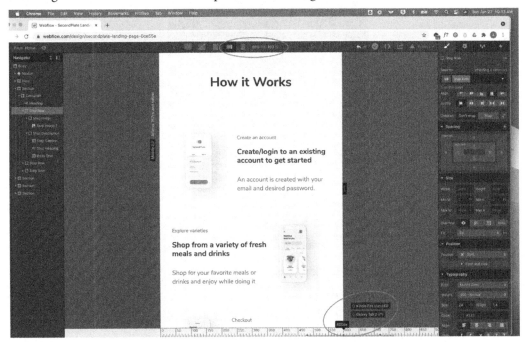

Figure 6.11 – At the Mobile Landscape breakpoint of 600px

Webflow conveniently lets us know that this breakpoint is commonly seen on non-HD Kindle Fire devices as well as the Galaxy Tab.

Notice that here, the screenshot of the device is becoming quite small and looks awkward compared to the text next to it. Therefore, we might be better off stacking the elements on top of each other, rather than putting them side by side.

Let's make that change now:

1.  Select the **Step Row** element. Recall that we have it set to a layout of flex. Note though that until now it has been laid out horizontally. Change the **Direction** property to **Vertical**, as shown in *Figure 6.12*:

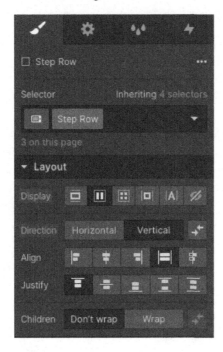

Figure 6.12 – Changing the flex Layout Direction from Horizontal to Vertical

2.  The elements in the **Step Row** element have now stacked on top of each other, which is what we wanted. But the image is now quite large, as seen in *Figure 6.13*:

Figure 6.13 – The stacked layout of Step Row

Select the **Step Image** element. Change its **Width** property to 80vw. This will ensure that the size of the image will always be 80% of the width of the viewport, that is, the screen size.

3. Note also that the rows are very close to each other, as seen in *Figure 6.14*:

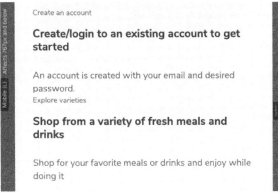

Figure 6.14 – The row elements are stacked too close to each other

Let's fix this. Select any of the **Step Row** elements. Change its bottom **Margin** property to 80px. That looks better.

4.  Note also in *Figure 6.14* that the order of the content in these stacked rows is looking uneven. Specifically, in the first and third **Step Row** elements, the screenshot comes first and then the accompanying text. However, in the second **Step Row** element, the text comes first followed by the screenshot. This inconsistency feels jarring on mobile pages, so let's fix it. Select the second **Step Row** element. Give it a combo class (remember, this is done by simply adding a new class) called Second. Now, in the **Direction** property, we can change the orientation of the element by selecting the **Reverse** icon, as shown in *Figure 6.15*. The second **Step Row** element now is organized consistently with the other **Step Row** elements:

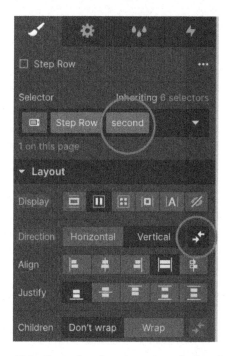

Figure 6.15 – Reversing the orientation of a flex element

And with that, we've now made the **How it Works** section responsive on mobile landscape views.

## Mobile Portrait mode

Let's finish off making it fully mobile responsive by tackling Mobile Portrait mode next.

1.  Switch to the Mobile Portrait breakpoint by selecting the *mobile portrait* icon in the breakpoint shortcut menu, as shown in *Figure 6.16*:

Figure 6.16 – Switching to Mobile Portrait mode

2.  You can optimize for any of the Mobile Portrait breakpoints, but the one I prefer is at 375px. Adjust the size of your screen to 375px. As seen in *Figure 6.17*, note that Webflow tells us this breakpoint covers devices from the **iPhone 11 Pro** all the way down to the **iPhone 6s**. At the time of writing, this presents a wide range of device screen sizes, so for the sake of simplicity, we'll be focusing on this size:

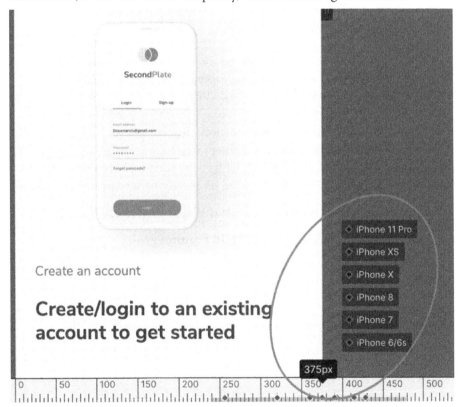

Figure 6.17 – Changing the Mobile Portrait breakpoint to 375px

3.  Scroll down to the **How it Works** section. The first thing we notice is that the **H2 Heading** of the section feels too big. Select it and change its font size to 32px.

4.  Next, it feels like the entire section might be a bit too narrow, which is causing the content to feel a little cramped from the sides. This is not necessarily bad, but we can try to optimize for space, especially since we're on a smaller screen. In the **How it Works** section, select the **Container** element. Change its left and right padding properties to 24px. That tweak looks better.

---

Tip

When designing in Mobile Portrait mode, just as in any other orientation, if you want to be as inclusive as possible to users using all types of screen sizes, it's a good practice to check your designs across the whole range of mobile breakpoints. In fact, as you drag the width of your screen up and down, you'll notice this range spans from Kindle Fire HD at the largest Mobile Portrait breakpoint of 479px all the way down to Nintendo entertainment systems at 256px. Since the number of screen sizes on mobile can be so numerous, a quicker way is to design primarily for the mid range (360px–375px) and then sanity-check it at the largest breakpoint (479px) and then the smallest (240px).

As always, it's best to think hard about who you think your primary audience is and what devices they would be typically using. Then, you can specifically make sure that your designs look optimal for their expected device types.

---

Now, as we look at the entire **How it Works** section, the changes we had made to the mobile landscape orientation have carried through well to portrait as well. The images are displayed stacked on top of the text content, with each individual **Step Row** element laid out consistently, and the font sizes all look good on these smaller screen sizes, too.

As such, we've now completed making the **How it Works** section fully responsive!

It's time to move on to the next section, the **Main Features** grid.

# Making the Main Features section responsive

Recall that on the base breakpoint, the **Main Features** section of the landing page was displayed in a large 3x3 grid of content cards.

In this part of the chapter, we'll cover how we can adapt these types of grids to other screen sizes.

Let's begin by viewing the **Main Features** section in the large-screen breakpoint of 1920px. Here, we can right away see that the grid items looks quite good already, as seen in *Figure 6.18*:

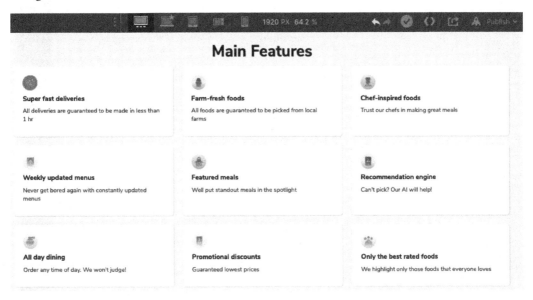

Figure 6.18 – The Main Features section on large screen sizes

As such, we can leave it at that and move on to tablet breakpoints right away.

# Tablet screens

Switch to the **Tablet** view in the breakpoint shortcut menu. At the smallest tablet breakpoint of 768px, we can see that the grid appears as shown in *Figure 6.19*:

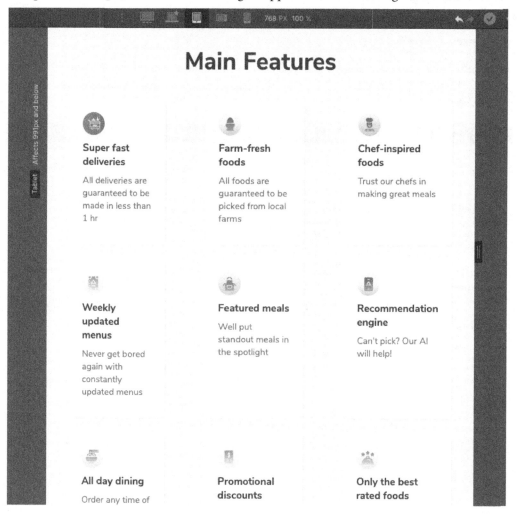

Figure 6.19 – The Main Features section in the Tablet view

For the most part, this is looking good already. But we can tweak this by reducing the gaps between the cards a little so that we give each card more real estate. Let's go ahead and do that:

1. Select the **Grid** element.

2. Click the red **Edit Grid** icon that appears in the grid or select the **Edit Grid** button in the **Layout** section of the **Style** panel, as shown in *Figure 6.20*:

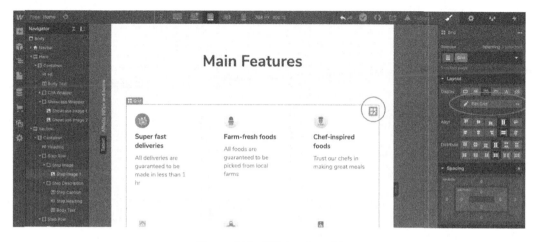

Figure 6.20 – Editing the grid

3.   In the **Edit** menu, change the **Gap** property to 40px, as shown in *Figure 6.21*:

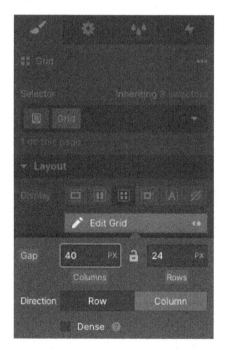

Figure 6.21 – Changing the grid gap size

4.   Hit the **Done** button to save your changes.

The cards in the grid now look better, with more of the real estate being used for the actual content and moving the individual cards a little closer to each other.

And with that, we were able to quickly edit the grid to make it appear a little nicer on tablet screens.

Let's move on to mobile screens, where things will start getting a little more interesting.

# Mobile screens

As before, let's begin by tackling Mobile Landscape mode. We'll see how the grid fares on these smaller screen sizes.

## Mobile Landscape mode

Go ahead and switch to the Mobile Landscape breakpoint. By default, it should switch you to a screen size of 568px. If not, go ahead and change it to that manually.

We note right away, as shown in *Figure 6.22*, that the grid content is beginning to overflow the screen:

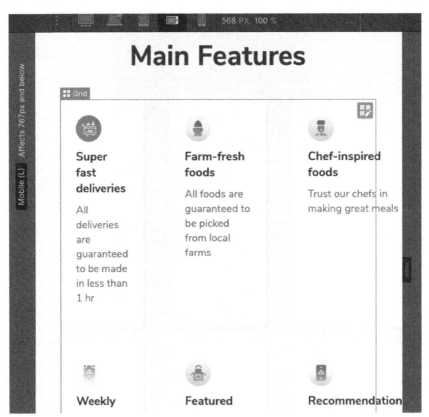

Figure 6.22 – The grid starts overflowing from the screen in Mobile Landscape mode

In order to try to adjust these content items to better fit this smaller screen size, we'll likely be better off not trying to fit three columns of cards. This way, we'll more comfortably fit the cards into the smaller screen. So, let's go ahead and tackle this:

1.  Select the **Grid** element.

2.  Click the **Edit Grid** option.

3.  In the **Grid Settings** menu, notice that there are three columns defined, each taking 1fr. In other words, each column is taking an equal ⅓ fraction of the available space. Now, go ahead and delete the third column. We now have two columns in the grid that the content cards are being organized in, with each of the columns taking half of the space available. It should resemble *Figure 6.23*:

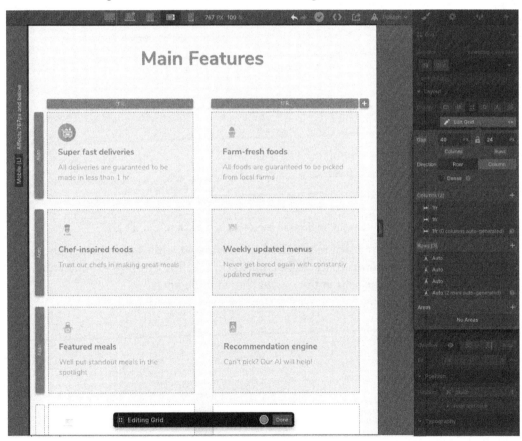

Figure 6.23 – Switching the grid from a three-column layout to two columns

4.  Hit the **Done** button to save your changes to the grid.

5.   Scroll to the bottom of the **Main Features** section. Since there were nine cards in this grid and we've now adjusted the grid to be two columns, we're left with a single card in the bottom row of the grid, as shown in *Figure 6.24*. We could leave it like this and live with this little inconsistency, but let's do one last thing to demonstrate another powerful feature of grids:

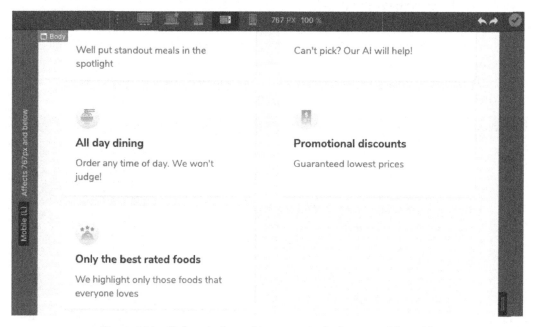

Figure 6.24 – Only a single card is present in the last row of the grid

6.   Select the last **Feature Card** in the **Grid** element. Now, while holding the right side of the card, drag it across to the right empty grid cell. The card will expand and gracefully fill both the cells in the row, as shown in *Figure 6.25*:

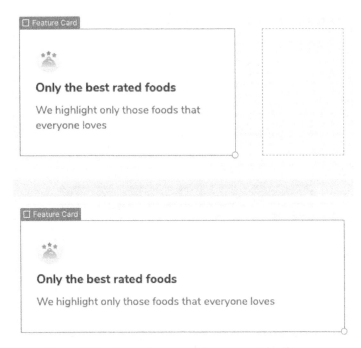

Figure 6.25 – Expanding a card from one grid cell to two

With a card that takes the entire bottom row, we now have a balanced-looking grid. While we're treating one card a little differently from the others, which may still not be the effect you want to go for, it demonstrates the powerful flexibility that grids can give you in laying out content. No matter the size of the grid, you can manually adjust how many cells vertically or horizontally to assign to most content in the grid by simply growing or shrinking the size of each grid cell.

And with that, we've now made the **Main Features** section responsive in Mobile Landscape mode.

## Mobile Portrait mode

Let's move on to Mobile Portrait mode:

1.  Select the mobile portrait view in the breakpoint shortcut menu.

2.  In the default view of 320px, notice that the grid appears as a two-column grid and not three. Recall that this is because we had configured the grid in mobile landscape view to be two columns, so those changes have cascaded down to smaller screens. While this is a good thing, unfortunately, at this screen size, even two columns is overflowing, as shown in *Figure 6.26*:

Figure 6.26 – The Main Features section overflows on Mobile Portrait mode

Select the **Grid** element. Since a two-column grid approach is likely going to be too cramped for Mobile Portrait mode, we can adjust this to a single column. One way we could do this is by editing the grid properties and removing one of the columns. Webflow will then arrange all the content into a single-column grid. You can try this and see for yourself. But using a grid layout to arrange content in a single column feels like overkill and doesn't make use of a grid's multi-column powers.

What other layout model can you think of that is better suited for arranging content along a single column or row? If you thought **flexbox**, then you're right!

3.  With the **Grid** element selected, change its **Display** property from **Grid** to **Flex**.

4.  Next, change its **Direction** property to **Vertical** so that we can arrange the cards in a column.

And now the **Main Features** section has shifted successfully from a grid layout to a more appropriate flex layout, and all the cards are stacked neatly in a single column, as shown in *Figure 6.27*:

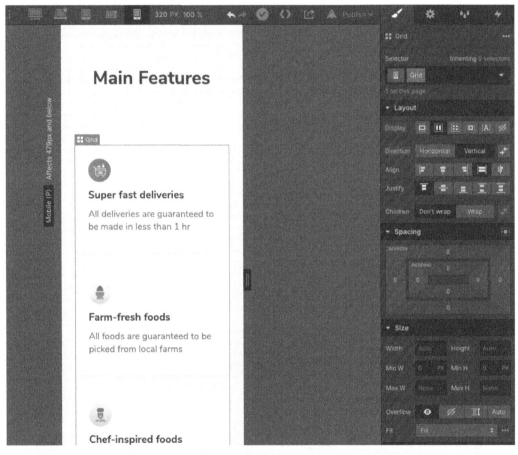

Figure 6.27 – Changing the grid element to a flex layout

Note that these layout changes are strictly active for these mobile portrait screen sizes. You can verify this by dragging the screen and expanding it alongside the mobile portrait sizes, and then by switching to either the Mobile Landscape, Tablet, or base breakpoints. You'll notice that each breakpoint adjusts accordingly.

This is the power of designing responsively in Webflow. Furthermore, this also highlights the importance of designing from the base breakpoint downward; a number of appropriate changes can cascade down while allowing us to override more specific properties in the individual breakpoints.

Let's now move on to the **Call to Action (CTA)** section, where we'll practice some more layout amendments.

# Making the CTA section responsive

If you switch back to the base breakpoint and scroll down to the **Final CTA** element, you'll recall that the section contained an image that was laid out using relative positioning and placed alongside some CTA texts and download buttons.

We'll explore how we may be able to adapt this section to smaller screens. We'll also leave it to you to explore adjustments you can make to the large-screen breakpoint.

Let's begin by switching over to Tablet mode.

## Tablet screens

Let's begin making this section responsive on tablet screens:

1.  Switch to the **Tablet** view and scroll down to the **Final CTA** section. At the breakpoint of 768px, the section should resemble *Figure 6.28*:

Figure 6.28 – The final CTA section on tablet screens

2. Select the **Left** element. Change its **Top Padding** property to 24px.

3. Next, select the **H2 Heading** element and change its font size to 24px. Also, change its **Height** property to 1.2-. Recall that doing this means that the spacing between the lines will always be 1.2 times the value of its font size.

4. Select the **Right** element. Remove its **Left** and **Right Padding** properties by setting them to 0.

5. Lastly, select the entire **Content Wrapper** element and change its **Top** and **Bottom Padding** properties to 40px.

With all said and done, the section should now resemble *Figure 6.29*:

Figure 6.29 – The updated section in tablet view

You can now verify that the section adapts well across the range of tablet screen sizes as you drag the screen to enlarge and shrink it.

As such, we didn't have to change much beyond simple tweaks to padding values and text sizes to get it to be responsive on tablet devices.

Let's now turn our attention to mobile screens.

# Mobile screens

As before, we'll be tackling both mobile landscape and portrait screens.

Because of the narrower screen sizes, we'll likely need to make some layout changes so that they are stacked in a single column, rather than being placed side by side.

## Mobile Landscape mode

Let's begin:

1.  Switch to Mobile Landscape mode. As before, if it doesn't switch you to 568px, you can do so manually. The section should resemble *Figure 6.30*:

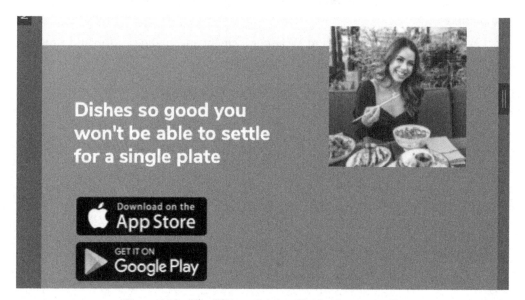

Figure 6.30 – The CTA section in tablet landscape mode

2.  We can start turning this section into a single stacked layout by first selecting the **Content Wrapper** element. Change its **Flex Direction** property from **Horizontal** to **Vertical**. Next, in order to have the image appear first, we can reverse the orientation of the **Content Wrapper** element. Do this by clicking the little **Reverse** icon that is next to the button for **Vertical** display. The section along with the properties should now resemble *Figure 6.31*:

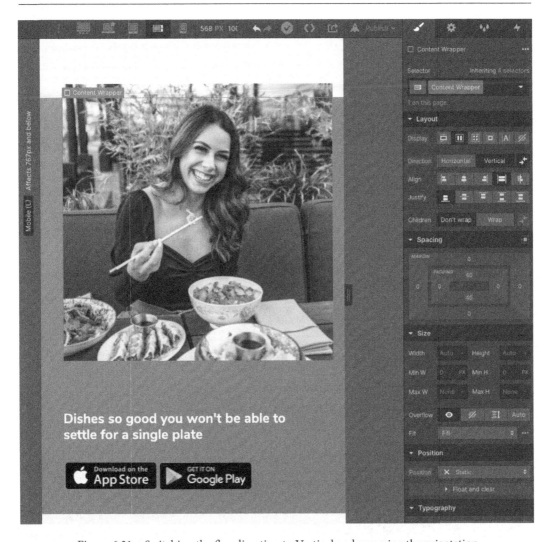

Figure 6.31 – Switching the flex direction to Vertical and reversing the orientation

3.  The section is already starting to look better. We can tweak it further by centering the text content, so it looks a little more balanced against the feature image. Select the **Left** element, and in the **Typography** section in the **Style** panel, use the alignment options to center-align the text.

4.  With the **Left** element still selected, remove all its padding so that we can make the best use of the real estate. Do this by changing the **Top Padding** and **Right Padding** properties to 0.

5.   Next, select the **CTA Wrapper** element and center-align that as we did with the **Left** element. As it happens, the alignment properties don't just apply to typography but can be used for most content items as well. The section should now resemble *Figure 6.32*:

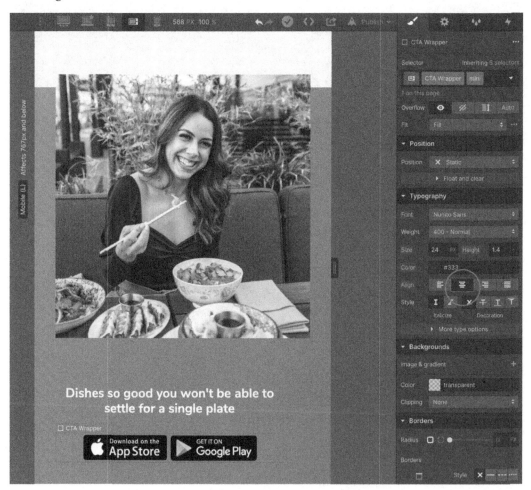

Figure 6.32 – Center-aligning content

And with that, the section is completely adapted to Mobile Landscape mode! You can verify this by checking the page out on various screen sizes in mobile landscape view.

Again, the main thing to note here was that we have the flexibility to change how we want to display, position, and lay out content on the different breakpoints so that each of them has an appropriately customized look.

## Mobile Portrait mode

Now, switch to Mobile Portrait mode. You should notice that the changes we had made to Mobile Landscape mode have, as expected, cascaded down to portrait mode as well, as shown in *Figure 6.33*. We don't need to make any further changes to this section:

Figure 6.33 – Mobile Portrait mode

With that, we've reached the final section of the page, the footer. Let's dive into how we can make it perfectly responsive.

# Making the footer responsive

To recap, we had built the footer on our base breakpoint as a collection of flex elements that were nested within each other. On smaller screens, we'll likely run into the same difficulty of fitting a number of items horizontally next to each other. As such, just as before, we'll be exploring ways we can stack them vertically instead.

Again, I'll leave it to you as an exercise to tackle the large-screen breakpoint.

For now, let's jump straight into Tablet mode.

## Tablet screens

When you switch to Tablet mode, the footer section should resemble *Figure 6.34*:

Figure 6.34 – The footer in tablet view

The footer already adapts quite well to tablet screens, and you can verify this across the range of tablet screen sizes by expanding and shrinking the screen. As such, we don't have anything more to do here, so we're already done!

Let's see how it fares on mobile screens.

## Mobile screens

As always, let's first jump into Mobile Landscape mode:

1.  Switch to Mobile Landscape mode from the breakpoint shortcut menu.
2.  Scroll down to the footer. It should resemble *Figure 6.35*; as you can see, the footer is looking cramped:

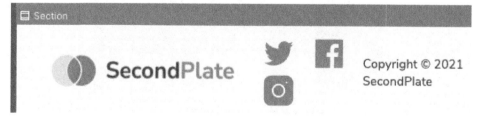

Figure 6.35 – The footer in Mobile Landscape mode

3. Select the **Footer Logo** element. Click on the **Settings** icon to reveal its sizing properties. Change its **Width** property to 140px, as shown in *Figure 6.36*:

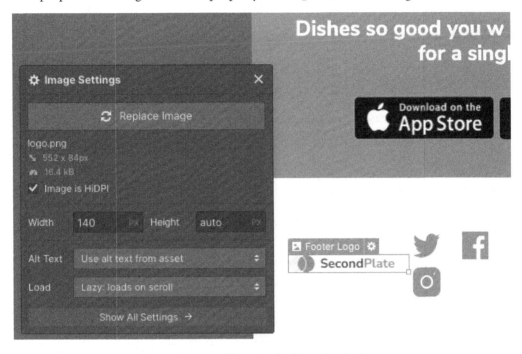

Figure 6.36 – Changing the footer logo's size

4. The social media icons are still cramped. Select any one of the **Social Link** elements. Change its **Width** property to 24px. Since all three social media icons are inside a **Link Block** element that shares the class name of Social Link, all three icons are updated at once. The footer should look a lot better now, as shown in *Figure 6.37*:

Figure 6.37 – The updated footer

5. We can tweak this a little further. Select the **Copyright** element and change its font size to 11px.

And with that, the footer is now responsive in Mobile Landscape mode as well! Luckily, we didn't have to change much besides some resizing of elements.

Let's move on to Mobile Portrait mode:

1. Switch to Mobile Portrait mode from the breakpoint shortcut menu. On the breakpoint of 320px, the footer resembles *Figure 6.38*:

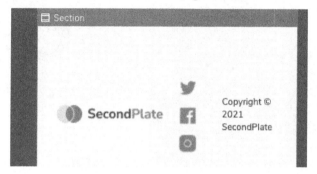

Figure 6.38 – The footer in Mobile Portrait mode

While it's not exactly terrible looking, we can do better. Since the screen size is quite narrow, it may not be wise to try to fit so much in a single horizontal line. Instead, let's stack them vertically. Can you think of how we can do this? That's right – we'll use the flex properties.

2. Select the **Footer Wrapper** element. In its **Flex Layout** properties, change its **Direction** property from **Horizontal** to **Vertical**. The footer should now resemble *Figure 6.39*:

Figure 6.39 – Making the footer vertically aligned

3. Let's add some breathing room between the items, as they're looking cramped. Select the **Footer Logo** element. Add a bottom **Margin** amount of 24px.

4. Next, select the **Social Icons** element and also give it a bottom **Margin** amount of 24px.

The completed footer in Mobile Portrait mode should now resemble *Figure 6.40*:

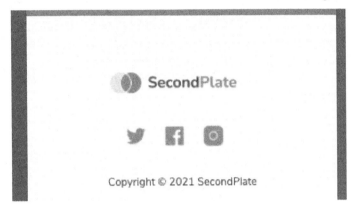

Figure 6.40 – The completed footer

And with that, we're done!

Congratulations – you now have a beautiful, fully responsive landing page completed! SecondPlate would be proud (and so should you).

## Summary

In this chapter, we completed turning the rest of the SecondPlate landing page into a fully responsive website, all built without code.

We took responsive design concepts that we were introduced to in *Chapter 4, Building Above the Fold*, and repeated a lot of it here, with some new twists.

Specifically, we saw how our changes cascade from larger breakpoints to smaller ones and how they can be overridden as needed.

We also saw how flex and grid layouts can be adjusted at different breakpoints as well. Flex layouts can have their orientations changed from being horizontal to vertical and vice versa, which helps with adapting to different sizes of screens. The order of their content can also be reversed as appropriate.

Grid layouts, as we saw, can also be customized by adding and removing columns and rows, or by expanding the space taken by a cell. These flexibilities allow us to create multiple types of layouts that can fit different breakpoint sizes.

We repeated a number of these basic concepts in multiple ways, hopefully giving you an appreciation of the flexibility and power that you have at your fingertips to create responsive websites in Webflow.

The next chapter explores concepts that can excite and potentially intimidate many people – interactions and animations. We'll learn how we can add these to our SecondPlate landing page in order to make it come alive and feel modern. As always, we'll start simple and build on top of it gradually. Before long, you'll see how Webflow makes modern-looking animations easy and powerful.

# 7

# Introduction to Interactions and Animations

By now, you've built a complete and fully responsive landing page for SecondPlate, a fictional food delivery service. While many landing pages can typically be ready to launch at this stage, we can take it the extra mile and give it an additional level of polish. In this chapter, we'll see how we can begin to achieve this by using Webflow's powerful interactions and animation tools. As always, it will all be done without code.

Specifically, we'll cover the following topics in this chapter:

- Basic concepts and principles of interactions and animations that will underpin everything we do in this chapter and *Chapter 8, Advanced Interactions*

- Creating simple hover effects and transitions on multiple element properties

- Using Webflow's interaction tool to add simple element-based triggers that result in elements smoothly animating onto the page

- Creating a custom interaction that moves elements on the page as the page scrolls up and down

- Reusing interactions on other elements

Let's begin by covering some basic principles of interactions and animations.

# The basics

You may have already seen websites that showcase slick animations and flashy transitions. When used properly, they can add a level of polish that instantly elevate the feel of the website and take it from a stale, static page to a lively and exciting one. At best, these animations and effects can also improve the user experience of the website by aiding the visitor in better understanding and navigating the site.

Typically, these animations and transitions are created by using complex JavaScript code and third-party plugins. Webflow, however, puts the power of many of these types of animations in your hands without needing to write a single line of code. It does this through its deep interaction capabilities.

In Webflow, interactions are composed of two main parts: an event or trigger usually initiated by the user (for example, a click, hover, or scroll); and a resulting animation or transformation (for example, moving, hiding, shrinking, and changing). *Figure 7.1* shows a simple visualization of this:

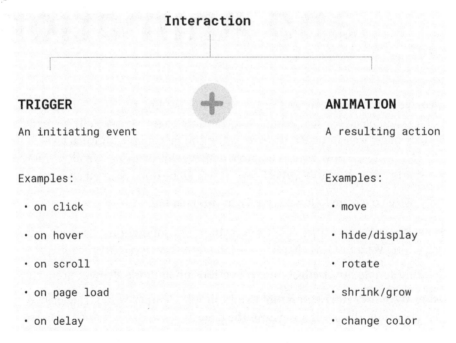

Figure 7.1 – The anatomy of an interaction

In general, there are two different types of interactions that Webflow allows us to create:

- **Element-level interactions**: Element-level interactions are applied when a specific element is triggered in some way.

- **Page-level interactions**: Page-level interactions are triggered when the larger page is affected.

All interactions are configured in the **Interactions** tab to the right side of the **Style** panel, as shown in *Figure 7.2*:

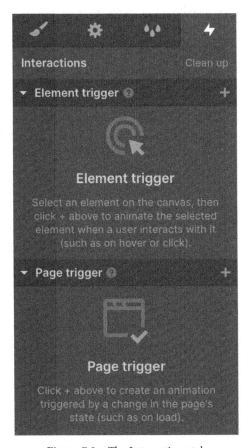

Figure 7.2 – The Interactions tab

However, not all interactions need to be created in the **Interactions** panel. Several basic pre-built animations can be added as simple but robust transitions that we can define on the element using its **Transition** property.

In this chapter, we'll create a few simple interactions on the SecondPlate landing page and demonstrate how quickly we can achieve great-looking effects without much effort. Rather than spending too much time upfront on the details of how everything works, we'll learn as we go along by putting them into practice.

Let's start simple and tackle basic transitions first. Then, we'll layer our knowledge on top of that as we explore increasingly more complex interactions. Let's start with one of the most common animation types on the web: hover effects.

# Animating transitions on hover

One of the most common types of transitions you might have seen on websites is simple animations when you hover over buttons. In order to signify that the user is hovering over a clickable button, we can make the button change color, grow, cast a shadow, and a whole host of other effects.

To achieve this, we need to specify three things:

- What does the element in question look like in its initial state?

- What does it look like in its final state?

- Are there any transition effects we want in order to take the element from its initial state to its final state?

Typically, this would have required us to write custom CSS, but Webflow allows us to do this visually without code.

In our case, we're going to add simple transition effects onto the download buttons that are on the **Hero** section of the SecondPlate landing page. We'll shift from a non-active state to a hover state, and in doing so, we'll move the button slightly up to indicate that the user has hovered over it. We'll also cast a little bit of a drop shadow to add some depth.

Let's begin:

1. Select any of the two CTA button elements.

2. In the **Style** panel, click the dropdown in the **Selector** field and select the **Hover** state, as shown in *Figure 7.3*:

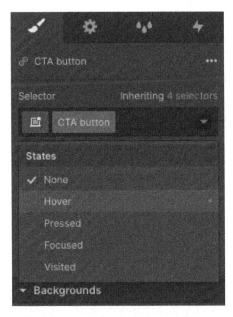

Figure 7.3 – Switching to the Hover state

3.   Next, scroll down to the **Effects** section in the **Style** panel and add a new **2D & 3D transform**. Since we want the button to move upward slightly when hovering over it, pick the **Move** transform type. Moving upward means we need to move it against the *y* axis, so we give it a value of -5px. Hit *Enter* to save your changes. *Figure 7.4* shows how these steps should have played out:

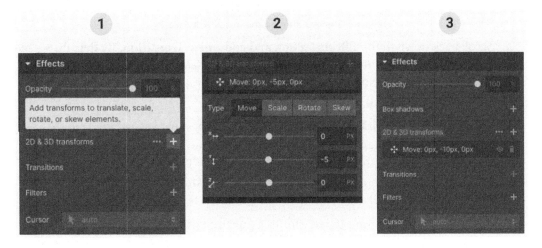

Figure 7.4 – Adding a Move transform type to the hover state

Notice that you should be able to see this effect immediately as you hover over the download buttons; the button should move upward a little. However, the movement is abrupt, which feels a little jarring. This is where adding an animated transition effect comes in to help smooth out the transition from a non-hover state to a hover state.

4.   To add transitions, we have to switch back to our initial state. In the **Selector** field in the **Style** panel, click on the dropdown once again and switch back to the **None** state, as shown in *Figure 7.5*:

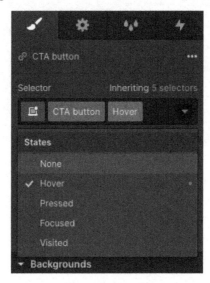

Figure 7.5 – Switching to the initial None state

5.   Scroll back down to the **Effects** section and add a new **Transition**. By default, it's set to **Opacity**, but that's not the effect we're going for. Select the dropdown to reveal the full list of transition effects. You'll notice right away that the list is quite large! Which one should you pick?

For a transition to work, it needs to match the changes that we had made to the end state of that element. In our case, in our end state (which was the **Hover** state), we had moved the button up along the *y* axis using a **Transform Move** action. As a result, the appropriate transition type here is **Transform**. Go ahead and select it from the list.

6.   By default, the **Duration** property for this transition is set to 200ms, and the **Easing** property is set to **Ease**. Throughout this chapter and *Chapter 8, Advanced Interactions*, we'll use more easing types, but for now, go ahead and hover over the button to test this out. It should feel a lot less abrupt than before! That's the transition effect working.

> **Tip**
>
> We could devote a lot of time to easing transitions, but it will likely not be the best use of time in this book. As you can see, Webflow provides a variety of easing types. What's most important to understand about easing is that it is a common way to control the timing and smoothing of animation transitions. And the best way to get a hang of how easing works is to test them out, which Webflow luckily allows us to do very easily. Now that you know how basic interactions work, it should be fairly easy for you to give the various easing options a test and see which effects work well for what you're looking for. For our purposes, we will mostly be using the basic **Ease In Out** transitions, which effectively ease the transition of the elements in question at its beginning and end.

7. Let's slow this down a little. Change the **Duration** property from 200 MS to 400 MS. This essentially slows it down by half the speed it was at. Test it out by hovering over the button again. You can continue tweaking this to your preference, but we'll leave it here for our purposes. See *Figure 7.6* to see an overview of these steps:

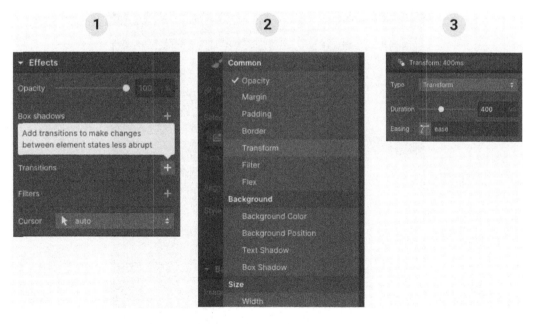

Figure 7.6 – Adding a transition effect of the Transform type

Notice also that both of the download buttons behave the same since they both have a class name of CTA button.

This transition is already looking good, but what if we wanted to add a box shadow as well?

Luckily, Webflow allows us to add multiple transitions and effects to the same element. Let's go ahead and try this right now:

1.  Select any one of the CTA button elements again.

2.  Remember, we need to define what the element will look like in its end state. So, like before, in the **Style** panel, click the dropdown in the **Selector** field and switch to the **Hover** state.

3.  Since we want to add a drop shadow, scroll down to the **Effects** section and add a **Box Shadow**. Change its **Blur** property to 10px, and its **Size** property to 5px. Then, while keeping the color of the shadow at its default, **Black**, reduce its opacity to 50. *Figure 7.7* shows how all these settings should appear in the **Hover** state.

4.  You can test out this transition now by hovering over the app download buttons. The drop shadow is subtle and present, which is what we want. But it's also appearing abruptly when you hover over the button. What do you think is missing? That's right – we haven't set a **Transition** effect yet.

Figure 7.7 – Adding a box shadow to the Hover state

5. Remember that all **Transition** effects need to be defined on the initial state. Let's do that now. Click on the dropdown in the **Selector** field and select the **None** state.

6. Scroll down to the **Effects** section in the **Style** panel. Add a new **Transition** property. This time since we're looking to make a box shadow appear on hover, so select the **Box Shadow** transition type, as seen in *Figure 7.8*:

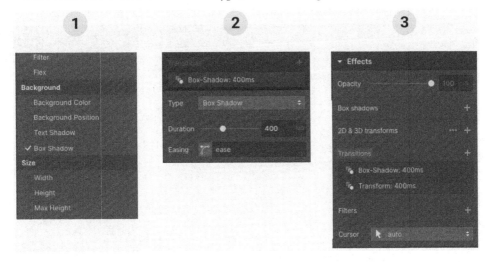

Figure 7.8 – Adding a Box Shadow transition type

7. Switch to **Preview** mode and test it out by hovering over the app download buttons. The effect is subtle, but should look quite good now, as seen in *Figure 7.9*:

Figure 7.9 – Comparing the None state with the Hover state of the download button

We've now explored how to easily add hover transition effects. In fact, you can use these same principles to add effects for any state-based transitions. With these basics covered, you should be armed with enough knowledge now to create simple but impactful transitions across state changes.

Next, we'll tackle how to create some simple element-triggered effects with Webflow's **Interaction** features.

# Simple element-triggered animations

You will recall that the **Hero** section of the SecondPlate landing page contains some introductory text, download buttons, and a couple of attractive screenshots of the app, as seen in *Figure 7.10*:

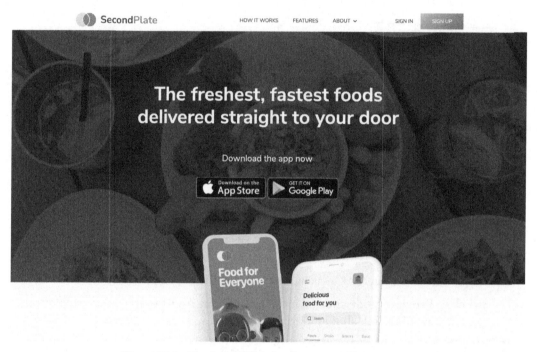

Figure 7.10 – The SecondPlate landing page – Hero section

We've already added subtle hover effects on the buttons, but we can take this a step further. A common animation seen on landing pages is a subtle fade-in or move-in transition for the elements on the page. When done with restraint, they can add a nice welcoming touch. Subtle movements can also indicate to users a sense of momentum that invites them to explore further.

In our case, let's add a simple effect where the content in the **Hero** section slides in once the page loads.

Let's explore how we can achieve this:

1.  Select the **Container** element in the **Hero** section.

2.  Access the **Interactions** tab to the right of the screen.

3.  Click the + icon under the **Element trigger** section and select the **Scroll into view** option, as shown in *Figure 7.11*:

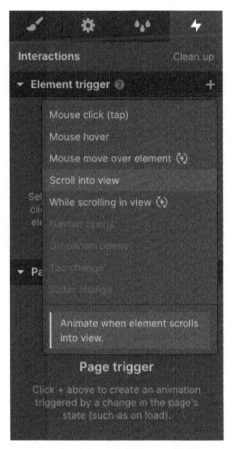

Figure 7.11 – Adding an interaction when the element scrolls into view

We're effectively defining the trigger to be the event when the **Container** element is scrolled into view, after which an interaction will take place. We'll shortly define what that interaction is.

4.  Next, we're asked to define whether we want to start the interaction when it is scrolled into view or out of view. In our case, we want to animate the **Container** onto the screen as soon as it's in view. Click in the **Select an Action** dropdown under **When scrolled into view** and select the **Slide** action. Note also that this trigger is set to occur by default across all devices, including desktop, tablet, and mobile devices.

5.  Now that we've selected the **Slide** action, we see that, by default, it's set to slide onto the screen from the left. Go ahead and change this so that it slides in from the bottom. Refer to *Figure 7.12* to see these steps laid out:

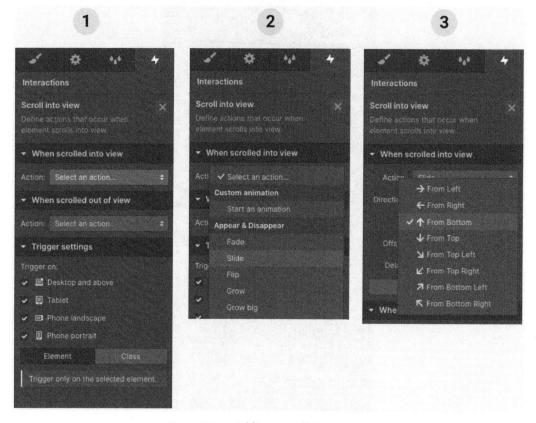

Figure 7.12 – Adding a scroll interaction

6.  Hit the **Preview** button to see the interaction in action so far. It should work, but it might look better if we delayed it a little so that it's not too immediate. Change the **Delay** property to 200ms.

7.  Hit **Preview** again. You might not see much of a difference yet. To get the full effect, preview the entire website with the **Toggle Preview** button on the top left of the screen. Now you'll notice that the **Container** slides in after a slight delay. This feels better.

And with that, you've completed your first simple interaction in Webflow! We learned how to initiate an element-based trigger, selected a corresponding action, adjusted it to our liking, and previewed it. These are general steps and principles that you'll repeat with almost any interaction you create.

Let's create one final interaction in this chapter that uses the principles we've covered above and takes it a couple of steps forward. Specifically, we'll see how we can create an effect where we can progressively slide an image as the screen scrolls up and down.

Let's jump in!

# Creating custom page scroll interactions

Sometimes, we may want to animate objects on the page as the page is being scrolled through. This effect can lend some fun depth to the page and guide the user's eye in interesting ways.

Let's build upon what we've already learned and create a custom interaction that moves images around as we're scrolling through the page. Specifically, we'll be animating the app screen images in the **How it Works** section.

Let's start:

1. Scroll down to the **How it Works** section and select the **Step Image 1** element.
2. Select the **Interactions** tab.
3. Create a new **Element** trigger.
4. Select the **While page is scrolling** option, then add a **Play scroll animation** action, and then add a new scroll animation, as in *Figure 7.13*:

Figure 7.13 – Adding a page-level scroll animation

> **Important**
>
> In this exercise, you may have noticed that we're using an Element trigger again and not a Page trigger. While we could have used a Page trigger, using an Element trigger will be more appropriate as it will allow us to focus the interaction on specific elements on the page. Had we used a Page trigger, we would have had to take into account the state of the entire page, which would have made things a little more difficult. If you want to see this for yourself and by way of a good exercise, try implementing this as a Page trigger once you're comfortable creating it as an Element trigger.

5.  We now are given the chance to name this new interaction. Call it `Enter from Left`.

6.  Select the **0%** mark in the **Scroll Animation** section and select **Move** as in *Figure 7.14*:

Figure 7.14 – Adding a Move animation

We're essentially stating that we want to initiate a **Move** action at the beginning, in other words, at the **0%** mark of this interaction.

You will observe that a few things have happened. We see a **Move** action being added for the **Step Image 1** element at **0%**, and note also that there is another **Move** action for **Step Image 1** added at the **100%** mark. Webflow does this automatically because you will recall that every interaction needs an initial state and a final state for it to work. By default, **100%** is considered that final state. Now we need to enter the exact specifications of this element at those two states.

7.  Select the **Step Image 1 Move** action at the **0%** mark. We want this image to move onto the screen from the left as we scroll down the page. As such, we're going to have to move the image further to the left so that once we scroll down, it will move in place to the right. Go ahead and enter -15% in the *x* axis. This is essentially positioning the image 15% to the left of its default position we had set initially.

8.  Now we need to set the corresponding **x** value for the end state. Select the **Step Image 1** entry at the **100%** mark. In the **x axis** property, change it to **0%**. This is essentially saying that by the time the **Step Image 1** element has scrolled 100% off the page, we want the image to finally rest at its default position. *Figure 7.15* shows what your **0%** and **100%** setting should look like:

Initial state: 0%  End state: 100%

Figure 7.15 – Setting the initial value of the element

9.  Now let's preview this interaction. Turn on the **Live Preview** toggle and start scrolling the page up and down. You'll notice that the image is moving in from the left to the right as you're scrolling down, and then goes in reverse, from right to left, when scrolling up. Webflow is smart enough to make reverse interactions for you in some cases, this being one of them. Fantastic!

10. Notice, however, that the image is continuing to move even as you scroll down past the image. This is because 100% here refers to the image going fully out of the view of the page, as we mentioned in *Step 8*. To ensure that the image makes its way to its final resting spot before it scrolls out of view, we can set the final state to be something earlier than 100%. While still in **Live Preview** mode, note that when the marker is at 50%, the content on the page seems like an ideal spot for the image to stop moving, as shown in *Figure 7.16*:

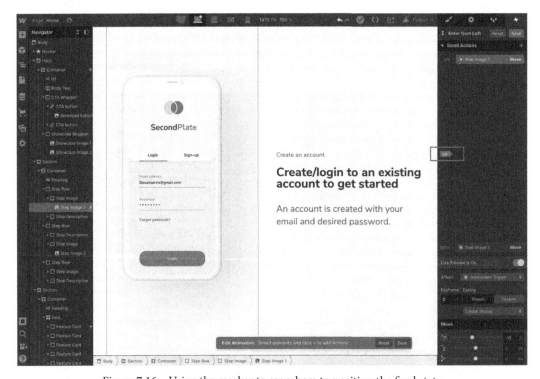

Figure 7.16 – Using the marker to see where to position the final state

11. Drag the **Step Image 1** entry that is currently at the **100%** mark so that it is now at the **50%** mark, as in *Figure 7.17*:

Figure 7.17 – Setting the final state to be at 50%

12. Turn on **Live Preview** again and test out the interaction by scrolling up and down. Now you'll notice that the image stops before it is scrolled out of view. This is what we were looking for!

13. However, now you'll probably notice that the image stops abruptly in place at its final state. This is because the **Easing** type is set to **Linear**. To put it simply, this is stating that the element in question is going to start and stop exactly in direct correlation with the scrolling of the page. We can change this so that it feels a little more natural by changing **Easing** to **Ease In Out**, as in *Figure 7.18*:

Figure 7.18 – Changing Easing to Ease In Out

14. Turn on **Live Preview** again and test the scroll effect. The change is subtle, but you should notice that easing it in and out is literally doing just that; it's easing the start of the movement and the end of it so that the effect doesn't feel as abrupt.

15. Hit the **Save** button to save your new interaction.

16. Finally, let's change the **Smoothing** property from its default value of 50 to 80 as in *Figure 7.19*. The higher the **Smoothing** value, the slower the element will be to respond to the scrolling of the page. This may seem like an undesirable effect, but when you preview the page, you'll appreciate that it lends a little bit of realistic weight and inertia to the element.

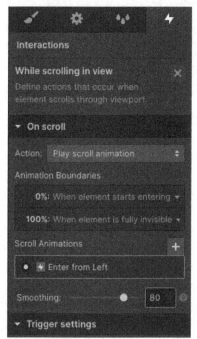

Figure 7.19 – Changing the smoothing of the interaction

Now that you've created an interaction for the one image, what about the other two images in the **How it Works** section?

Note that the first and last images in the **How it Works** section are oriented on the left of the screen. This means the last image can use the same interaction we created for the first one.

Let's do that now:

1. Select the **Step Image 3** element.

2. Go to the **Interactions** tab.

3. Add a new **Element** trigger and select the **While scrolling in view** option just like last time.

4. Now, you'll notice that under the **Scroll Animations** section, there is an **Enter from Left** option, as shown in *Figure 7.20*. This is the interaction we have just saved; select it.

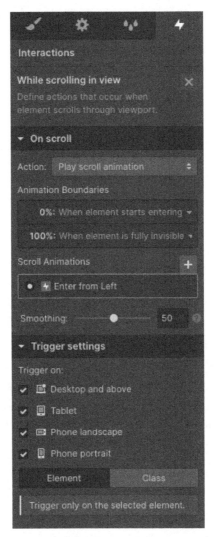

Figure 7.20 – Selecting an existing interaction

5. Just as before, let's increase the smoothing on this interaction to 80.

And just like that, we've reused an interaction we had already created, thereby saving us a ton of time.

Now that the first and third images in the **How it Works** section are animating properly, what do we do about the second image? That one is oriented on the right of the page, so transitioning it from the left will likely not look great. Instead, we'd want to move it in from the right to the left.

This will require us to create a new interaction that we'd likely call **Enter from Right**. We'll leave it to you as an exercise to create it. All you'd need to do is repeat the initial steps we went through to create the **Enter from Left** interaction. However, this time, you will need to move the image in from the opposite side along the $x$ axis.

## Summary

In this chapter, we learned the basics of how to create and customize simple animations and interactions. More broadly, we learned that all interactions consist of two things: a trigger and a resulting action or animation. Moreover, all animations require an initial state, a final state, and a way to transition between them.

We started by showing how we can create simple transitions between an element's states, specifically when hovering over it.

Then, we showed how to create some element-triggered interactions using Webflow's powerful interactions tool. We looked at how to use deliberate and subtle animations to liven up elements on the SecondPlate landing page. We learned how to add actions, how to customize them, how to relate them back to the page's scroll properties, and how to use basic easing properties to make smooth and fluid animations.

We also learned how we can reuse interactions on other elements on the page, saving us a lot of time and making our workflow more efficient.

With these basics in place, we'll be ready to dive into more advanced interactions in the next chapter. We'll create parallax effects and custom page-level triggers to create layered and modern interactions that look good and improve the experience of using the page.

I hope you're excited to jump in!

# 8
# Advanced Interactions

The previous chapter introduced you to the basics of creating transitions, interactions, and animations. In this chapter, we'll take this a couple of steps further and practice how to build more complex and useful interactions.

Specifically, we'll cover the following topics:

- Creating parallax effects
- Hiding and showing the top navigation bar when scrolling up and down
- Creating a fixed page element that allows the user to go back to the top of the page quickly

Each of these will display the versatility of Webflow's interaction capabilities and hopefully arm you with enough knowledge and confidence to try building custom interactions of your own.

Let's begin by jumping straight into creating one of the most popular effects you'll see on the web today: parallax effects.

# Building a parallax effect

If you've been surfing websites over the last few years, then you've undoubtedly come across parallax effects. Simply put, this is an effect where objects in the foreground appear to move at a different speed than objects in the background as you're scrolling down the page. These differences in movements create an interesting perception of depth that lends visual interest and a little bit of fun to a page.

Functionally, however, they typically don't make any measurable improvements to the usability of a page. Moreover, when overused, they can feel disorienting. Nevertheless, with restraint, subtle parallax effects can make a page feel instantly interesting.

By implementing our version of a parallax effect on the **SecondPlate** landing page, we'll also learn a little more about how to quickly create complex custom interactions from scratch. The parallax effect we'll create is going to focus on the two app mockup images in the **Hero** section. As the user scrolls down the page, we'll make the two move at slightly different speeds to each other so that they appear to be floating in space. This will serve to create a visually interesting first impression to new visitors, which may help give the website a more polished experience.

And don't worry if it's hard to picture the effect we're going for! In a few minutes, you'll see exactly how it'll look. Let's begin!

1.  In the **Hero** section, select the **Showcase Image 1** element.
2.  Select the **Interactions** tab.
3.  Add a new **Element** trigger and select the **While scrolling in view** type.
4.  Click the **Action** dropdown and select the **Play scroll animation** option.
5.  Add a new **Scroll Animation**.
6.  Give the new **Scroll Animation** a title of `Parallax`.
7.  Select **0% position** and add a **Move** transform. Notice that this creates a **Move** transform on both the **0%** and **100%** marks.
8.  Select the **Move** transform that is on the **0%** mark. Change its **y-axis** property to **50%**. This will move the **Showcase Image 1** element 50% lower on the page from its original placement. What we're looking to do is move it back to its original placement as the user scrolls down the page. We'll get to that soon.

9.  Next, select the **Showcase Image 1 Move** transform that is on the **100%** mark. Change its **y-axis** property to **0%**. This will ensure that the image will return to its original position by the time it has scrolled fully off the page.

> **Important**
>
> When using properties in interactions, make sure you are consistent about your units. So far, we've been using percentage units for placement properties in the start states and end states. If we use percentages in the start state and pixel units in the end state, for example, Webflow won't be able to tell that we're referring to the same properties and will be unable to close the interaction between the start and end states. To demonstrate this, try changing **y-axis** of the **Step Image 1** element at the **100%** mark to 0px rather than **0%**. You'll find that the **Move** transforms show a warning icon and that the interaction will stop working.

10. Now, select the **Showcase Image 2** element.

11. Again, select the **0%** start state mark and add a **Move** transform. You should now have two **Move** transforms at the **0%** mark – one for **Showcase Image 1** and another for **Showcase Image 2**. The following screenshot shows what you can expect to see:

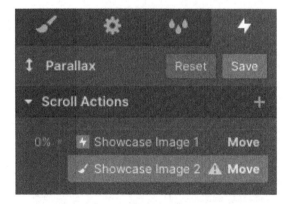

Figure 8.1 – Adding transforms for multiple elements at the start state

12. Now, for **Showcase Image 2**, let's configure this interaction so that this image will appear to move a little slower than **Showcase Image 1**. Recall that **Showcase Image 1** was displaced **50%** down the y-axis. So, for **Showcase Image 2**, change its **y-axis** property to something smaller. Let's change it to **25%**.

13. Next, with the **Showcase Image 2** element still selected, select the end state of the **100%** mark and add a **Move** transform to that as well. As we did previously, change its **y-axis** value to **0%** so that it returns to its original position by the time it completely scrolls off the page. The following screenshot shows what the properties of **Showcase Image 2** at the **100%** mark should look like.

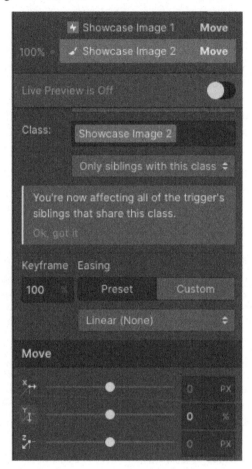

Figure 8.2 – The y-axis value of Showcase Image 2 at its end state of 100%

14. With those in place, you can now turn on the **Live Preview** toggle and start seeing the parallax effect in place as you scroll up and down the page. You'll notice that the two images are moving at different speeds to each other, as expected. Already, this effect should look quite interesting.

15. But we can make it even more interesting. What if we rotated the images a little as they scrolled? Let's give it a shot. Select the **Showcase Image 1** element again.

16. Select its **0%** start state but this time, add a **Rotate** transform type.

17. Select its **z-axis** and give it a rotation of `-15` degrees, as shown in the following screenshot:

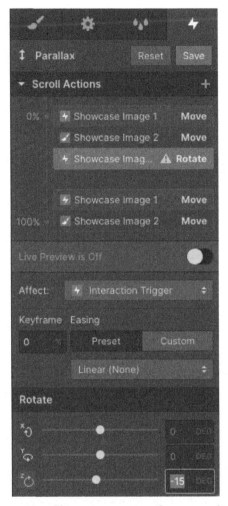

Figure 8.3 – Adding a rotation transform to an element

18. Next, select the end state of **100%** and add another **Rotation** transform. Finish the interaction by giving it a **z-axis** value of 0 degrees.

19. Turn the **Live Preview** toggle on and preview the interaction by scrolling up and down. You should see **Showcase Image 1** rotate in and out of place as you scroll up and down. Pretty cool!

20. Now, let's do the same for **Showcase Image 2**, except we'll rotate it in the opposite direction instead. Select **Showcase Image 2** and select the **0%** start state. Add a **Rotate** transform.

21. Give it a **z-axis** rotation of 10 degrees.

22. Next, with **Showcase Image 2** still selected, select the **100%** mark and add a **Rotate** transform action.

23. Change its **z-axis** value to 0 degrees.

24. Preview the page again and preview the interaction by scrolling up and down the page. The parallax effect should have the two images scrolling and rotating at different speeds, giving a great first impression to visitors.

All said and done, the parallax effect should look like what you can see in the start and end states shown in the following screenshot:

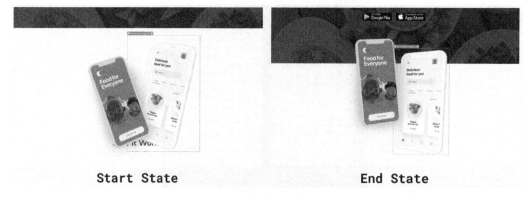

Figure 8.4 – The start and end states of the parallax effect

With that, you've successfully created a custom and visually interesting parallax effect that gives the page some depth. You've learned how to create multiple transforms on multiple elements, all within the same interaction.

> **Tip**
>
> There are many more ways in which we can add to this interaction, and you're encouraged to experiment and try them out. For instance, we haven't added any easing properties to the interactions in this chapter so far. Recall from *Chapter 7, Introduction to Interactions and Animations*, that easing allows us to create smooth transitions that can give elements a sense of natural inertia. Currently, the easing properties of the transforms are set to their default values of **Linear**. As an exercise, try changing them to any of the other ones Webflow makes available, such as **Ease In** or **In Out Cubic**. Experiment to see how each easing type differs from the others and settle on one that you're most comfortable with.

# Animating the menu on scroll

In our current version of the **SecondPlate** landing page, the top menu is only visible and accessible if you're at the very top of the page. Once you scroll, the menu is out of reach.

But what if we wanted the menu to always be visible so that it's in easy reach, regardless of where on the page the visitor is? We could achieve this by fixing the menu to the top of the page so that it sticks there as you scroll. This could be handy, but making the menu always visible may take up too much valuable attention and real estate, especially on smaller screens such as mobile phones.

This is where a simple interaction could come to the rescue.

What we can do is hide the menu when the user scrolls down the page and make it reappear whenever the user begins to scroll back up. This is a type of anticipatory design; we show elements to users only when we anticipate that they might want to see them.

Let's begin by making the menu fixed to the top. Then, we can layer on some interactions to give the disappearing and reappearing effect we mentioned previously:

1.  Select the **Navbar** element, as shown in the following screenshot:

Figure 8.5 – The Navbar element

2.  In the **Style** panel, under the **Position** section, change its **Position** property to **Fixed**. You'll instantly notice that the **Navbar** shrinks, as shown in the following screenshot. This is because, by default, it is taking the top left of the screen as its origin point and choosing to stay as close to that origin point as possible while keeping its contents intact:

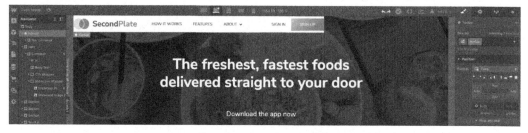

Figure 8.6 – Changing the position of Navbar to Fixed

Also, note that when you scroll down the page, the **Navbar** element stays fixed to the top of the page. This is the effect we expect.

3.  Let's adjust the width of the **Navbar** element. Under its **Position** properties, select the icon that fixes it to the top edge of the screen and stretches it to the full width of the page. You'll notice that the menu covers the entire width of the page again, as we intended. The following screenshot shows what it should look like:

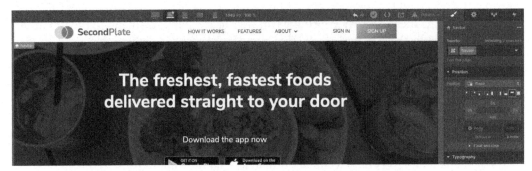

Figure 8.7 – Making the fixed Navbar stretch to the full width

Just as before, when you scroll down the page, you'll notice that the menu stays fixed to the top of the page.

4.  With the **Navbar** element still selected, change its z-index property to 1000. Recall that setting a high z-index value will ensure that the element always remains on top of all the other elements on the page, so long as it's the highest z-index value on the page.

5.  With the **Navbar** element still selected, go to the **Interactions** tab and select a new **Page trigger**. We are selecting a page trigger this time rather than an **Element** trigger because we want the overall scrolling of the page to be the trigger that sets off this interaction.

6.  Select the **Page scrolled** trigger type from the dropdown.

7.  Next, under the **When scrolled down** section, add an action and select **Start an animation**. The following figure sums up these steps:

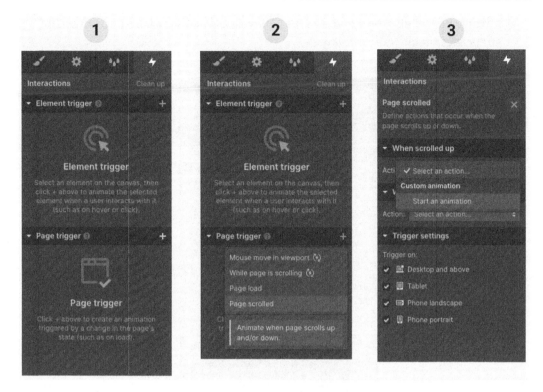

Figure 8.8 – Adding a new Page trigger element for scrolling down the page

8. Add a new **Timed Animation** and call it `Hide Nav`.

9. Click the start state of **0.00** and select **Move**.

10. Set the **y-axis** value to `-64px`. This ensures that when the user scrolls down the page, the **Navbar** element will move up and out of view.

11. Press the play button to preview it. As you can see, the interaction works as expected, but it's feeling a little too plain.

Change its **Easing** property to **In Out Cubic** to give it a smoother transition. The properties should look as follows:

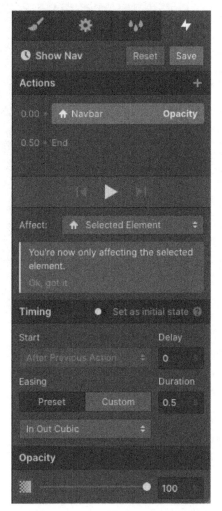

Figure 8.9 – The properties for the Hide Nav interaction

12. Click the **Save** button.

13. Now, let's do the opposite so that the Navbar menu appears back into view when the page scrolls up. Instead of recreating the interaction from scratch, though, let's reuse what we've got so far and tweak it. Just as we did previously, go back to the **Interactions** menu and add a new **Page scrolled** interaction. This time, under the **When scrolled up** section, select **Start an animation**. You'll notice that our previously created Hide Nav animation appears. Right-click this and select the **Duplicate** option from the pop-up menu, as shown in the following screenshot:

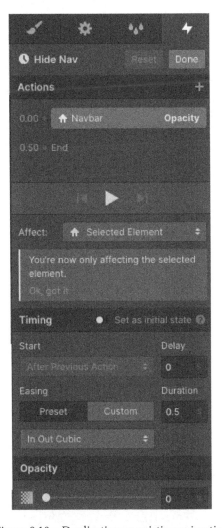

Figure 8.10 – Duplicating an existing animation

14. You should see that a duplicate animation has been created called **Hide Nav 2**. Double-click this to start configuring it.

15. You should notice that the original **Hide Nav** animation's settings have been copied over. But since we want our new animation to show the navigation bar when the page is being scrolled back up, we'll just have to reverse these properties. As such, select the **Move** action that's on the **0.00** start mark. Change its **y-axis** value from -64px to 0px. This will ensure that the Navbar returns to its original point.

16. We'll leave the **Easing** and **Duration** properties as-is since they've been copied over and will work just fine for this animation. In essence, we're just reusing work we've already done, saving us time in the process.

17. Finally, change this animation's name from `Hide Nav 2` to `Show Nav`. The final interaction should look as follows:

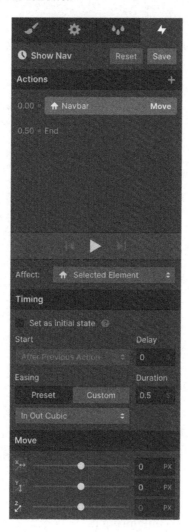

Figure 8.11 – The properties for the Show Nav interaction

18. Now, you can preview the page and test the interaction by scrolling up and down the page.

You should see that as you scroll down the page, the navigation menu slides out of view (since we're anticipating that the user won't need the menu because they're more likely focused on the content of the page). Conversely, when you scroll up the page, the menu should slide back into view (since we're anticipating that the user might want to access the menu as they're retracing their steps). This is working as expected!

In the preceding steps, we learned how to create page-level triggers that are scroll-based. We also learned how we can duplicate an existing animation and configure it to our needs, saving us some time and effort.

The last interaction that we'll create will combine a lot of the principles we've covered so far. It will build upon them to produce an effect that is useful and a little more complex than what we've covered so far. You'll soon develop an appreciation for how much we can accomplish by combining these simple but powerful capabilities.

# Creating a custom floating button

A floating button is simply a button that floats above the page in a fixed position while the page is scrolling. Why would we want this?

In our case, we're going to create a button that quickly takes the user to the top of the page rather than having them manually scroll back up. Many websites make use of something like this as it saves the user's time and effort to scroll through long pages.

Our action plan is going to look like this:

1.  Create the **Back to top** button and set its **Position** to **Fixed**.
2.  When the user clicks on the button, it will take the user back to the top of the page.
3.  Hide the button when the user is at the top of the page.
4.  Show the button when the user scrolls down to a certain position on the page.
5.  When the user hovers over the button, make it react in some way so that it stands out.

The following diagram shows the floating button we'll be creating, along with what the hover effect will look like. As you can see, it'll require changing the size of the element and showing/hiding some text:

Figure 8.12 – The hover effect on the floating button

With the action plan laid out, let's get started:

1.  Select the **Body** element.
2.  Add a new **Link Block** element. Give it a class name of Floating Button.

3.  With the **Floating Button** element selected, add an **Image** block to it. Select the up-arrow.png image from the **Assets** menu. With the settings popup still open, give it a **Width** and **Height** of 32px each.

4.  Next, in the **Style** panel, give the **Floating Button** element a **background color** of **white**, a **border radius** of 100px (to make it look circular), and padding of 16px on all four of its sides.

5.  You'll have already noticed that the element is taking up the entire width of the page. This is because it's a block-level element. Recall from *Chapter 2, The Web in a Nutshell*, that, unless specified otherwise, block-level elements will try to occupy all the width that's available to them. To make the element take up less space, we can specify an explicit size, but let's do something a little easier to fix this.

6.  With the **Floating Button** element selected, change its **Display** type from **Block** to **Inline-block**. Immediately, the element will look round and small. With **Inline-block** selected, the element is only taking up the amount of space that it needs. In this case, this is the space required for the up-arrow.png icon that is nested inside it.

7.  Now, let's make the button float over the page in a fixed position. Under the **Position** section in the **Style** panel, change its **Position** from **Static** to **Fixed**. Inconveniently, the element has now likely disappeared off the page. Fix this by selecting its positioning to be at the bottom right of the page using the appropriate positioning selection, as shown in the following screenshot:

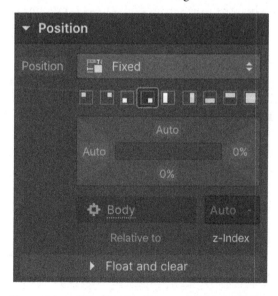

Figure 8.13 – Setting the position of the Floating Button element to the bottom right of the page

8. The **Floating Button** element now reappears and is stuck to the bottom right of the page, as expected. Let's give it some breathing room between the edges of the page. Change its **Bottom** positioning property to **10%** and the **Right** positioning property to **5%**.

9. As you scroll up and down the page, the **Floating Button** element should be fixed in its place, **10%** above the bottom edge of the page and **5%** off from the right edge, as expected. To give it more of a floating effect, let's give it a drop shadow.

10. With the **Floating Button** element selected, scroll to the **Effects** section in the **Style** panel and add a **Box Shadow**. Give it a distance of 6px, a **Blur** property of 16px, and an **Opacity** value of **10%**. The element should now look like it's floating above the page in its fixed position, as shown in the following screenshot:

Figure 8.14 – The Box Shadow properties of the Floating Button element

Let's pause here and recap:

- We added a **Link Block** element and gave it a class of Floating Button.

- We added an up arrow inside it and styled it to look like a white floating button.

- We gave it a position of **Fixed** and adjusted its positioning properties so that it is to the right of the page.

- We finished by giving it a nice drop shadow so that it looks like it's floating.

Great! Before we move on to creating the interaction, let's ensure that clicking this button takes the user back to the top of the page.

# Creating the interaction

Let's quickly do this:

1.  When the user clicks the **Floating Button** element, we want them to be taken to the **Hero** section of the page. So, we need to create an anchor in the **Hero** section. Select the **Hero** element and navigate to the **Settings** panel on the right. In the **ID** field, enter any identifier – let's say, hero. The following screenshot shows where you can find this:

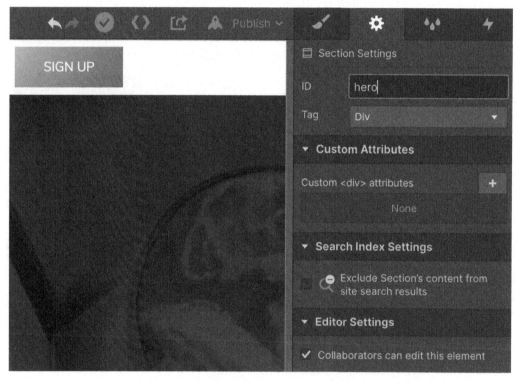

Figure 8.15 – Giving the Hero section an ID under Section Settings

2.  Now, select the **Floating Button** element. Click on the **Settings** icon and select the **Page Section** icon. In the **Section** drop-down menu, you should see the identifier you added earlier called **hero**. Select it, as shown in the following screenshot:

Figure 8.16 – Selecting the page section anchor that we want to link to

Now, you can preview the page and test it out. Try scrolling further down the page and clicking the floating button. It should smoothly scroll you back up to the top of the page, as expected. Good job!

## Adding the interaction

Now, let's add the interactions so that the floating button is hidden out of view when the user is at the top of the page already and reappears when the user scrolls further down the page:

1.  Select the **Floating Button** element.

2.  Go to the **Interactions** tab and select a new **Page trigger**. Select the **While page is scrolling** trigger type.

3.  Add a new **Scroll Animation** and call it `Floating Back to Top`.

4.  Select the **0%** mark, which is the point that represents the very top of the page.

5.  Since we want the **Floating Button** element to be hidden when we're at the top of the page, select the **Opacity style** property.

6.  Set its **Opacity** value to **0%**. The element should now be hidden from view.

7.  Let's say that we want the visitor to be able to see the **Floating Button** element when they're halfway down the length of the page. As such, select the end state of the **Floating Button Opacity** action from its current spot of **100%** (that is, the bottom of the page) and drag it to the **50%** mark.

8.  Here, give it an **Opacity** property of **100%**.

9.  Now, you can toggle on **Live Preview**, scroll to the top of the page, and test it out. As expected, the **Floating Button** element should be hidden when you're at the top of the page and appear as you scroll further down the page, as shown in the following screenshots:

Figure 8.17 – Hiding and displaying the Floating Button element at different sections of the page

10.  However, notice that the **Floating Button** element starts appearing as soon as you start scrolling down the page. What if we wanted to only let it start appearing at, say, a quarter of the way down the page?

    We can adjust this easily. Instead of starting the **Opacity** action at the **0%** mark, select it and drag it down to the **25%** mark. Now, when you preview it, you'll notice that it will stay hidden until you've scrolled down a quarter of the way down the page. It is only then that the element will start appearing and by the time you're halfway down the page, it will be fully in view.

We've made a lot of progress so far. We've learned how to add and style a floating button. We've also learned how to fade it in and out of view as you scroll down and up the page with a page-level trigger, as well as how to manipulate the starts and ends of the interactions so that they only start and end when we want them to.

## Displaying text on the floating button

We're left with one last part of this interaction that will help us improve upon it a little more. Recall that when we started this section, we said that the **Floating Button** element would also show the text **Back to top** whenever a user hovers over it. Let's tackle this now:

1.  Select the **Floating Button** element. Add a new **Text Block** element to it and type `Back to top` as its text. Rename its class to `floating link`. Change its font color to **Text Gray** or give it a **HEX** value of #727272.

2. With the **Floating Button** element selected, change its **Display** property to **Flex** and make sure you've chosen to center align it. Change the **Font** size to 14px. The following figure shows what the button should look like now:

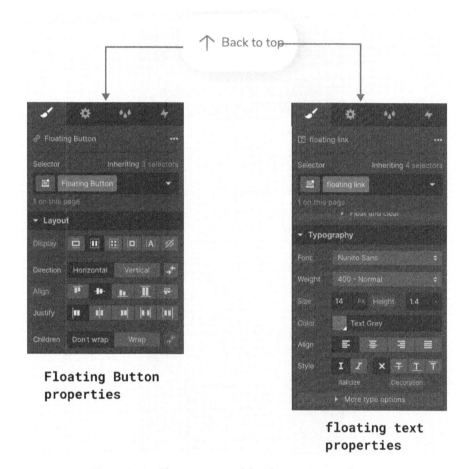

Figure 8.18 – The properties of the Floating Button element

3. But we don't want the text to appear until someone hovers over it. So, select the **floating link** text element. Change its **Display** property to **None**. This will hide it from view.

4. Now, let's add an interaction. Select the **Floating Button** element and go to the **Interactions** tab. Since we want this interaction to take place upon hovering over the specific element, add a new **Element** trigger and select the **Mouse hover** trigger type from the dropdown.

5. Under the **On Hover** section, add a new custom animation and call it Show Back to top.

6.  Next, make sure to select the floating link text element from the **Navigator** menu. With it selected, click the **0.00** mark. From the drop-down menu, select the **Hide/Show** animation type under the **Miscellaneous** section, as shown in the following screenshot:

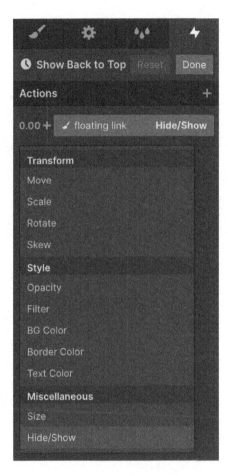

Figure 8.19 – Selecting the Hide/Show animation type for the floating link element

7.  Next, change its **Display** property to **Inline-block**. This will ensure that when the user hovers over the floating button, the floating link text will come into view. Click the **Done** button to save the interaction.

8.  Just as we did previously, we could duplicate our interaction, but let's go under the **On hover out** section add a new custom animation as well. Call this `Hide Back to top`.

9.  Just as we did previously, make sure to select the **floating link** element. Next, click on the **0.00** mark and add a **Hide/Show** action.

10. Since we want to hide this element when the user hovers away from it, change its **Display** property to **None**. The following screenshot shows the properties for the **Hide back to top** interaction:

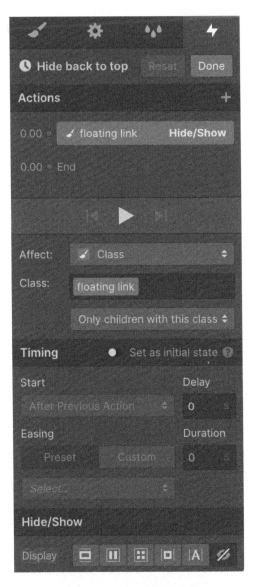

Figure 8.20 – The properties of the Hide back to top interaction

11. Click the **Done** button to save it.

12. The last thing we want to do is set this interaction to not happen on tablet or mobile
    devices. This is because touch devices do not typically have hover-type interactions.
    So, in the **Interactions** menu, under the **Trigger settings** section, make sure to
    deselect the **Tablet**, **Phone landscape**, and **Phone portrait** checkboxes so that only
    the **Desktop and above** checkbox is selected, as shown in the following screenshot:

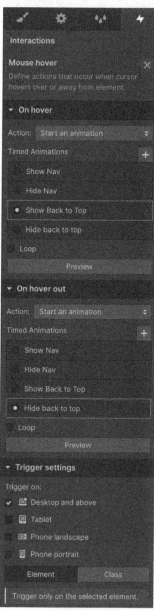

Figure 8.21 – Setting the trigger on only Desktop and above

Now that this is all said and done, you can put the page into **Preview** mode and interact with it. You should notice that as you scroll up and down the page, the **Floating Button** element hides and displays and that as you hover over the button, it expands to show the **Back to top** text. Conversely, if you hover away from the button, it hides the text and shrinks. This is what we expected.

# Summary

In this chapter, we took the basics of what we had learned about interactions and animations in *Chapter 7, Introduction to Interactions and Animations*, and built upon it. We created three advanced and custom interactions that showcased multiple capabilities, as well as how we can quickly build interactions that not only give a level of polish and dynamism to a web page but that also elevate the user experience.

The first interaction was a parallax effect, where we learned how to manipulate the movement of elements on the page in relation to each other to give an effect of depth and inertia. We also learned how to stack several actions or effects on top of each other in the same interaction.

The second interaction introduced us to page-level triggers. We created one to hide and show the top navigation menu when the user scrolls up and down the page. This is a type of anticipatory design that assists the user when we feel they might need the help of the menu and get it out of the way otherwise.

Our third and last interaction was the most complex. We learned how to create a floating button by using **Position** properties and then added multiple interactions to it to bring it to life. We saw how to hide it from view when the user is at the top of the page and only fade it into view when the user scrolls down to a certain position on the page. Then, we added hover-on and hover-out interactions that grow and shrink the floating button. Finally, we learn how to turn on triggers on some device sizes and turn them off on others, as appropriate.

All in all, *Chapter 7, Introduction to Interactions and Animations*, and this one should have given you much more confidence in building custom interactions and animations. Webflow's interaction and animation capabilities are deceptively deep, so you are advised to continue experimenting and playing with them. Most excitingly, you can create all these complex interactions without writing a single line of code yourself and have Webflow build it all out for you under the hood.

This also marks the end of this project and the end of *Section 1* of this book! Congratulations on building your first landing page with Webflow!

*Section 2* will introduce us to a brand-new project. We will be devoting our time to Webflow's CMS capabilities by learning how to create collections of objects to create our very own curated library of content that is scalable and editable.

See you there!

# Section 3: Building a Dynamic Website with Webflow CMS

This section will teach you how to take advantage of the power of Webflow CMS to create and manage websites with dynamic content. We'll do so by creating a curation-based website that showcases some of the most interesting libraries from around the world.

We will cover the following chapters in this section:

- *Chapter 9, Getting Started with Webflow CMS*
- *Chapter 10, Creating Your First CMS Project*
- *Chapter 11, Creating Collection Pages*
- *Chapter 12, Managing CMS Projects*

# 9

# Getting Started with Webflow CMS

While Webflow is a tremendous tool for building custom and complex responsive static web pages, it can especially shine at building dynamic ones. From blogs to publications, portfolios to product listings, many of the websites you might have used online are dynamic. Specifically, they let administrators or users create, display, and edit the website's content on demand, depending on the nature of the website.

In this chapter, we'll provide a high-level overview of dynamic website creation and how Webflow can help us design and build one for ourselves, again without code. Specifically, we'll cover the following topics:

- Understanding **Content Management Systems (CMSes)** and their role in building dynamic content

- Taking a closer look at Webflow's own CMS solution and how it compares to other ones

- Getting an overview of and setting up our very own dynamic project, which we'll be building

- Understanding the structure and organization of our dynamic website

By the end of this chapter, we'll be ready to start building our first dynamic website using Webflow CMS.

# What is a CMS?

At the heart of it, a CMS allows us to create and manage content on websites. It can be done either by one person or a team of people. Sometimes, some of the control of content creation and management can even be given to the website's visitors.

Let's take an example we've seen before: CNN.com. This news publication website features constantly updating content multiple times a day, every day. These hundreds and thousands of pages would be too cumbersome to build from scratch daily.

This is where a CMS steps in. With a CMS, the content publishers of CNN can simply focus on writing the content itself; the CMS is then used to publish the right content to the right categories at the right time. And because the format of each of the pages has already been defined, the CMS just replicates those as new pages, greatly simplifying the process.

But you don't need to have thousands of pages of constantly updated content to want to use a CMS.

Imagine that you want to share your adventures in cooking. If all you wanted was to create a website that you knew you would hardly update, then a static website without a CMS would be a perfectly fine decision. But if you wanted to turn it into a blog with new weekly or monthly content, you would likely want to consider using a CMS to manage and publish that content.

Most CMS solutions allow you to write new content and take care of its publication for you. For each new blog post you write, the CMS would dynamically generate a new page without you needing to build it out from scratch each time. Moreover, if you were to change any of the content, the CMS would update it across the entire website where it is referenced.

And, as it turns out, Webflow is one of those tools that provide a CMS solution. But what makes it stand out from the crowd?

# Why Webflow CMS?

One of the longest-running and most popular CMS solutions is arguably WordPress, so it bears some consideration here.

WordPress is a CMS built on the PHP programming language and is purportedly being used to power more than a third of the websites on the internet. That's a lot of websites!

As such, WordPress has grown a large, dedicated, and prolific ecosystem of designers, developers, and third-party service providers. For some, this ecosystem and the support it provides is one of the main reasons to adopt WordPress as their CMS of choice.

While Webflow CMS may not have a community that large yet, it does offer several great benefits, most of which we've already seen. Specifically, Webflow makes it easy to customize your pages extensively without code, whereas WordPress requires you to know some PHP code to be able to do so. As such, WordPress will typically restrict you to templates. So, if you're looking to have control and flexibility over how your website is going to be designed, Webflow is generally the way to go. Its flexibility and ease of use are arguably its biggest differentiators from many other CMS solutions.

Furthermore, Webflow CMS makes it quite easy to set up your underlying content model in a way that makes sense for your project. Webflow CMS allows you to create object models that contain various types of data, from text to images, currency values, and even colors. In effect, Webflow CMS can end up feeling more like a powerful database of objects compared to WordPress' flat structure of pages. While you can extend WordPress' capabilities with add-ons and extensions, these typically require you to purchase third-party tools, each with non-standardized ways of doing things. With Webflow CMS, it all comes with the tool, making learning it a simpler exercise.

But the best way to appreciate the power of Webflow CMS is to take it for a spin yourself. Luckily, it won't take long to do so, so let's jump in and take a deeper dive into it right now.

# Webflow CMS – the basics

With the free plan of Webflow, you can create a Webflow CMS project. However, it will be restricted to two pages. This will be sufficient for our needs.

In Webflow CMS, all content objects are called **items**, which, in turn, are grouped into **Collections**. A Collection is Webflow's way of grouping content that is alike in some way. So, if, for example, you were creating a list of meals for a cookbook, each recipe could form a single item in the cookbook and altogether, they could be grouped in a Collection called **Recipes**.

An item in the Collection is then further broken down into individual units of data called **fields**. These fields are the bottom-most level of data you can have in the CMS and can take on multiple types, from plaintext to number values and even color codes.

> **Note**
>
> It is worth mentioning that Webflow has a limit of 30 fields per item in the Collection. And with the basic CMS Site plan, you're allowed to create up to 2,000 Collection items before you must upgrade to the Business plan.

So, to continue with the cookbook example, each item in the **Recipes** Collection can have multiple fields such as **Meal Name**, **Cooking Time**, **Image**, **Description**, **Type**, and more. The following diagram shows a visual breakdown of what the **Recipes** Collection may look like:

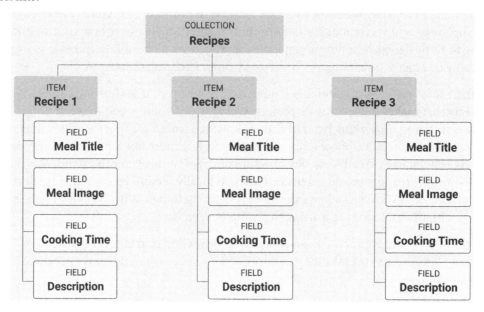

Figure 9.1 – A sample Collection, item, and Field breakdown in Webflow CMS

Once your Collection of items is structured and created, Webflow CMS provides you with two ways to display them on your website:

- **Collection Lists**: Once added to any of your pages, you can connect the Collection List to your Collection, which will instantly give your page access to all the items in the connected Collection. Furthermore, you can add sorting and filtering criteria to the Collection List so that you only pull certain items. Say, for example, we wanted to display some recipes on the home page of the cookbook. We would add a Collection List to the page and bind it to the cookbook Collection.

- **Collection Pages**: Unlike Collection Lists, where multiple items are displayed, a Collection Page is just that – a page devoted to a single item in the Collection. Conveniently, Webflow CMS dynamically and automatically creates unique pages for each item in the Collection, which you can then reference. These pages are typically called **templates** as they form the blueprint for the content's layout, which is then replicated across all Collection item pages.

Typically, you'll use Collection lists to display a list of objects. In our cookbook example, the main page might contain a list or grid of recipes that you can browse. Once you select a single recipe, you'll be taken to a Collection Page specifically for that recipe, as shown in the following diagram:

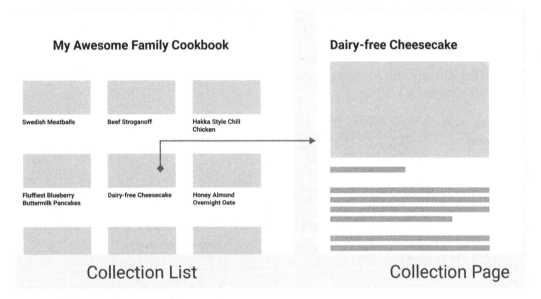

Figure 9.2 – Collection List versus Collection Page

As usual with Webflow, both Collection lists and Collection Pages are fully customizable with Webflow's design and development features, and all of this is done without code.

With that, we now know enough about the basics to start building on Webflow CMS. But first, let's take some time to introduce our next project, where we'll be using Webflow CMS to build a curation website dedicated to some of the most interesting libraries around the world.

# Project overview

Curation websites are becoming an increasingly popular type of website nowadays. There seems to be a curation site for anything, from marketing tools to online courses to famous designers. Their appeal is understandable too; for people interested in the subject matter, a website that can curate information can potentially save the visitor a lot of time searching for the items themselves across the web.

For our Webflow CMS project, we will build a curation website of our own. In our case, our website will serve as a curation of some of the most beautiful libraries around the world. Visitors can discover them on the website and learn more about them to appreciate their wonder and maybe even visit them one day. We'll aptly call it **Libraries of the World**.

We'll keep the design of the website minimal and simple since we want to mainly focus on learning about Webflow CMS, but you're encouraged to stylize the website how you like. The following screenshot shows the home page, which will feature a grid layout of libraries. Each library entry will showcase an image of the library, its name, and the city and country where it's located:

Figure 9.3 – The Libraries of the World home page

When the website visitor clicks on any of the libraries on the home page, it will take them to a details page that showcases more information about the library in question, as shown in the following screenshot:

# Toronto Reference Library

**Address:**   130 St George St, Toronto, ON M5S 1A5

**Opened:**   1971

**Books:**   4.5 million

**Visit website** ↗

The Toronto Reference Library is the largest public reference library in Canada with an extensive collection of books, manuscripts, microfilm, and other items. Most items in its collection are designated for reference-use only, with the public unable to borrow these items for use outside the library. In addition to providing access to its collection, the library also hosts a number of public reading events, as well as provide technical access and services to the public.

**More images**

**See more libraries**

**Austrian National Library**
Vienna, Austria

**New York Public Library**
New York City, USA

**Doha National Library**
Doha, Qatar

Figure 9.4 – The library details page

The library details page will contain the following key pieces of data:

- The name of the library

- A showcase image of the library

- The address of the library

- The library's year of construction

- The approximate number of books in the library

- A link to the library's website, if available

- A short description of the library

- A Collection of other images of the library, if available

To round out the page, we'll end with some quick links to other libraries in case the visitor wants to continue browsing.

Now that we've provided an overview of what we'll build, let's make sure we have all the assets we need to build the Collection of libraries.

## Technical requirements

Since our website is going to feature a Collection of libraries, we'll need to download some asset files that will accompany the information provided. You can find them all here:

```
https://github.com/PacktPublishing/Webflow-by-Example/tree/
main/Chapter09/Assets.
```

Download them all to your local drive. We will be uploading them to our CMS project in the next chapter.

Now that you've downloaded all the assets, let's spend a few minutes preparing the structure of our CMS Collection.

## Planning the CMS structure

Whenever you're about to start working on setting up Collections in Webflow CMS, it's always a good idea to take a few minutes to think through the data structure that you're looking to represent in your CMS and website. This not only gives you a good mental model of what data you'll need, but it will also assist you in thinking about what the website and its pages will look like.

In our case, since we're creating a curation site for libraries around the world, it stands to reason that we can call our Collection **Libraries**.

Within our Libraries Collection, we'll have a grouping of Library items. Each Library item will, in turn, have several fields, most of which we already mentioned in the previous section. The following diagram shows a visual breakdown of the data structure that we'll be setting up in Webflow CMS:

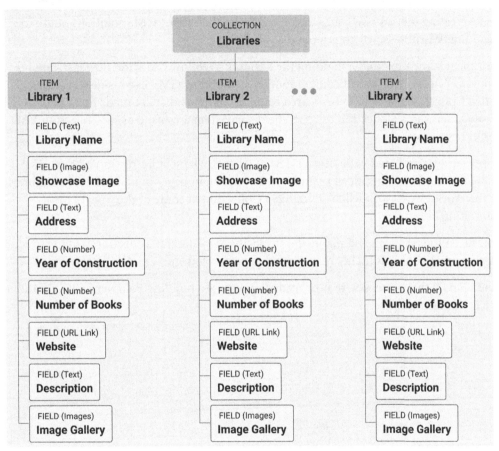

Figure 9.5 – The Collection structure of Libraries of the World

Armed with this information, we are now prepared to jump straight into building the project!

## Summary

In this chapter, we introduced you to the world of Webflow CMS. You saw what makes a dynamic website different from a static website and you learned that Webflow CMS can make creating dynamic websites easier and faster than many CMS solutions out there, including WordPress, which is a popular alternative.

You spent some time understanding the basics of Webflow CMS and how it structures content. You learned that all content models in Webflow CMS live inside structures called Collections, which, in turn, are groupings of items that are made up of fields. Once created, items in a Collection can then be displayed on a website using Collection Lists or Collection Pages.

You were also provided with an overview of what you'll be building on Webflow CMS using the free plan. Specifically, you looked at the main pages of a website called Libraries of the World, where you will be curating a Collection of some of the world's most interesting libraries.

You sliced the pages up and planned out specifically what the Collection is going to look like – a practice that is highly recommended before you start any CMS project.

And with all that done, you're now ready to jump into building your very own curation site in the next chapter!

# 10
# Creating Your First CMS Project

Now that we've had an overview of what we're going to build as our first CMS project, let's dive in and get building in this chapter!

We'll begin by creating a new CMS project, but rather than jumping into designing the web page, we'll start by defining our data model. That is to say, we'll start by setting up our CMS Collections. We'll then use this data to populate the home page of our dynamic website about libraries.

As such, we'll cover the following topics in this chapter:

- Setting up a new CMS Collection from scratch
- Adding new items to the Collection
- How to quickly populate a page with items from a Collection
- Dynamically updating the order of items shown by adding simple filters

With that, let's jump right into creating our CMS project!

# Technical requirements

If you haven't yet downloaded the project assets, now's the time to do so. You can download all the assets from the following link: `https://github.com/PacktPublishing/Webflow-by-Example/tree/main/Chapter09/Assets`.

When the time comes, we'll be uploading them to our CMS project as appropriate.

# Creating a CMS project

Remember that on the free plan of Webflow, you can create two projects, each with a maximum of two pages.

Since we've already used up one project with our previous SecondPlate landing page, let's go ahead and create a new project for our Libraries of the World CMS website:

1. Navigate back to your Webflow dashboard page.

2. Click the blue **New Project** button in the top-right corner of the page, as shown in *Figure 10.1*:

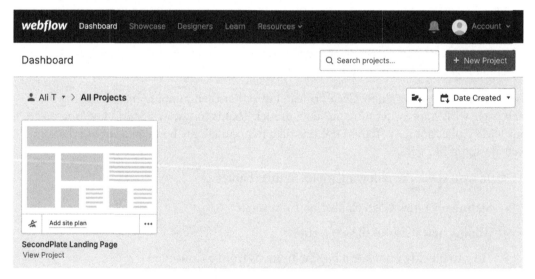

Figure 10.1 – Creating a new project

3. Select **Blank Site** on the template page and name it `Libraries of the World`.

4.  Once you've created the project, you'll land on a blank page. From the menu on the left, select the **CMS** menu item. Then, select the **Create** button to create your first Collection, as shown in *Figure 10.2*:

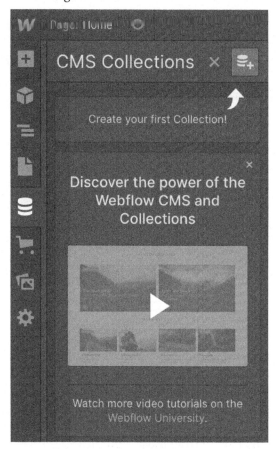

Figure 10.2 – Creating a new CMS Collection from scratch

You'll now be landed directly in the CMS Collections view. Admittedly, this page can feel a little overwhelming.

Let's break the page down into the four main sections that are worth paying attention to from the get-go, as shown in *Figure 10.3*:

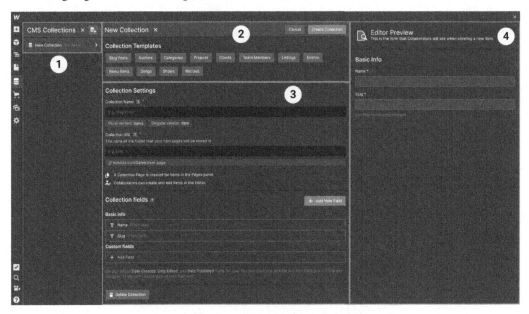

Figure 10.3 – The CMS Collections view

Now we will look at each section shown in the preceding screenshot:

1. **The Collections selector section**: Recall from *Chapter 9, Getting Started with Webflow CMS*, that CMS projects need to have at least one Collection. This Collection will contain all the items or data objects that we want to keep a record of. More complex CMS projects can have multiple Collections if it's required to keep records of very different types of objects. This section of the CMS page is where you'll be able to add or select from those multiple Collections. In our case, our project will only have one Collection, which we'll be creating soon.

2. **New Collection templates**: Webflow also provides some shortcuts to create a Collection to help you save some steps and time. If you were creating a blogging website or publication, for example, you might want a blog posts Collection. In that case, you could select the **Blog Posts** template and Webflow will automatically create some commonly used Collection fields and prepopulate it accordingly. For our project, however, we'll create our Collection from scratch, so we can skip the templates for now.

3. **The Collection Settings and Collection fields sections**: This is where we'll be spending most of our time, customizing our current Collection. We'll devote most of the rest of this chapter to creating a custom Collection of libraries here.

4. **The Editor Preview section**: Every CMS project can have multiple collaborators to help out with managing the content in CMS. In order to make this process of adding and editing CMS content easier, all collaborators will have access to a simple form that is made up of all the fields that are entered. This section shows a live preview of what that form will look like. We'll return to this later.

Now that we've had an overview of the CMS settings, let's dive in and create our first Collection!

## Creating a Collection

Since our website is going to showcase a Collection of libraries around the world, it stands to reason that the Collection we create should be about libraries. Let's go ahead and do this:

1. Under the **Collection Settings** section, enter the Collection name as Libraries. Note that the best practice for naming Collections is to make it a plural noun since it's likely going to hold more than one instance of that object. Also note that the name you give the Collection is automatically used as the URL (often called a **slug**) of that Collection on your website. In our case, the URL or slug is formed as http://website.com/libraries/library-page. You can always customize this, but we'll keep it as is. The **Collection Settings** section will now look like what you see in *Figure 10.4*:

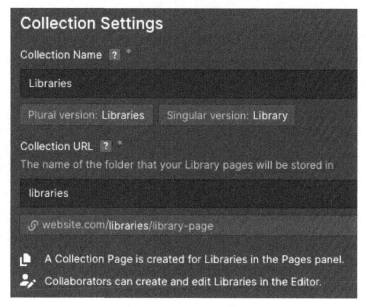

Figure 10.4 – Collection Settings for our Libraries Collection

2.  Next, let's create the Collection fields. Collection fields are essentially individual pieces of data about the object we're modeling. In our case, these include things such as the name of a library, where it's located, and any images of it. We'll be referring to *Figure 9.5* in *Chapter 9*, *Getting Started with Webflow CMS*, to help us create these fields.

3.  Under the **Collection fields** section, you'll notice that the **Name** and **Slug** fields are already filled in for us. Let's keep these as is.

4.  Let's add the first of our own fields, Showcase Image. This will be the main image that we want to display of the library in question.

    First, click the blue **Add New Field** button. Notice that Webflow allows us to create multiple types of fields. For this one, select the **Image** type, as shown in *Figure 10.5*:

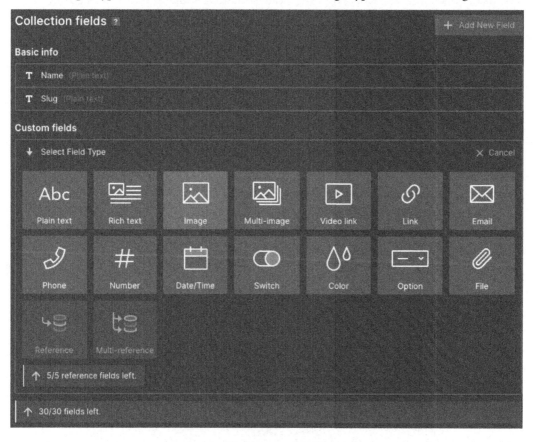

Figure 10.5 – Adding an Image field type

5.  Next, in the **Label** field, write Showcase Image. The **Help text** input field is where we can write some instructions for any users that we decide to add as collaborators on this project; we can leave it blank for now. Since we want all our libraries to have a showcase image, check the **This field is required** checkbox. Note that once we designate a field as mandatory, it will need to be populated, else the Collection will fail to be created. Hit the **Save Field** button to save our changes, as shown in *Figure 10.6*:

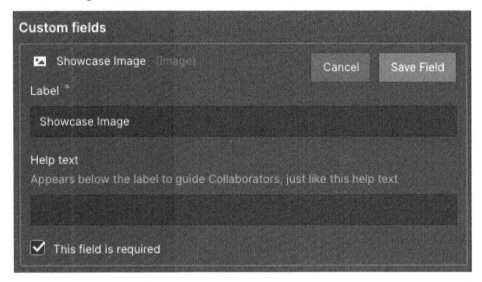

Figure 10.6 – Saving the Showcase Image field

Congratulations – you've now created your first collection field!

Let's repeat this for the following fields:

- **Label**: City

    **Select Field Type**: **Plain text**

    **Text field type**: **Single line**

    Required: Yes

- **Label**: Country

    **Select Field Type**: **Plain text**

    **Text field type**: **Single line**

    Required: Yes

- **Label**: Continent

  **Select Field Type: Plain text**

  **Text field type: Single line**

  Required: Yes

- **Label**: Description

  **Select Field Type: Plain text**

  **Text field type: Multiple line**

  Required: Yes

- **Label**: Address

  **Select Field Type: Plain text**

  **Text field type: Single line**

  Required: No

- **Label**: Year of construction

  **Select Field Type: Number**

  Required: No

- **Label**: Number of books

  **Select Field Type: Number**

  Required: No

- **Label**: Website

  **Select Field Type: Link**

  Required: No

- **Label**: Image Gallery

  **Select Field Type: Multi-image**

  Required: No

And that's it! In the end, your list of fields should look like what is shown in *Figure 10.7*:

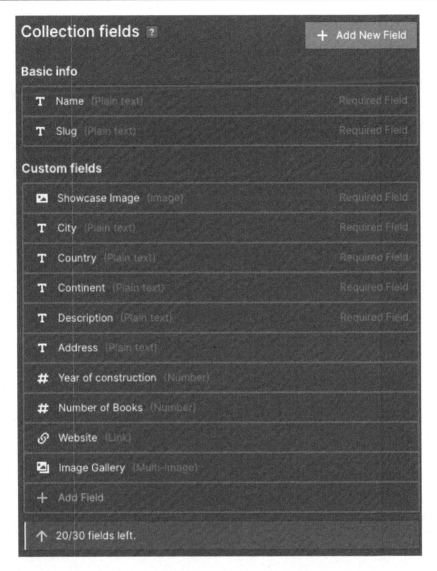

Figure 10.7 – The fields of the Libraries Collection

Now that we've created all our Collection fields, let's save this work by clicking the blue **Create Collection** button at the top of the page.

And with that, you've now created the skeleton of your first Webflow Collection! Now it's time to put some meat on that skeleton and add the data that's going to make the Collection come to life.

# Adding content to a Collection

Once you've created the **Libraries** Collection, you'll be brought to the main Collections page and will see a screen that looks as in *Figure 10.8*:

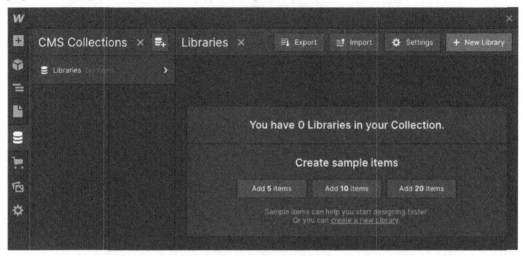

Figure 10.8 – Empty Collection

Since we haven't created any content in the Collection yet, Webflow is conveniently offering to generate some of the content for us. Note that the content likely won't look very real, but what it will enable for us is the ability to quickly populate and design our website so that we can start seeing how everything comes together. Once we're happy with the designs, we can then go back into the Collection and replace the content with real data.

Let's explore what this actually looks like. Click the **Add 5 items** button. After a moment, Webflow will have created sample content for you, and it will look something like *Figure 10.9*:

Figure 10.9 – Sample content added to the Libraries Collection

As mentioned, notice that the **Name** field is populated with randomized content. In fact, if you click on any of the row items, you'll notice that all the fields are randomized with gibberish.

Again, this is fine for now as we'll focus on presenting the data first. That said, since the look of the website is going to be heavily impacted by the actual content, it will be helpful to update at least one of the library items so that we have a reasonably realistic version of a library that we can present on the website.

Let's go ahead and do that:

1.  Click on the first-row item.
2.  In the **Name** field, change it to `Toronto Reference Library`.
3.  In the **Slug** field, change it to `toronto-reference`.
4.  For **Showcase Image**, you'll be using an image you downloaded from the project asset files. Use the file picker to find the file titled `TO_Ref_Library.jpeg` and select it.
5.  Change the **City** field to `Toronto`, the **Country** field to `Canada`, and the **Continent** field to `North America`.
6.  For the **Description** field, again you can write anything you like here; try to make it a few lines long. You can use the following text if you like:

    *The Toronto Reference Library is the largest public reference library in Canada with an extensive collection of books, manuscripts, microfilm, and other items. Most items in its collection are designated for reference-use only, with the public unable to borrow these items for use outside the library. In addition to providing access to its collection, the library also hosts a number of public reading events, as well as provide technical access and services to the public.*

7.  Change the **Address** field to `789 Yonge St, Toronto, ON M4W 2G8`.
8.  Set the **Year of construction** field to `1977`.
9.  Change the **Number of books** field to `375,000`.
10. Set the **Website** field to `https://www.torontopubliclibrary.ca/ torontoreferencelibrary/`.
11. You can leave the images as is or use the additional images for the Toronto Reference Library provided in the project link at the beginning of this chapter.
12. After updating the fields, be sure to hit the **Save** button.

You've now successfully added your first library item! We can now begin to design and dynamically display these items on the website's home page.

# Designing a CMS home page

We've created our **Libraries** Collection and added some library items to it. Even though most of the entries are not quite real yet, we can still design our home page to get a feel for how the page will come together. Especially now that we've updated one of the items to display some more realistic data, it can give us a better sense of the website's design.

So, let's go ahead and start designing the home page. Our end goal is to make the home page look similar to *Figure 10.10*, displaying libraries in a two-column grid and allowing users to filter the libraries dynamically by continent:

Figure 10.10 – The Libraries of the World home page

Taking a step back, notice that the home page will be divided into two areas: the left navigation that will contain the filters and the main content area on the right. We'll need to keep this in mind when we build this page out.

So, with that, let's begin!

1.  Select the **Pages** icon on the left menu to go back to the home page. You should see a blank white canvas.

2.  Make sure you're on the **Base Breakpoint** size of 1440 **PX**.

3.  Select the **Body** element, and make sure the class is set to **Body (All Pages)**. Then, change **Font** to **Georgia**. Give it a size of 18 **PX** and a height of 1.2-.

4. With the **Body** element still selected, add a new **Section** element and give it a class name of `Section`. This is what we'll encapsulate the entire home page under.

5. Select the **Section** element. Add a **div** element and give it a class name of `Side Panel`. This is the container that will contain the website logo and the filters.

6. With the **Side Panel** element selected, give it a width of `20%` and a height of `100vh`. This will ensure that the panel will only ever take up 20% of the screen's width and will always cover the full height of the page. Next, give it left and right padding values of `32` **PX**.

7. Again, while you've still got the **Side Panel** element selected, add a **Heading** element and make it **H1**. Set the heading as `Libraries of the World`.

8. Remove the class name of the heading that exists by default and select the purple **All H1 Headings** class name. This will ensure that any H1 headings we add to the website will get the properties we set here.

9. With the **Side Panel** element selected, change **Font** to **Impact**.

   We won't be adding any filters just yet until we have all the library items on the page. So, for now, let's move on to building the main content area.

10. Select the **Section** element. Add a new **div** element and give it a class name of `Main Content`.

11. You'll notice that this new **Main Content** div element was added to the bottom of the page. We want it to be sitting to the right of the **Side Panel** element. To do this, select the **Section** element and change its **Display** property to **Flex**. Since **Flex Direction** is set to **Horizontal** by default, the **Main Content** element is now oriented horizontally alongside the side panel as we expected, as shown in *Figure 10.11*:

Figure 10.11 – Orienting the Side Panel and Main Content elements

12. Select the **Main Content** element. Now add a new element called **Collection List**.
    This is a Webflow-specific element that allows us to pull and display data from our
    CMS Collections. You'll now see a **Collection List Settings** popup that will show a
    **Source** dropdown. Here, select the **Libraries** Collection, as shown in *Figure 10.12*:

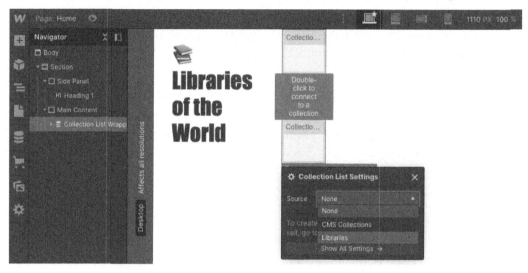

Figure 10.12 – Connecting the Collection list to the Libraries Collection

13. Next, in the same popup, choose the two-column layout setting. Then close the
    settings popup.

14. In the Navigator, you can now see that Webflow has created a **Collection List
    Wrapper** element. Nested under it is a **Collection List** element and nested under
    that is a **Collection Item** element. All these elements are specifically generated by
    and for Webflow CMS and all appear in purple.

15. Select the first **Collection Item** element in the Navigator. Inside here, we're going
    to add the showcase image for a library. To do this, first add an **Image** element. The
    **Image Settings** popup should appear and right away, you should see the addition of
    new purple-colored settings. These settings allow us to pull data directly from any
    CMS Collections by referring directly to any fields we have created. As such, select
    the checkbox for **Get Image from Libraries** and select **Showcase Image**, as shown
    in *Figure 10.13*:

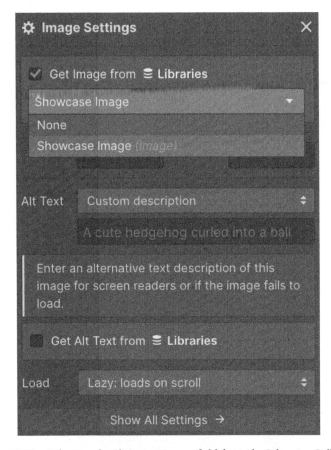

Figure 10.13 – Selecting the Showcase Image field from the Libraries Collection

16. Immediately, you'll notice that several images have populated the home page. These are all the showcase images of the individual Collection items that we had created.

We still need to add the library names and their locations.

17. Select the **Collection Item** element again. Now, add a **Heading** element and set it to **H2**. Check the **Get text from Libraries** checkbox and select the **Name** field, as shown in *Figure 10.14*:

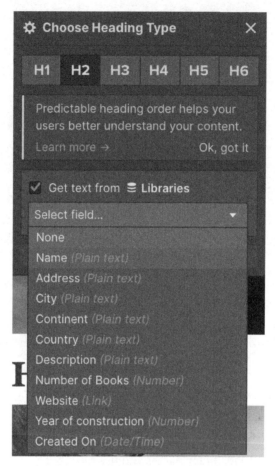

Figure 10.14 – Selecting the Name field

Just as before, you should now see the names of the libraries automatically get populated across all the library items.

18. With the **H2** element selected, make sure to choose **All H2 Headings** as its class. Now change **Font** to **Impact**. The home page should be looking as in *Figure 10.15*:

**Libraries of the World**

**Toronto Reference Library**

**Asperiores Quisquam**

**Vitae Aliquid Doloremque Placeat**

**Architecto Aut Numquam Placeat**

Figure 10.15 – Populating the home page with library titles

19. By now, you should be noticing a powerful feature of Webflow CMS: when you make a change to a Collection list item, it flows through to all the other Collection list items.

20. Let's now add the **City** and **Country** fields as well. Select the **Collection List Item** element again. Add a **div** element and give it a class name of `Location`. Next, add a **Text Block** element, select the **Get text from Libraries** checkbox, and select the **City** field. Select the **Location div** element again, then add another **Text Block** element, select the **Get text from Libraries** checkbox, and select the **Country** field this time.

21. Select the **Location** element and name it `Display of Flex`. This will now horizontally align the **City** and **Country** fields.

22. Select the **Country Text Block** element and give it a left margin of 8 **PX**. Next, select the **More text options** button under the **Typography** section. Select the **Capitalize** option.

23. Next, change the font color to #6e6e6e and the font size to 26 **PX**. The
    **Typography** settings should look as shown in *Figure 10.16*:

Figure 10.16 – The Typography settings for the Country field

After all these steps, the home page should now be featuring five library items, the
first with an image, its name, its city, and its country and the rest with placeholders.
It should look similar to *Figure 10.17*:

Figure 10.17 – The updated home page

Remember, we updated the fields of only one of the library items—the one about the Toronto Reference Library—so the others are starting to look a little strange with their randomized content. Again, this is expected as we only wanted to use the other fields temporarily in order to understand how the design would come together. Now that we have that idea, it's time to populate the rest of the data so that the other library items look a little more realistic as well.

But instead of going in and individually updating each of the library items, we'll look at how we may be able to speed up this process a little.

# Importing mass content

Occasionally, when you're working on managing CMS Collections and keeping them updated, you'll need to update or add new Collection items. You could do this by adding them individually, but this can end up taking a lot of time if you need to do this for large amounts of data.

Alternatively, we can also upload content in batches. Let's do this now to add a number of libraries to our Collection:

1. Go back to the **CMS** section and while you have the **Libraries** Collection selected, hit the **Import** button, as shown in *Figure 10.18*:

Figure 10.18 – Importing data into a Collection

2. Select the comma-separated file titled `libraries_of_the_world.csv` from the project assets you downloaded at the start of the chapter.

3. Webflow will usually detect that the first row in the import file has headings. If you create your own import file, make sure that each of the headings maps back to a Collection field in your CMS Collection. In this case, the import file should have headings that match the fields we already created in the **Libraries** Collection. Once you make sure that you've selected the **Yes, this is the header** selection, click the blue **Continue** button.

4.  Next, you'll be shown a preview of the data you're about to import, as shown in *Figure 10.19*:

Figure 10.19 – Previewing the import

You can double-check each of the entries to ensure they are sound. You can use the left and right arrow buttons along the top of the page to traverse through all the library items, each of which corresponds to a row from the import file. Go ahead and click the blue **Import** button as is shown in the top-right corner of the preceding screenshot.

5.  If all goes well, the five libraries should now be added to your Collection. Now
    we can go ahead and delete all the items in the Collection that were previously
    randomized. Hit the **Select** button and then check off the items that we no longer
    need. Then hit the **Delete** button. It should look similar to *Figure 10.20*:

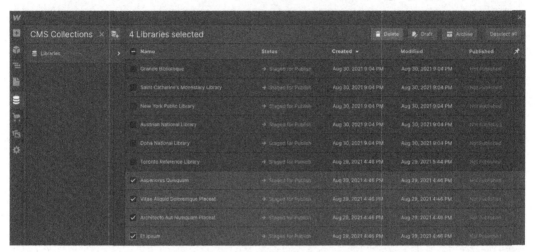

Figure 10.20 – Deleting the items that we no longer need

You can now go back to the home page and view the libraries you've just uploaded. And
that's it. You've now imported content in a batch using an external data source.

# Finishing touches

Now that we've uploaded some libraries into our CMS, we can view them on the home
page in all their glory! Right away, you should find that looking at real data makes the
page look far better. But you may also notice some things look a little off. Let's add some
finishing touches to fix these.

First, as seen in *Figure 10.21*, some of the library entries aren't aligned properly with each other:

Figure 10.21 – Some library entries appear misaligned on the home page

This is because the images we had uploaded as showcase images for the libraries don't all have the same dimensions. We can quickly fix this by adding some consistency to the dimensions of the images.

Select one of the showcase images. Then, set its **Width** property to 500 **PX** and the **Height** property to 350 **PX**. You'll notice that now all the showcase images get a uniform width and height, which aligns all the libraries cleanly in place, as seen in *Figure 10.22*:

Figure 10.22 – Making all images the same width and height

This is looking a lot better! We can make another small change so that the library entries have some vertical white space and don't feel too cramped together.

Select one of the showcase images again. Now give it a top margin of 56 **PX**. The libraries are now nicely spaced out from each other.

There's one last thing we can do. Notice that the content on this page is pressed right up against the top and right edges of the screen. Let's give it some breathing room.

Select the **Section** element. Give it top and right padding values of 40 **PX**, as shown in the following screenshot:

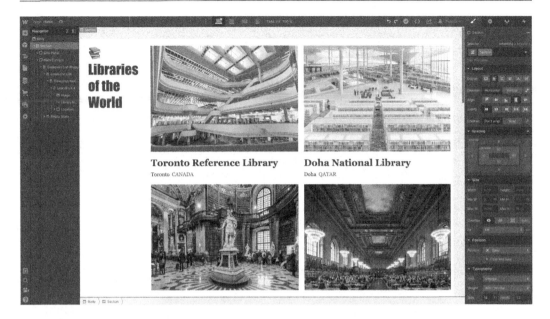

Figure 10.23 – Adding top and right padding to the page

These tweaks are small but already make a better impression.

We'll stop this here for now, but you're encouraged to continue tweaking this page to your heart's content. Try changing fonts or adding colors. If you're adventurous, you can even try adding some animations and interactions to make the library images come to life upon hovering.

> **Important**
>
> Notice that we haven't at all explored making this page responsive across multiple device sizes. We'll leave it to you as an exercise to explore accomplishing this.

# Summary

We covered a lot in this chapter!

We created a CMS project and created our **Libraries** Collection by adding fields. We also saw how Webflow can generate randomized content for us to help speed up the design process. We took advantage of this to quickly put together our home page.

Then, we updated one of the library items directly in the CMS to reflect some real data. This helped us get an updated view of the home page, which helped make things more contextually real.

Next, we uploaded a number of new library items by importing a CSV file that contained data that we mapped back to our CMS. Each row in the CSV file corresponded to a new library item in the CMS.

Finally, we made some last adjustments to the design of the home page to ensure that the library items were being displayed well.

In the next chapter, we'll continue building the website out. What happens when a user selects one of the libraries? How do we allow users to filter the view of their libraries so that they are viewing them based on which continent they're in?

We'll answer these questions and more by continuing to explore more of Webflow CMS's powerful collection and filtering features.

See you in the next chapter!

# 11
# Creating Collection Pages

In the last chapter, we went through the process of creating our first Webflow CMS Collection from scratch. We populated our Collection with a number of libraries, and we made great progress in creating the home page of our Libraries of the World project.

In this chapter, we'll continue where we left off. Right now, visitors who arrive on the home page will see names and pictures of various libraries around the world. But wouldn't it be great if we could also let them click into each of the libraries to see further details about it? In this chapter, we're going to do just that.

To that end, we'll be covering the following topics:

- Unlocking the power of Webflow Collection Pages to build multiple pages in one shot
- Binding CMS fields to a Collection Page
- Using filters to update the view of libraries in a Collection list
- Linking to a Collection Pages from the home page

By the end of this chapter, you will appreciate the power and flexibility of working with Webflow CMS for building large dynamic websites. And we'll have covered enough of the features of Webflow CMS for you to be able to build a CMS project of your own.

So, let's begin!

# Project overview

As usual, let's first take a look at what we'll have built by the end of this chapter. *Figure 11.1* shows the Collection Page that we'll be building out:

 Back

## Toronto Reference Library

| | |
|---|---|
| **Address:** | 130 St George St, Toronto, ON M5S 1A5 |
| **Opened:** | 1971 |
| **Books:** | 4.5 million |
| **Visit website** ↗ | |

The Toronto Reference Library is the largest public reference library in Canada with an extensive collection of books, manuscripts, microfilm, and other items. Most items in its collection are designated for reference-use only, with the public is unable to borrow these items for use outside the library. In addition to providing access to its collection, the library also hosts a number of public reading events, as well as provide technical access and services to the public.

**More images**

**See more libraries**

**Austrian National Library**
Vienna, Austria

**New York Public Library**
New York City, USA

**Doha National Library**
Doha, Qatar

Figure 11.1 – The Library Collection Page

Users will be able to click into any library from the home page and access a details page that shows more information about that specific library. These extra details will include things such as the library's address, a link to its website if available, a short description of the library, and a gallery of pictures showing more of that library.

We'll also take a look at how to create quick links to other library pages as well. This is typically a good idea to include because it will assist the user in browsing through other pieces of content on the website.

Most impressively, we'll be building this page only once. We'll see how the page design will propagate throughout all our library pages. Again, all of this will be achieved without code.

So, with that outline, let's dive into Collection Pages.

# Building the Library Collection Page

The first thing to realize about Collection Pages is that Webflow always creates one for us whenever we create a new **Collection**.

We can see this ourselves by clicking on the **Pages** menu item on the left of the page. As shown in *Figure 11.2*, you should see a section at the bottom called **CMS Collection pages**. Under it, you'll see an entry called **Libraries Template**. Any Collection we create in the CMS will automatically get its own Template page and you'll see it here. Because we have only one Libraries Collection, we see a corresponding Libraries Template page here:

Figure 11.2 – Locating the Collection Pages

Go ahead and click on the **Libraries Template** page.

You'll notice we're presented with a blank page. We'll design our library details page from scratch, and we'll see how this page's design then gets propagated to all the libraries automatically.

> **Important Note**
>
> Just as in *Chapter 10, Creating Your First CMS Project*, for the purposes of this chapter, we'll only be designing this page on its base breakpoint for desktop screens. As a personal challenge, we encourage you to try designing for the other breakpoints as well so that it becomes fully responsive.

We'll design this page by splitting it up into two sections. First, we'll tackle the top section of the page, which we'll call the **Main** section. This will contain details about the library, including its name, address, year of construction, the number of books it has, a website link, a short description, and a featured image. To end this section, we'll have a gallery of additional images of the library.

The second section of the page will contain links to other libraries in this Collection. We'll see how we can populate this section dynamically by using some of Webflow CMS' built-in features. We'll call this section **Other Libraries**.

Let's begin designing the **Main** section now.

# Building the Main section of the Library page

Recall that we had added all the details of the libraries into our Libraries Collection in *Chapter 10, Creating Your First CMS Project*. Now is our chance to start binding our page to these details and start displaying them to the user. Let's go ahead and do this:

1.  Select the **Body** element and add a **Section** element. Give the **Section** element a class name of Main. Select the **Main Section** element and add a **Container** element to it. Give this **Container** element a class name of Container.

2.  With the **Container** element selected, add a **Link Block** element. In its **Settings** popup, click the **Page** button and set the **Page** to **Home**, as shown in *Figure 11.3*:

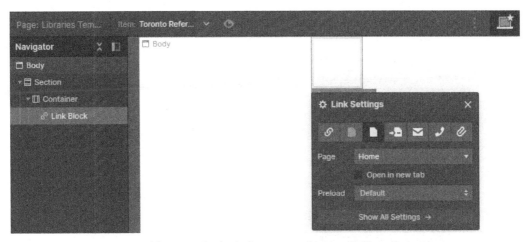

Figure 11.3 – Adding a Link Block element to take users back to the home page

3. Next, give the **Link Block** element a class name of `Back`. This is the element that will allow users to navigate back to the home page.

4. With the **Back** element selected, add a **Text Block** element. Rewrite the text inside of it to `Back to Home`.

5. We want to remove the default blue color of the text. So, select the **Link Block** element and give it a color of `#333`.

6. Let's give this page a little bit of breathing room at the top. Select the **Section** element and give it a top padding value of `64px` – much better! The page should now look like *Figure 11.4*:

Figure 11.4 – Updating the Library Collection Page

7. Now, let's move on to the actual content section of the page. Select the **Container** element and add a **Heading** element. Set it to **H1**.

8.  Check the **Get text from Libraries** checkbox and select the **Name** field, as shown in *Figure 11.5*:

Figure 11.5 – Binding the H1 text to the Libraries' Name field

We've now successfully bound the **H1** element to the **Name** field in our Libraries Collection, as we can see from the updated name that it has pulled. We'll be repeating this essential binding process throughout the page.

9.  Next, let's create the grid that will contain the details of the library in question. The container will hold some additional details about the library. Select the **Container** element and add a **Grid** element to it. Give the **Grid** element a class name of `Details Grid`.

10. With the `Details Grid` element selected, reduce the size of the first column down to `0.5fr`. Next, in the first cell of the **Grid** element, add a **Text Block** element and write out the `Address` label. Give it a class name of `Label`. Change its **Font Weight** to **700 Bold**.

11. Next, add a **Text Block** element in the second column and, this time, bind it to the Collection field of **Address**. It should automatically populate the address of the library. Give it a class name of `Value`. The page should now be looking like *Figure 11.6*:

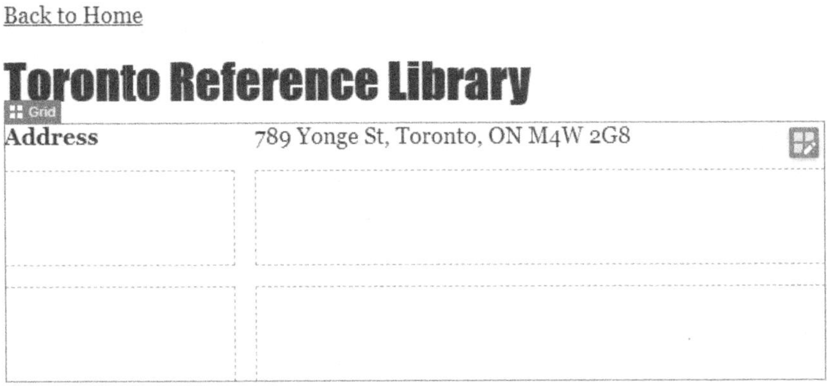

Back to Home

# Toronto Reference Library

| Address | 789 Yonge St, Toronto, ON M4W 2G8 |
|---------|-----------------------------------|
|         |                                   |
|         |                                   |

Figure 11.6 – Adding the Address field to the Library page

12. Now, let's move onto the second row. Add a **Text Block** element and reuse the class name that we created in *step 10*. In the text input, write out **Opened**. In the second column, add a **Text Block** element and bind it to the **Collection** field called **Year of Construction**.

13. Repeat *step 11* so that you have added another **Label** element called `Books`. Add a corresponding **Text Block** element that binds to **Number of books**.

The last field we want to show here is the website URL, if it exists. For this, add a **Text Link** element. As shown in *Figure 11.7*, in the **Link Settings** popup that appears, check the checkbox that allows you to get the URL from the Libraries Collection and select the **Website** field. Make sure to also select the checkbox to open the link in a new tab:

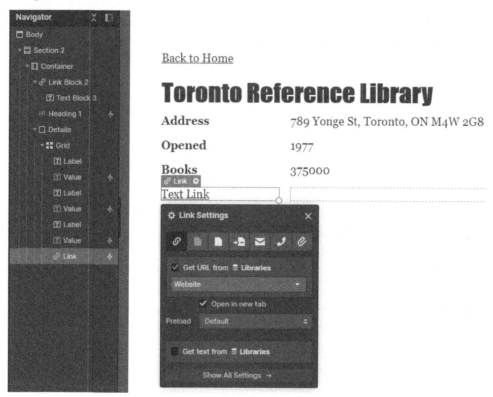

Figure 11.7 – Binding the Website URL field

14. Next, rewrite that text link to say **Go to Website**. Now, whenever a user clicks on this link, it should open a new window taking them to the library's website.

15. Let's finish this section by styling the **Details Grid** element a little. Select the **Details Grid** element. Under the **Borders** section in the **Style** panel, give the border a solid style, set its **Width** property to 2px, and give it a border radius of 8px, as shown in *Figure 11.8*:

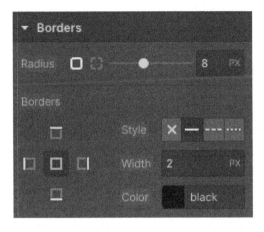

Figure 11.8 – Setting border properties on the Details Grid element

16. With the **Details container** element still selected, give all of its sides padding values of 24px. We've now wrapped up the details of the library with a nice border, setting it apart from all else on the page.

17. Let's now add a short description of the library to the page. Select the **Container** element. Add a **Paragraph** element, check the **Get text from Libraries** checkbox, and select the **Description** field to bind to it, as shown in *Figure 11.9*:

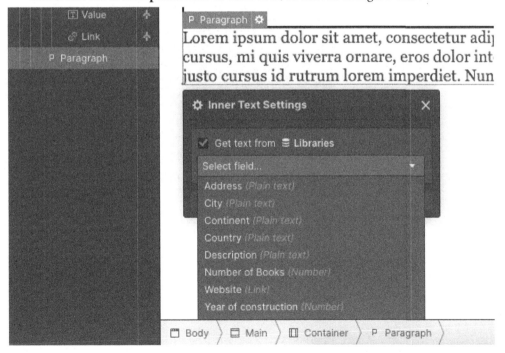

Figure 11.9 – Binding to the Description field

Lastly, give the **Paragraph** element a **Top Margin** property of 32px.

This is looking really good. We've bound our Library page details to a number of fields in our Collection and it's already pulling all the data. We still need to add a showcase feature image, though. Let's add that now.

18. In order to show the feature image, we'll be dividing the content into two sides. The details and description content will be on the left of the page and the feature image will be on the right.

    Select the **Container** element and add a new **Div Block** element. Give this a class name of Left. Then, move the **Details Grid** and **Paragraph** elements under the **Left** div element. Next, select the **Container** element again and add another **Div Block** element. Give this one a class name of Right. The Navigator should now look like *Figure 11.10*:

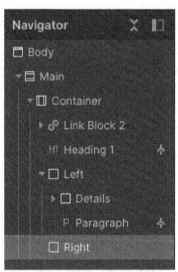

Figure 11.10 – Organizing the elements in the Navigator

19. Select the **Right** div element. Add an **Image** element to it. In the **Image Settings** popup that appears, bind the **Image** element to the **Showcase Image** field, as shown in *Figure 11.11*:

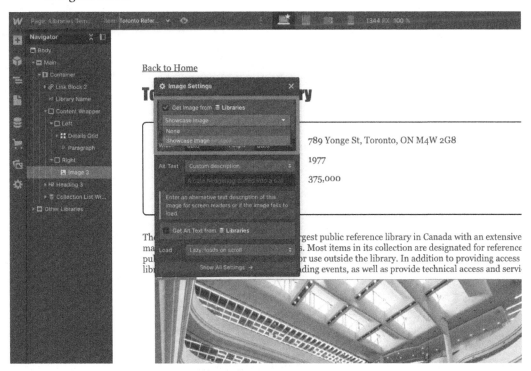

Figure 11.11 – Binding to the Showcase Image field

The image is automatically populated but the content is still stacked. Do you remember how we can align content so that it is horizontally grouped? That's right – Flex to the rescue!

20. Before we use Flex though, let's wrap the **Left** and **Right** div block elements into a content wrapper so that we can apply the **Flex** property to them specifically. So, go ahead and select the **Container** element again. Add a **Div Block** element and give it a class name of Content Wrapper. Move the **Left** and **Right** elements so that they are both nested under the **Content Wrapper** element, as shown in *Figure 11.12*:

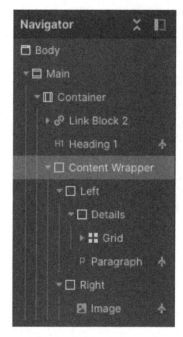

Figure 11.12 – Wrapping the content into a Content Wrapper element

Now, select the **Content Wrapper** element and change its **Layout Display** property to **Flex**.

21. The content should be horizontally aligned now, but you may notice that the image could be looking disproportionate. This is because we haven't explicitly set any sizes for the content items yet. There are a number of ways we can fix this, and you are encouraged to try them. For now, however, we'll just select the **Left** div block element and set its **Width** property to **100%**.

22. Let's add some breathing room to the Showcase Image. Select the **Right** div block element and give it a **Left padding** value of 24px. The **Content Wrapper** element should now be looking like *Figure 11.13*:

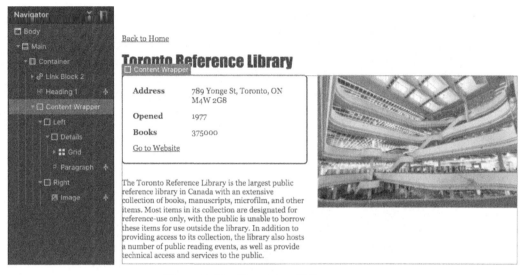

Figure 11.13 – The updated Library page

23. This is looking good! But we can tweak the Showcase Image one more time to make it appear a little more balanced with the text. Select the Showcase Image and set its **Width** property to 800px and its **Height** property to **100%**. Then, set its **Fit** property to **Cover**. Now, the image will always span a width of 800px while filling the space provided with its height, ensuring that the dimensions never look off.

24. We have one thing left in the **Main** section of the Library page: the image gallery. Select the **Container** element again and, this time, add a **Collection List** element. Select **Source** to be **Image Gallery** and change the **Layout** property to **3 columns**, as shown in *Figure 11.14*:

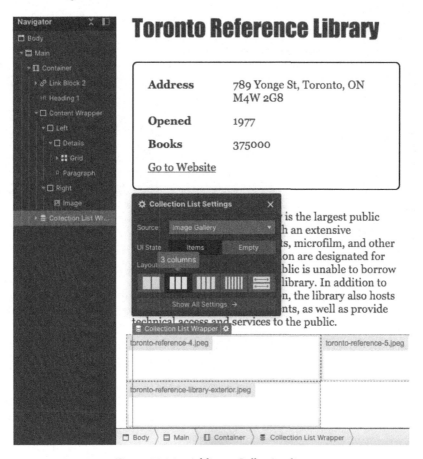

Figure 11.14 – Adding a Collection list

Like on the home page, a Collection list essentially allows us to list a number of items from a Collection in a single place. In this case, we're binding to the **Image Gallery** field in order to pull any images that were uploaded.

25. Note, however, that after setting this property, even though we're able to see the image names in the placeholders, we're not seeing the images themselves yet. This is because we still need to add an **Image** element.

Select any of the **Collection List Item** elements that we just added and add an
**Image** element to it. Make sure to bind the **Image** element to the **Image Gallery**
field, as shown in *Figure 11.15*:

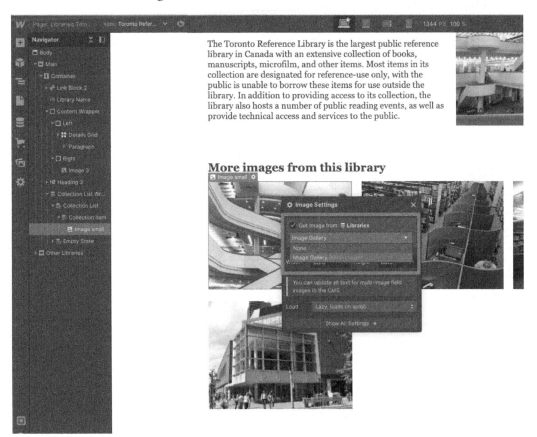

Figure 11.15 – Binding to the Image Gallery field

26. Note, however, that since the images aren't of a uniform size, they end up feeling randomly placed. We can fix this. Select any of the images and change its **Width** property to 300px and the **Height** property to 220px. Next, change its **Fit** property to **Cover**. Let's also set the **Bottom** margin to 24px so that if the images overflow onto an additional line, there is some vertical whitespace between them. Note also that the class name of this **Image** element is set to Image 2, since this is a new instance of the **Image** element. Go ahead and rename it to Image small. With all said and done, the **Image** settings should look like *Figure 11.16*:

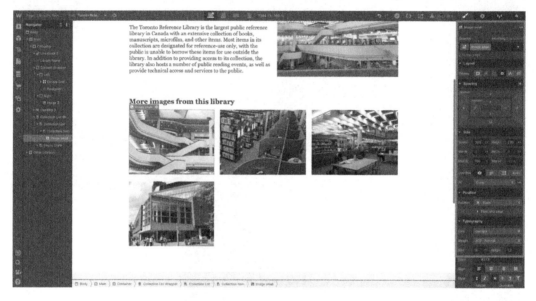

Figure 11.16 – Making the images appear uniform in the image gallery

Finally, let's add a heading to this Image Gallery. Select the **Container** element and add a **Heading** element and set it to **H2**. Move the **H2** element above the **Image Gallery** section and rewrite the text as More images. Next, give it a **Top margin** property of 24px.

With that, we've now completed putting together the **Main** section of the Library page! Your page should be looking a lot like *Figure 11.17*:

Figure 11.17 – The Main section of the Library page

Now enters a powerful feature of Webflow CMS. At the top of the page, you can use the Item selector dropdown to cycle through all the other Collection items that have been created, as shown in *Figure 11.18*:

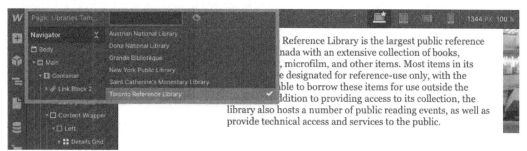

Figure 11.18 – Cycling through all the Collection items

And as you choose any of the others, you'll notice that all the pages are automatically updated with their own unique data.

In essence, what we've done here is build a single Libraries Template page that is being used to display all of our Library items – one page for potentially hundreds of items. Furthermore, let's say we wanted to update the page to have an additional field, or we want to style it differently. All we would have to do is update it once on this Template page and it will update all the Library items. The time saved here can be enormous!

Now, let's finish designing the Library page by adding the second and last section of the page: some quick links to other libraries.

## Building the other libraries section

As mentioned earlier, it's typically a good idea to provide users with quick links to other related items in a Collection as it can ease the browsing experience. In our case, we'll build a small section that will include the names and showcase images of other libraries in the Libraries Collection. We'll see how we can achieve this dynamically, and we'll also see how we can leverage work that we've already done to save us time.

Let's begin:

1.  Select the **Body** element and add a new **Section** element. Give this a class name of Other Libraries. Give it a **Top** margin of 64px.

2.  With the **Other Libraries** section element selected, add a **Container** element and give it the existing class name of Container.

3.  Select the **Container** element and add a **Heading** element, and set it to **H2**. Change its text to say Other libraries.

4.  We'll be needing to add a new **Collection List** element here to list out some of the other libraries in our Collection. Recall that in *Chapter 10, Creating Your First CMS Project*, we had already created a Collection list to showcase all the libraries on the home page. It turns out that we can reuse this and save ourselves some work.

5.  Go to the home page and select the **Collection List Wrapper** element.

6.  Hit *Ctrl + C* if you're on a PC, or *Cmd + C* if you're on a Macintosh, to copy the element.

7.  Next, select the **Libraries Template** page again and select the **Container** element that is nested under the **Other Libraries** section.

8.  Hit *Ctrl + V* or *Cmd + V* to paste the **Collection List Wrapper** element here. And, as simple as that, you should now see that the same collection of libraries that was seen on the home page is now visible on the Libraries Template too, as shown in *Figure 11.19*:

□ Other Libraries

## Other libraries

### Grande Bibliotèque
Montreal  CANADA

### Saint Catherine's Monestary Library
Sinai  EGYPT

□ Body 〉 □ Other Libraries 〉

Figure 11.19 – Pasting a copy of the Collection list onto the Library Template page

9.  Let's tweak this Collection list a little so it looks more appropriate for this section. With the **Collection List Wrapper** element selected, give it a class name of `Other Libraries List`.

10. Access **Collection List Settings** for the **Other Libraries List** element. Change its layout to the three-column layout, as shown in *Figure 11.20*:

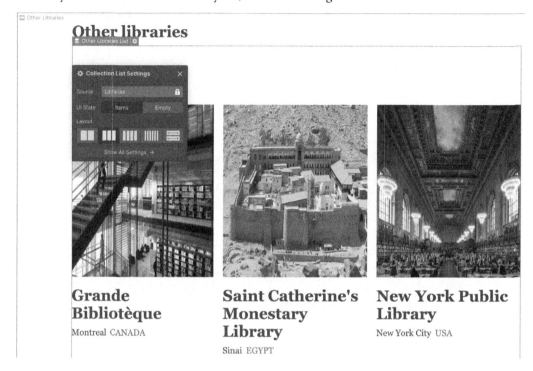

Figure 11.20 – Changing the layout of the Collection list to a three-column layout

11. We only want to show three libraries in this list, though, rather than the full list of libraries. With the **Collection List Settings** popup still open, click the **Show All Settings** button. Webflow will display some additional settings on the right-hand side that we can use to dynamically control what we want to display in this Collection list. Next, check the **Limit items** checkbox and set the **Show** field to **3**. This will limit the Collection list to only ever display three items at a time.

12. Next, add a new **Filter** element. Set the **Name** dropdown to **Library** and the **Equals** value to **is not Equal**, as shown in *Figure 11.21*. This filter ensures that the Collection list does not show a Library Item that the user is currently on, since that would be redundant and unhelpful:

Figure 11.21 – Creating a new filter so that we do not display an item that the user is currently viewing

13. The images are looking out of proportion. This is because they are still using the same properties of the images on the home page. Let's fix this. Select any of the images in the **Other Libraries List** element. Change its class name to our previously created class name of `Image small`.

14. Lastly, select any of the library name **Heading** elements and change it from **H2** to **H3**.

With that completed, the **Other Libraries** section should now look similar to what you see in *Figure 11.22*:

Figure 11.22 – The updated Other Libraries section displaying a Collection list

We want these libraries to be clickable, though, so that the user can navigate to them if needed. Let's do that now.

15. With any of the Collection items selected, add a **Link Block** element. Select the **Collection Page** tab, and under the **Choose a collection page** dropdown, select **Current Library**. This will ensure that if the user clicks on the **Link Block** element, they will be taken to the Library page of the specific library that it is binding to. So, go ahead and move all **Image**, **Heading**, and **Text Block** elements into the **Link Block** element so that it looks like *Figure 11.23*:

Figure 11.23 – Binding the Link Block element to the Library Item it is currently showing

16. Notice also that the link colors have now changed to the default blue, since that's what was set on the **Link Block** element. Feel free to change it to anything you want. In this case, we're going to set the **Typography Decoration** property on the **Link Block** element to **None**, and we'll set the font colors on the **Heading** and **Text Block** elements to #333.

17. Next, we can set the **Bottom padding** value of the **Other Libraries** section to 100px in order to give it some vertical whitespace from the bottom of the page.

18. Finally, let's make this section stand out a bit more visually from the rest of the page. Since it's not as important as the details of the current library, let's make its background a bit more muted. Select the **Other Libraries** section element and give its background a #f3f3f3 color. With the section still selected, give it a **Top padding** value of 64px.

With all said and done, the final **Other Libraries** section should look like *Figure 11.24*:

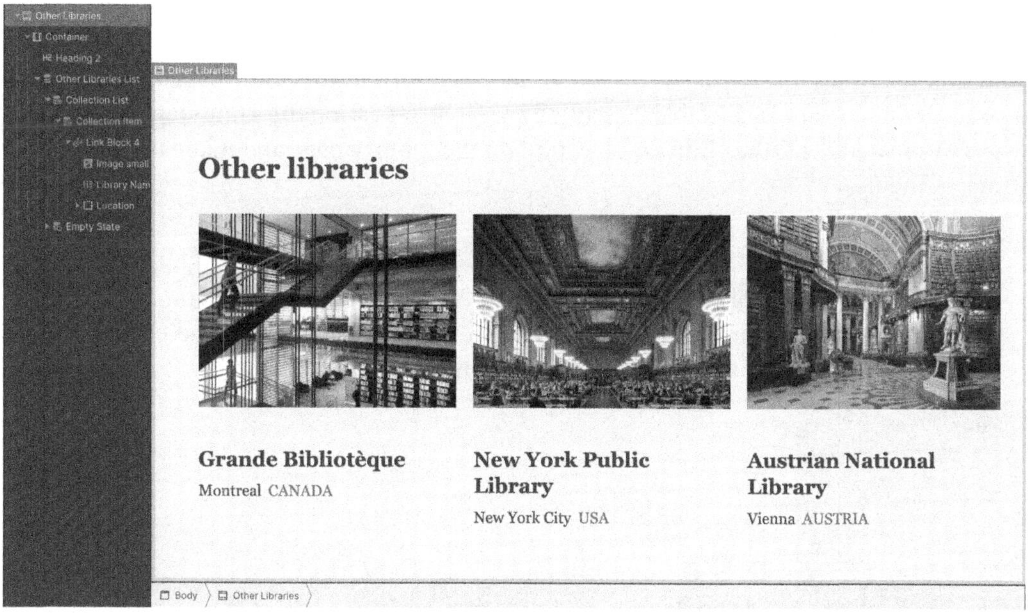

Figure 11.24 – The final look at the Other Libraries section

Just as before, you can now cycle through the Library pages to see how this **Other Libraries** section looks in each of them. You should notice that it will always display three libraries, each of which you can click on to navigate to that Library's specific page. Neat!

And with that, the Library page is completed! We covered how to design a Collection Page by adding elements onto the page and binding them to Collection fields. We also saw how to create Collection lists to pull multiple image items. Lastly, we saw how we could create a dynamic and filtered Collection list to display other Collection items as quick links to those Collection item pages.

But, most importantly, however, we learned that Webflow CMS allows us to create a Collection Page once and then applies it automatically to all the available Collection items. This is a big timesaver, especially if we have large numbers of items in our Collections.

And now that we've created and seen how the Library pages get dynamically updated to show each of their respective details, we still have one big piece of the website to complete. Specifically, we need to return to the home page and make sure each of the libraries is clickable so that users can navigate to their now-completed Library pages.

# Putting the finishing touches to the home page

And now that our Library page is complete, we can return to the home page to complete it so that each Library is clickable. Essentially, we'll be repeating the same steps we took when we created the **Other Libraries** section on the Library page and made use of **Link Block** elements.

Let's do that now:

1.  Select any of the Collection item elements. Add a **Link Block** element, and in the **Link Settings** popup that appears, select the **Collection Page** tab and use the **Page** dropdown to select **Current Library**, as shown in *Figure 11.25*:

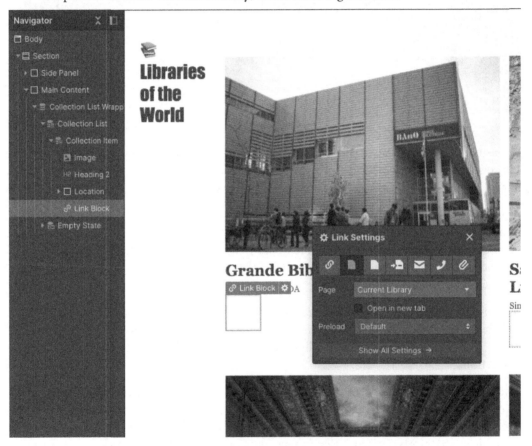

Figure 11.25 – Binding the Link Block element to the current Library item

2.  Move the **Image**, **Heading**, and **Location** elements into the **Link Block** element, as shown in *Figure 11.26*:

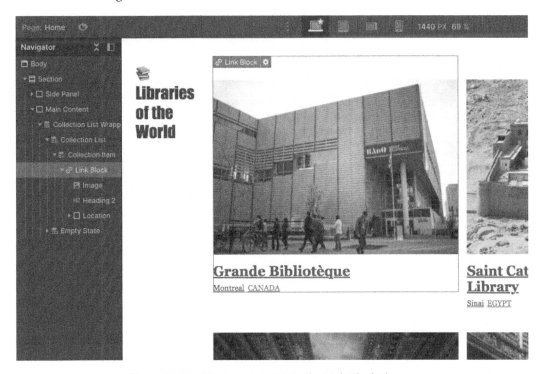

Figure 11.26 – Moving content into the Link Block element

3.  Select the **Link Block** element again and set its **Decoration** property to **None**.

4.  Next, select the **Heading** element and set its color to #333. Do the same for the **Location** element. You may have to set it to a different color before changing it back to #333, as it may still be inheriting the color from the default **Link Block** setting.

You can now preview the page, and try clicking on any of the libraries to view their detailed Library pages. The final home page should look like *Figure 11.27*:

Figure 11.27 – Updated home page

Congratulations! You've now created your first dynamic website using Webflow CMS and many of its powerful features. There's a lot more that can be done to refine and add to what you've already built. Perhaps you want to add animations and interactions. Maybe you want to create an input box that allows people to enter their own items. These are beyond the scope of this book, but, believe it or not, you have already learned all the required basics for creating customizable and dynamic CMS-based websites.

> **Tip**
>
> One of the most important features of CMS-based websites is the ability to filter data with the click of a button. Imagine, for instance, that we wanted users to be able to see only those libraries in North America. Or maybe they want to see libraries that were built after 1950. Similar to how on retail websites you can filter products by various characteristics, such as price, location, and type, so too can content in a CMS be filtered.
>
> However, in order to do this in Webflow, at the time of writing, it is best implemented by using third-party tools such as the MixitUp JavaScript library, Finsweet, and Jetboost.io. Going through these would be out of scope for this book, but you are encouraged to look these tools up and try them out for yourself.

# Summary

Over the last three chapters, we've been slowly building our CMS muscles. When we started this chapter, we had a CMS Collection created and had imported a number of Library content items into it. We had also created a first pass of the home page to display our Library items; however, we didn't have a way for a user to navigate into a detailed view of each library.

In this chapter, we were introduced to Collection Pages or **Collection Template Pages**. We learned that these are created automatically by Webflow for any Collection we create.

We then designed the Collection Template page for our Libraries Collection so that it could display detailed information about each library.

We saw how to create and bind various page elements to the Collection fields we had created in *Chapter 9, Getting Started with Webflow CMS*, and *Chapter 10, Creating Your First CMS Project*. Included in this was how to bind to more complex fields, such as **Multiple Images**. We achieved this by using Collection lists.

We also learned how to add filters to Collection lists in order to create a section of quick links to other Collection items. This way, we were able to show users links to other Libraries from within the Library pages themselves so that it's easier for them to navigate and browse through the website.

We also learned and previewed how designing and creating the Collection Template page once saves us a lot of time, since it is propagated throughout all the Collection items.

We finished off the chapter by putting some finishing touches to the home page and making each of the Library items clickable. We previewed the full website to demonstrate a fully working CMS-based project that is usable and useful.

In the next chapter, we'll take a look at how to use the CMS Editor to manage the data inside the CMS quickly, with or without collaborators.

See you there!

# 12
# Managing CMS Projects

If you've followed *Chapter 10, Creating Your First CMS Project*, and *Chapter 11, Creating Collection Pages*, you should have built a functional dynamic website that makes use of some of the most important features of Webflow CMS. So far, we've been focusing on the creation and web design side of things. In reality, a CMS and its content are likely meant to exist and evolve over time. As a data store, a CMS can be seen as a living, breathing repository of information that can be used and reused in a variety of ways.

If this repository becomes large enough (think hundreds and maybe even thousands of data items), then it's likely that you'll need some help to manage the CMS and its Collections.

As such, we'll devote this chapter to exploring some of the features and functions of Webflow CMS that will help make our lives a little easier when it comes to managing CMS projects. We'll cover the following topics:

- Collection Page settings, including optimizing them for various ways of consumption

- Editing Collections and individual fields and changing the structure of Collections

- Changing the states of items from published to draft and more

By the end of this chapter, you'll have built enough knowledge to manage your living, breathing Collection with confidence.

# Managing Collection Page settings

Recall that Collection Page templates are created automatically by Webflow for any Collections we create. In *Chapter 11*, *Creating Collection Pages*, we used this to build the Library page so that each library in our Libraries Collection gets a page that displays its unique data. In essence, we built the Collection Template Page once and Webflow dynamically generated it for the individual Collection items.

All Collection Page templates have a few settings that we can configure to manage the page a little. Let's take a look at a few of the most useful ones here.

## Making Collection Pages SEO-friendly

Eventually, we're likely going to want to publish this website on the web and make it accessible to visitors. We can edit the page's settings so that it dynamically generates page tiles and descriptions that appear on search engines and browsers appropriately. This will not only ensure that the pages appear more descriptive in search results but that they will also be optimized for searchability across various search engines.

Let's learn how to achieve this:

1.  Go to the **Pages** screen using the left menu.

2.  Under the **CMS Collection Pages** section, hover over the **Libraries Template** row to reveal the **Settings** icon, as shown in the following screenshot. Click it to access the **Settings** screen:

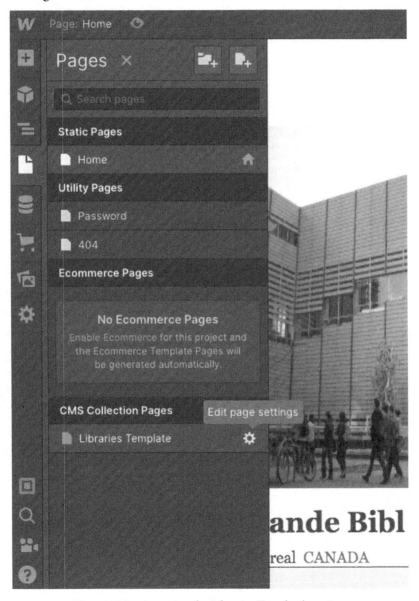

Figure 12.1 – Accessing the Libraries Template's settings

3.  Under the **SEO Settings** section, you can preview how the page would appear if it were to show up on a search results page on any given search engine, such as Google or Bing. In the **Title Tag** and **Meta Description** input fields, you can enter any descriptor text you want. However, since this is a dynamically generated page, it is highly recommended that you take advantage of Webflow's CMS binding features to display Collection fields here directly. You can do this by clicking on the purple **Add Field** text that appears next to the fields. For example, the following screenshot shows what this would look like if you added the **Name** field to the **Title Tag** input, along with some static text that said `Libraries of the World`. Likewise, we can add the **Description** field to the **Meta Description** input as well:

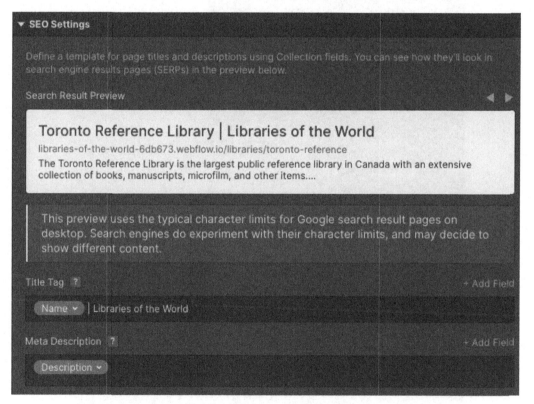

Figure 12.2 – Configuring and previewing SEO Settings

4.  Hit the **Save** button.

# Making Collection Pages ready for social media

It's not only on search engines that someone may use to find a website. Often, websites are shared by people on social media sites such as Twitter, Facebook, LinkedIn, and so on. Thankfully, we can set some properties to help ensure that the pages appear properly on such social media channels. Let's do this now:

1. On the same **Collection Page Settings** page, scroll down to the **Open Graph Settings** section. In the **Open Graph Title** input, click the **Add Field** option and add the **Name** field. Then, add to it the text | Libraries of the World. If you have already set up the **SEO Settings** section, you could also check the box that says **Same as SEO Title Tag**.

2. In the **Open Graph Description** input, add a field called **Description**. Alternatively, you can select the **Same as SEO Meta Description** checkbox to reuse the corresponding setting from the **SEO Settings** section.

3. Lastly, from the **Open Graph Image** dropdown, select the **Showcase Image** option.

4. Hit **Save**.

The preview should show what this page would look like if it were to be shared on social media, as shown in the following screenshot:

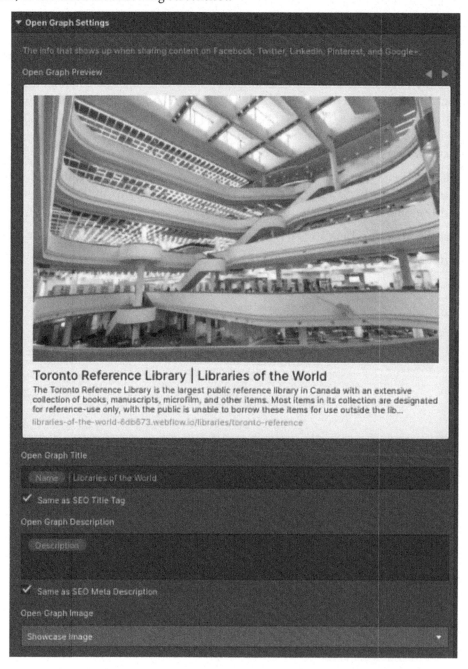

Figure 12.3 – Setting the social Open Graph Settings for a Collection Page

# Setting up an RSS feed for a Collection Page

If you expect your CMS project to be constantly updated with new content, you may want to consider making it an RSS feed that users can subscribe to. Many users use RSS readers to do this so that they don't miss any new updates.

Again, Webflow makes it easy to configure the Collection for such a need. The following steps will show you how:

1.  On the **Collection Page Setting** page, scroll to the **RSS Feed Settings** section. Enable it so that it is turned on.

2.  In the **Channel Title** input field, enter `Libraries of the World`.

3.  For **Channel Description**, enter a concise description of what this publication is about: `A constantly updated collection of some of the most interesting libraries around the world`.

4.  For the **item Title** field, select the **Same as SEO Title Tag** checkbox.

5.  For the **item Description** field, select the **Same as SEO Meta Description** checkbox.

6.  For the **item Image** field, select **Showcase Image**.

7.  Leave **item Publication Date** set to **Published On**.

8.  Change **Channel Refresh Time** to **1440 minutes** so that RSS readers pick up changes once every 24 hours. Then, hit **Save**.

All said and done, you should be able to preview what the publication will look like on an RSS feed, as shown in the following screenshot:

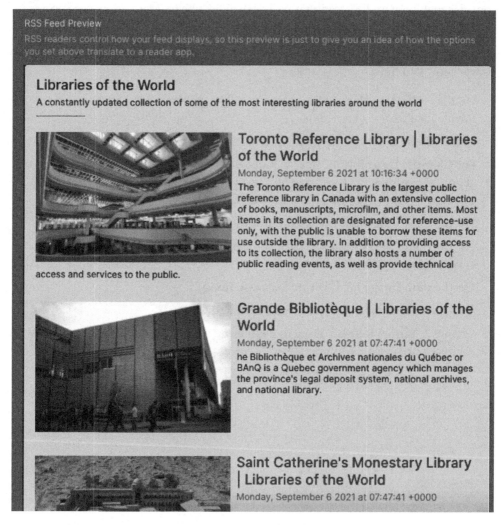

Figure 12.4 –RSS Feed Preview of the project

With those changes, our pages are now ready to be discovered and viewed on the web through search engines, social media, and RSS feeds.

The other page settings are not relevant to our project here and not as frequently used, but you're encouraged to explore them on your own for future needs.

Now that we've learned how to update the Page Settings, let's turn our attention to how to manage and update Collection fields.

# Updating Collections

When we created our Libraries Collection in *Chapter 10, Creating Your First CMS Project*, recall that we had created several fields that we then populated with data. This included fields such as the library's **Name**, **Address**, **Description**, **Showcase Image**, and more. Going forward, we may want to update either the data that is stored in the fields or the structures of the Collection fields themselves.

Let's begin by learning how to update the data in the fields.

## Updating data in Collection fields

Recall that we had populated data in the Collection by using a data import file in *Chapter 10, Creating Your First CMS Project*. We could reimport data using a similar technique, but what if you just wanted to update a single or a handful of field data? Using an import file may be too tedious. As you might expect, Webflow gives us a simple way to do just that.

You may have already noticed that when we imported the data, some of the fields were missing. If you haven't seen this yet, check out the page for the New York Public Library, as shown in the following screenshot:

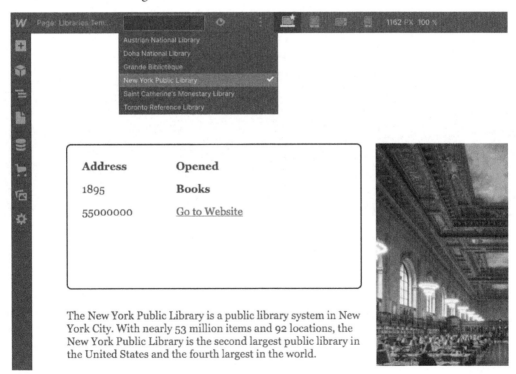

Figure 12.5 – Some pages are missing some data

As you can see, the layout of this page doesn't look quite right. That's because **Address Field** is empty, which is causing the rest of the elements on the page to shift around, causing a bit of a mess.

Let's go ahead and update this field with an address:

1. Navigate to the CMS page from the menu, click the Libraries Collection, and select the row for the **New York Public Library** Collection item, as shown in the following screenshot:

Figure 12.6 – Selecting the New York Public Library Collection item

2. Scroll down to **Address Field** and enter `476 5th Ave, New York, NY 10018, United States`, as shown in the following screenshot:

Figure 12.7 – Entering a value into the Address field

3. Hit the **Save** button.

Now, when you preview the page for the New York Public Library, the address should appear. Furthermore, that change also fixed the layout of the rest of the page, as shown in the following screenshot:

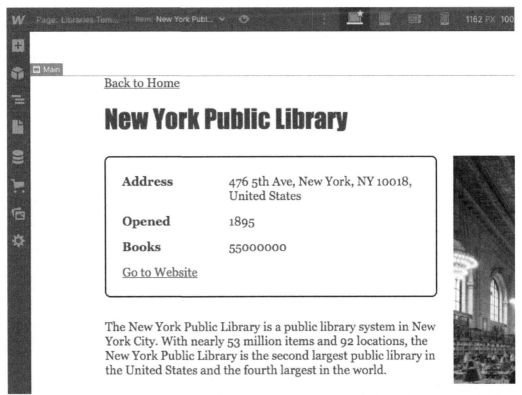

Figure 12.8 – Previewing the fixed version of the New York Public Library page

As an exercise, try going through the rest of the pages and finding some more missing fields. Then, go into the Libraries Collection settings and update them manually. It doesn't matter whether you update them with accurate data – just get the hang of how to update individual fields.

> **Tip**
>
> Here's a quick way you can quickly look at fields across all Collection items. Go to the **CMS** menu item, click on the Libraries Collection to view all the Library items, and then click on the pin icon to the far right of the page. This will reveal a popup that allows you to add as many fields as you want. Each will appear as a column that will allow you to quickly see what each data field looks like across the entire Collection. The empty ones will be blank, as shown in the following screenshot:

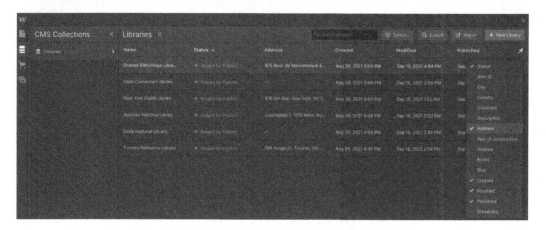

Figure 12.9 – Adding field columns to the Collection view

# Updating the structure of fields

Sometimes, it's not the data in a Collection that you might want to update but the structure of a field.

Take, for example, the **Number of Books** field in our Libraries Collection. Notice how, on the **New York Public Library** page, the number of books is shown as **55000000**. This would be a lot easier to read if it had a few commas to break out the number. When we first created this field, we set it to be of the Number type. As it happens, the Number type in Webflow does not support commas. We would need to use the plaintext type instead. Unfortunately, however, once you create a field of a specific type, Webflow doesn't allow you to change it. We'll need to create a new field of the Plain Text type from scratch.

In the next few steps, we'll look at how we can disconnect an element on the page from a field, after which we'll create a brand new field. We'll make this new field of the Plain Text type so that we can use commas. We'll end by reconnecting the new field to the web element on the Library Page. Let's begin:

1.  Click on the **CMS** menu item on the left to reveal the Libraries Collection. Hover over the **Libraries** row to reveal a cog icon for the **Settings** page, as shown in the following screenshot, and click it:

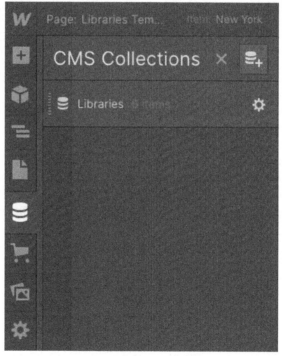

Figure 12.10 – Accessing the Libraries Collection Settings page

2. Scroll down and click on the **Number of Books** field to expand its view. We can choose to delete the field right now and it will remove any links it has on any page on the website. But let's achieve this another way. Click on the chain icon, as shown in the following screenshot:

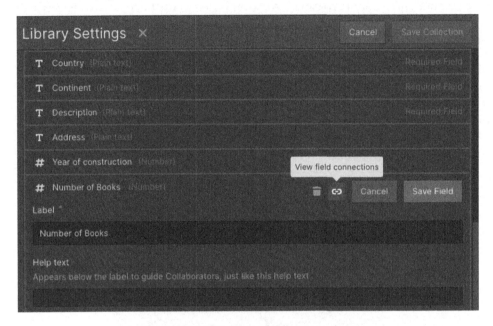

Figure 12.11 – Viewing a field's connections

3. The popup that appears shows all the pages and instances where this field has connections. In this case, for example, you can see that the **Number of Books** field is connected to a **Text** element on the Libraries Template page. Hover over the **Text** row from the dropdown and click the **Disconnect** icon, as shown in the following screenshot, to disconnect it from the page:

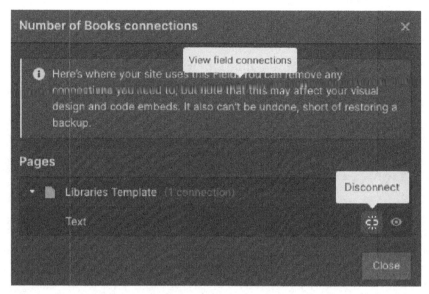

Figure 12.12 – Disconnecting a field from a web page

Now, if you view any of the Library Pages, you should notice that the number of books is no longer shown.

4.  Back on the **Library Settings** screen, click the blue **Add New Field** button. Select the **Plain Text** type, as shown in the following screenshot. This will allow us to enter numbers, text, and symbols. And yes, that includes commas:

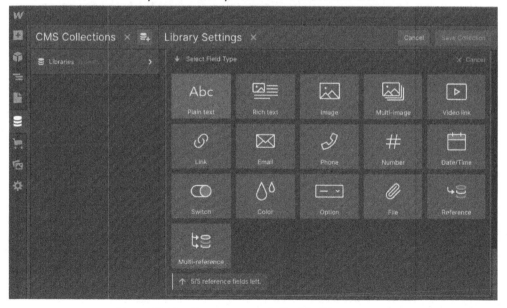

Figure 12.13 – Creating a new field of the Plain text type

5.  Give this new field a label of Books and hit the **Save Field** button.

6.  Hit the **Save Collection** button.

7.  Now, let's select the **New York Public Library** row. Scroll down to the **Books** field and type in 55,000,000, remembering to insert the commas, as shown in the following screenshot:

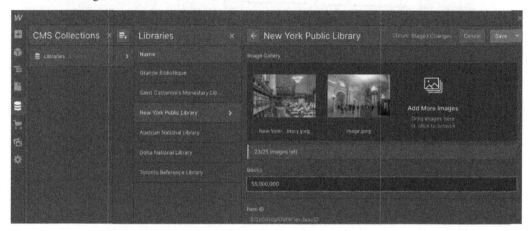

Figure 12.14 – Populating the Books field

8.  Hit **Save**.

9.  Go back to **Pages** and view the **New York Public Library** page. Select the unpopulated text block next to the **Books** label. Click on the **Settings** icon and select the **Get text from Libraries** checkbox. Use the dropdown to select our newly created **Books** field, as shown in the following screenshot:

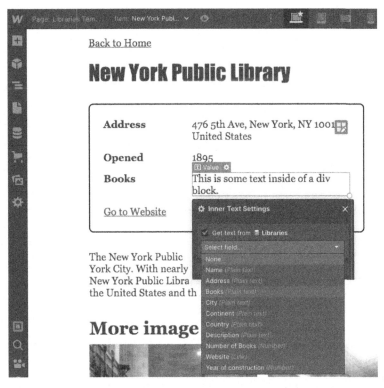

Figure 12.15 – Binding the text block to the new Books field

Now, it should update to show our updated data, complete with two commas, making for a much easier read.

Now that we've created and bound to the new **Books** field, go ahead and enter values into the other **Library items' Books** field so that all the pages are updated. Conveniently, you can copy the value from the original **Number of Books** field and paste it into the new **Books** field, adding a comma where necessary.

After updating all the Library Collection items, you can go ahead and delete the old **Number of Books** field since we longer need it, as shown in the following screenshot:

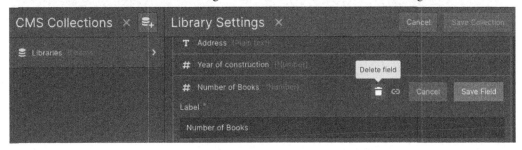

Figure 12.16 – Deleting the Number of Books field

When all is said and done, you can preview each of the Library pages to see the updates.

With that, we've learned how to update data in a field and how to update the fields themselves.

> **Note**
>
> So far, we've been managing the CMS Collections all by ourselves. But what if this project becomes quite large and we wanted some extra help?
>
> Webflow allows us to invite collaborators to a project. However, you must sign up for a CMS Site plan to add them. We will not accomplish this here as we're using the free plan, but if you ever decide to upgrade, then you can go to the **Project Settings** page from the main menu and go to the **Editor** tab. Scroll down to the **Collaborators** section to add others to your team.

## Managing Collection item states

Throughout the lifetime of a CMS project, the various Collection items we create may need to exist in various states. Imagine, for example, that we were to add more libraries to our Libraries Collection. We may not be ready to publish all of them from the get-go, so we will likely want to put some in a sort of draft state until we're ready.

First, you would've noticed by now that the libraries in our Libraries Collection are all in a **Staged for Publish** state, as shown in the following screenshot:

Figure 12.17 – Having items as Staged for Publish

In the **Staged for Publish** state, the item will be published and go live as soon as the website itself is published. We'll cover more about publishing a project in *Chapter 13, Publishing Projects to the Web*. For now, you can assume that any item in the **Staged for Publish** state is ready to go live.

But let's say we didn't want an item – say, **Doha National Library** – to go live when the website is published. In that case, the following steps can help us achieve this:

1. Go to the Libraries Collection on the **CMS** page to view all the available Collection items.

2. Hit the **Select** button at the top of the page. This will switch the page to **Select** mode. Select **Doha National Library**, as shown in the following screenshot:

Figure 12.18 – Selecting an item in Select mode

3. Next, hit the **Draft** button. You will be asked to confirm that you want to move it into the **Draft** state and essentially exclude it from being published. Go ahead and confirm this by clicking the **Draft item** button.

4. You'll notice that the **Doha National Library** item is put into the **Draft** state, as shown in the following screenshot:

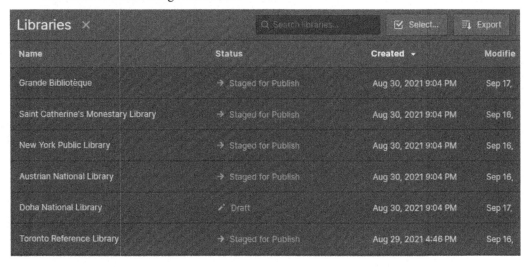

Figure 12.19 – Confirming that the Doha National Library is in the Draft state

5.  Now, whenever you're ready, you can hit the **Select** button again, select **Doha National Library**, and hit the **Stage for Publish** button to move it back into a publish-ready state.

An alternative way to achieve the same effect is by selecting any of the items and hitting the drop-down arrow next to the **Save** button at the top right of the page. This will reveal alternative states that you can save your item in, as shown in the following screenshot:

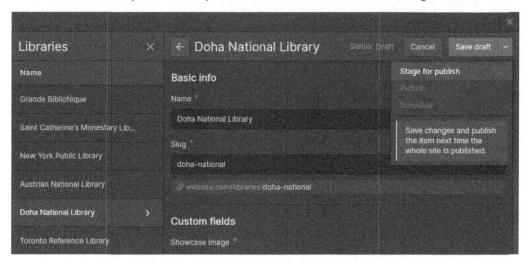

Figure 12.20 – An alternative way to save an item in a different state

> **Tip**
>
> In the preceding steps, we only selected a single item from the **Select Mode** screen for which we changed states. In reality, we could have selected multiple items and changed all their states at the same time. Apart from switching between the **Staged for Publish** and **Draft** states, you can also archive items that you know you no longer want to publish but still wish to keep in your records. Lastly, you can also outright delete items that you no longer want at all.
>
> Also, keep in mind that at the time of writing, Webflow allows up to 2,000 Collection items under the CMS Site plan. The **Published**, **Staged for Publish**, **Draft**, and **Archived** items all count toward this limit, while deleted items do not.

# Summary

In this chapter, we covered several smaller details and features that will help us manage our CMS projects. Specifically, we learned how to use the Collection Page settings to make a CMS-based website optimized for search engines, social media, and RSS feeds.

Next, we looked at how to update individual fields and put this into practice by updating the addresses of some of the libraries in our Libraries Collection.

We then saw how to create new fields from scratch. This involved us finding the connections that an existing field had, disconnecting those connections, adding a brand-new field, and reconnecting it to an element on the page. In the process, we saw how a field of the `Number` type is different from a field of the `Plain Text` type; the former only allows numbers to be used, whereas the latter allows letters and symbols to be used as well.

Finally, we took a brief look at some ways Collection items can be published. Specifically, we saw that an item can be moved to a **Draft** state and a **Published** state. We looked at some simple workflows to update and view their states.

And even though we've now covered two full Webflow projects, we have yet to launch any into the wild! In the next chapter, we'll do a deep dive into how to publish a website onto the web and how we can edit it in (almost) real time.

See you there!

# Section 4: Additional Topics

In this section we'll go over some essential topics that will round out the development process in Webflow.

We will cover the following chapters in this section:

- *Chapter 13, Publishing Projects to the Web*
- *Chapter 14, Using Webflow Editor to Update Websites*

# 13
# Publishing Projects on the Web

If you've been following this book, you should now be the proud creator of two Webflow projects. The first was a fully responsive single-page website, while the second was a CMS-based website that allowed dynamic content to be displayed.

One thing we have yet to do, however, is publish them on the web. We want others to enjoy the fruits of our labor, so, to that end, in this chapter, we'll explore the ins and outs of publishing a Webflow project on the web.

Specifically, we'll cover the following topics:

- Configuring the project settings to prepare to publish a website
- Using Webflow Audit to find and fix accessibility issues on a website
- The different workflows of publishing a website, both on a Webflow subdomain and a custom domain, and making it available for other Webflow developers to clone and build off
- Exporting the code of a Webflow project so that you can publish it yourself

For the sake of convenience, in this chapter, we'll focus on publishing the **Libraries of the World** project that we built in *Chapter 9, Getting Started with Webflow CMS*, through *Chapter 12, Managing CMS Projects*. This will allow us to demonstrate some extra capabilities that apply specifically to Webflow CMS. We'll then leave it to you, as an exercise, to try publishing the SecondPlate project on your own.

By the end of this chapter, you'll be on your way to publishing your Webflow projects and sharing your creativity and hard work with the world!

For now, let's start by looking more closely at some important project settings.

# Publishing a Webflow project

Before we publish a project on the web, we need to ensure some basic project settings have been configured properly.

## Configuring the project settings

As we mentioned previously, let's step through the settings of our Libraries of the World project:

1.  Open the **Libraries of the World** project in the **Designer** view, click the Webflow menu at the top left of the page, and click on **Project Settings**, as shown in the following screenshot:

Figure 13.1 – Accessing Project Settings

2.  In the **General** tab, type in any name for the project in the **Name** field. This is the internal name of the project and has no bearing on what people on the web will see.

3.  As shown in the following screenshot, in the **Subdomain** field, type in the name you'd like the web URL to have. Here, we've written it out as `librariesoftheworld.webflow.io`, so chances are, you won't be able to use that. This is the URL that a user will see for the website if it's published without a custom domain:

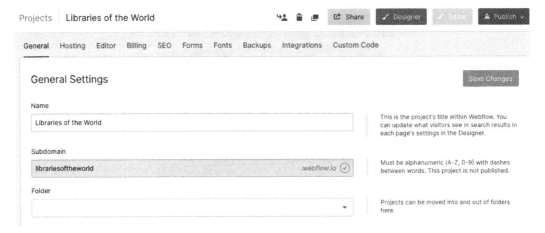

Figure 13.2 – Providing a subdomain

---

**Tip**

Using a Webflow subdomain is useful in many instances. It's free and quick, so it makes for a great way to test a website out or launch a side project before having to invest in a custom domain or hosting solution.

---

4.  Next, scroll down to the **Icons** section of the page and hit the **Upload** button for **Favicon**. You can use any images of size 32px x 32px that you want. We'll use the file called `lotw_favicon.png`, which should be located in the original **Project Files** area. Favicon is the tiny icon that appears in the browser's tab, so it's advised to keep it simple.

5.  Hit the **Save Changes** button.

With that, we've now got the basic settings ready for us to publish our project! We'll do that next.

## Publishing the project

With the project settings saved, click the **Designer** button to go back to our Home Page and click on the **Publish** button at the top of the page. This will reveal two ways in which we can publish a project, as shown in the following screenshot; we can publish it to the subdomain we created earlier, or we can use a custom domain:

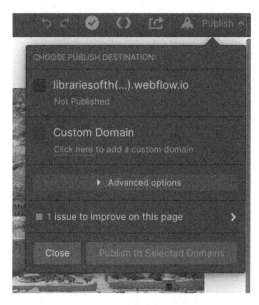

Figure 13.3 – Publishing a project

However, before we go ahead and publish this, note that Webflow is telling us that it has identified one area where we can improve the page. Click on it and you will be greeted by a panel called **Audit** that slides in from the left of the page, as shown in the following screenshot:

Figure 13.4 – Revealing the Audit accessibility panel

At the time of writing, this is one of the latest offerings that Webflow has rolled out. With Audit, Webflow is continuing its efforts to make finding and fixing accessibility issues easier than ever. Let's take a closer look at Webflow Audit now and see how we can use it to identify and address accessibility issues before we publish the site to the web.

With the **Audit** panel open, notice that it has automatically evaluated several areas with accessibility requirements and laid those out into areas that require attention and those that have passed. Our links, for example, are all adequately descriptive, so they pass the accessibility requirement. Likewise, the headers on the page are structured sequentially, so they are also in line with the accessibility requirements.

However, where the accessibility on the page has been compromised is in the note that reads **Missing alt text**. Click on this to expand it. Webflow will provide a brief explanation that states the requirement for all the images to have alt text. Screen readers use alt text descriptions to help viewers who are visually impaired understand what is on a page. Thus, it serves us and our viewers well to ensure that all the images have appropriate alt text descriptions in place.

In this case, however, the image in question is being pulled from the CMS. If you click further into the **Image** field, it will reveal a popup that describes how the issue can be fixed: by adding a new **alt text** field to our Collection that corresponds to the image, as shown in the following screenshot:

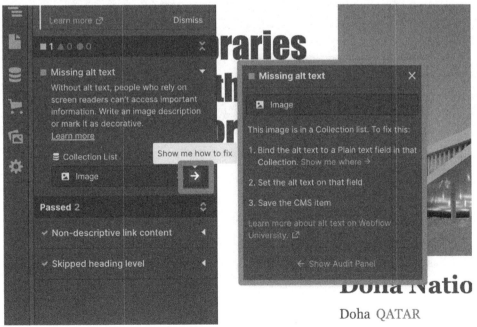

Figure 13.5 – Fixing missing alt text for an image that is being pulled from a Collection

Let's go ahead and add this alt text field now:

1.  Navigate to the CMS menu, click on the **Library Collection Settings** page, and click the **Add New Field** button, as shown in the following screenshot:

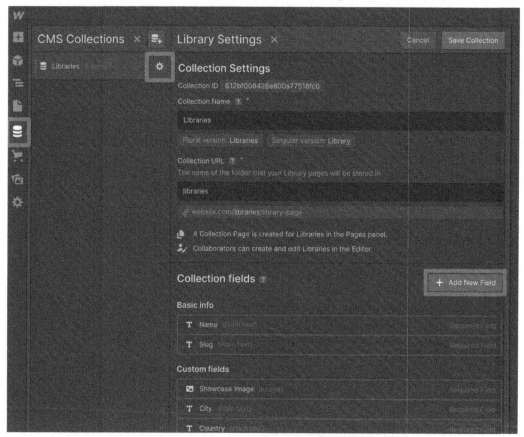

Figure 13.6 – Adding a new field to the Libraries Collection

2.  Choose a **Plain Text** field type.

3.  Call the new field `Showcase image alt text`.

4.  You can now choose to drag and drop the new field right underneath the **Showcase Image** field so that they are conveniently close to each other for easier viewing.

5.  Click the **Save Collection** button.

6.  Now, proceed to each library and add an appropriate alt text description of the showcase image to each. For instance, for **Doha Public Library**, your alt text field could read **Front of the Doha Public Library**.

7.  Once you've entered the alt text descriptions to all the Library items, navigate back to the Home Page. Select any of the images on the page and access the **Element Settings** panel on the right. Check the **Get Alt Text from Libraries** checkbox and select the **Showcase image alt text** field from the dropdown, as shown in the following screenshot:

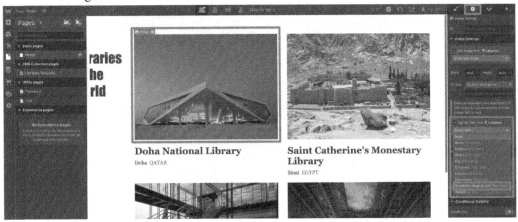

Figure 13.7 – Binding to the Showcase image alt text field

Now, when you click on the **Publish** button again, you'll notice that there are no longer any warning messages letting us know of any accessibility issues. Fantastic!

8.  With the **webflow.io** domain selected, go ahead and click the **Publish to Selected Domains** button. After a short moment, you should see a success message, similar to the one shown in the following screenshot, and the project should officially be published on the web! You can then click on the URL or type it into the browser to visit the site:

Figure 13.8 – Publishing a project successfully to a Webflow subdomain on the web

Now, any time you make a change to the website, you can hit the **Publish** button directly from the **Designer** window to quickly publish the changes live, making it easy to test and view changes.

> **Tip**
> Don't want your website or project to be viewable on the web anymore? No problem! Just click the **Unpublish** button, which appears when you open the **Publish** popup. If you don't see the **Unpublish** button, you must remove it from the **Showcase** area through **Project Settings** first.

Also, note that in *Chapter 12, Managing CMS Projects*, we spent some time making the **Libraries of the World** project's SEO and Open Graph ready so that search engines and social networks can read and process them properly. Going forward, every time you're looking to publish a site, it is good practice to ensure that all of your pages are also optimized for SEO and Open Graph.

> **Important**
>
> Publishing to a custom domain may be something you are very keen on doing, and for good reason; it will personalize it to the branding of your choice. As it turns out, the process is a little more involved than what we can cover here because a good chunk of it relies largely on how your domain registrar is set up. As such, rather than spending a lot of time here writing technical instructions that may not be relevant to a lot of you, you're encouraged to read Webflow's documentation on it at `https://university.webflow.com/lesson/connect-a-custom-domain`.

## Exporting project code

Sometimes, you may not want to host a project directly on Webflow. Instead, what you could do is export the code and host it on your website. Thankfully, Webflow allows you to do this, albeit with some caveats:

- You need to be on a paid **Site Plan** to be able to export code.

- Exported code from a CMS project will not include any of the Collection data. The CMS project needs to be hosted on Webflow to be able to take advantage of Webflow CMS' features and capabilities. As such, if you export the code of a CMS project and host it on your website, all the references to Collection items such as those in a Collection list will, unfortunately, appear blank.

If these caveats don't matter to you and you've gone ahead and signed up for a **Site Plan**, you can follow these steps to export your website's code:

1. Open the **Libraries of the World** project in the **Designer** view.

2. Click the **Export code** button at the top of the page, as shown in the following screenshot:

Figure 13.9 – Exporting your project's code

3. A popup should appear that shows your website's code across HTML, CSS, and any JavaScript. Click on the **Prepare ZIP** button.

4.  After a moment, you should have a ZIP file packaged up and downloaded onto your computer for you to use as you please to host on your site.

> **Important**
>
> It's worth mentioning that all the code that you export can be edited further if you're inclined to do so. Keep in mind, however, that because Webflow creates some custom code for its components, you may risk breaking some of its functionality.

There's no limit to how many times you can export code, but note that at the time of writing, there is no way for you to export only a single page or part of a page. If you want to export code, you have to export the whole site. Depending on how big the project is, this could take a while, especially if you have a lot of image and video assets.

Either way, having the flexibility to export and use the code any way you like is certainly great added value.

Now that we've covered publishing a project, let's look at one of Webflow's coolest features: its ability to showcase projects.

# Showcasing a project

One of the most helpful features of Webflow is its ability to showcase and clone projects. Essentially, this allows anyone in the Webflow community to view others' projects and reuse them or build upon them for their projects. Think of it as community-based remixing. Not only is this a great way to display your skills, but it also turns out that this is a great way to learn how others have built their websites, components, and interactions, making it a great resource for further inspiration.

To that end, now that we've published our project, let's go ahead and showcase it as well so that others can benefit from it (and, OK, so that you can show it off a little):

1.  Go back to the **Project Settings** page of the **Library of the Worlds** project.

2.  In the **General** tab, scroll down to the **Showcase** section. Turn the toggle **ON**.

3.  You'll be taken to a page where you can enter some more details about the project. This is what the public will see in the Webflow community. As such, make sure the title is descriptive and that the **Description** field explains the project a little more for the benefit of others. Finally, add some tags that will help others find the project. The following screenshot shows what this could look like:

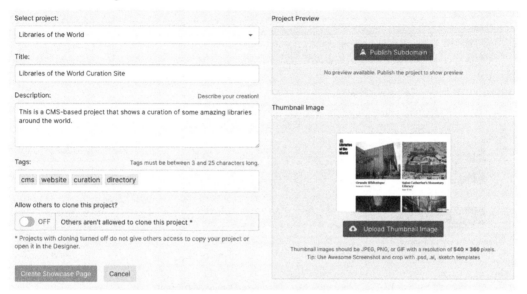

Figure 13.10 – The project's Showcase details

4.  Note that this is where you can choose to turn on the **Clone Project** toggle. Doing so will allow members of the Webflow community to copy your project to their accounts so that they can view how the site was created. It also gives them permission to create a copy of the site and remix it to their heart's content. We'll leave it to you to decide whether you want it to be cloneable or not.

5.  The previews should show you a glimpse of what the project will look like to others in the community. Go ahead and click on the **Create Showcase** page.

Now, when you go to your profile page, you can view all the projects you are showcasing, as shown in the following screenshot:

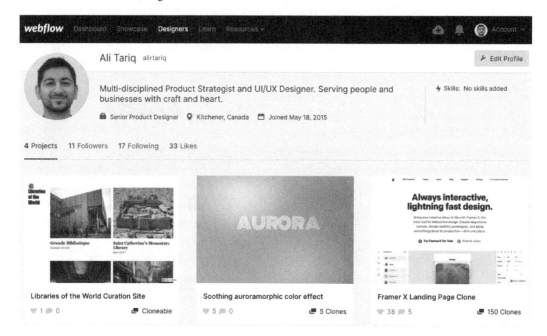

Figure 13.11 – Viewing your showcased projects on your profile page

> **Tip**
>
> If you haven't noticed by now, both projects we created in this book are also cloneable. If you haven't cloned any of them to take a closer look at their structure yet, you're encouraged to do so. And regardless, you're strongly encouraged to go to the Webflow **Showcase** page and explore all the great projects the community has been sharing, many of which are graciously cloneable. Looking under the hood at how others have built their websites is a fantastic way to learn.

Congratulations – you've officially published your first Webflow project into the wild! Now is a good time to share your website with your family, friends, and network. You deserve the spotlight!

# Summary

In this chapter, we closed the loop in our Webflow development process by learning how to publish our websites and projects to the web.

Specifically, we learned how to configure some key settings fields for the page before publishing it. We also quickly saw how to use Webflow Audit to identify and address accessibility issues on the page.

We then went ahead and published our **Libraries of the World** project to a Webflow subdomain quickly and for free. We also learned how to add a project to the Webflow Showcase page and how to allow others to clone the project for them to build off.

Finally, we quickly looked at how to export the code of a Webflow project. This could come in handy if you want to host a website on your hosting service.

Often, however, our work isn't complete at the initial launch. Depending on the nature of the website, we may want to continue editing it going forward. In the next and final chapter, we'll explore how to do just that using the Webflow Editor, a special tool that makes it easy to update websites without having to know how to use Webflow Designer.

That's right – we'll be able to get non-Webflow developers to update the website too. See you there!

# 14
# Using Webflow Editor to Update Websites

Now that we've published our project on the web, we may want to edit it to keep it updated going forward. While it's possible to do this via the Designer and republish any changes, an easier way to accomplish this is by using **Webflow Editor**. In this chapter, we'll take a closer look at Webflow Editor, a seamless way to update published content either by ourselves or in collaboration with others.

In this chapter, we'll cover the following topic:

- Why using Webflow Editor can be very helpful?
- Using Webflow Editor to configure and update website settings for SEO and Open Graph
- Using Webflow Editor for static and dynamic content on a live Webflow website

Since we published our **Libraries of the World** project in *Chapter 13, Publishing Projects to the Web*, we'll continue to use that project to demonstrate how we can use Webflow Editor to update it.

Let's take a closer look.

# Using Webflow Editor to update a website

While publishing a project to the web is a good cause for celebration, for many web projects, it doesn't end here. Keeping the website updated can be critical to its success going forward.

This is especially true if you intend on handing over the website to a client so that they can manage their content or if you plan on having collaborators for your project. In either of these cases, it may be asking too much of others to expect them to be well-versed in using Webflow Designer to keep their content updated.

Luckily, this is where Webflow Editor steps in. In essence, Webflow Editor is a tool that has the flexibility for content creation and editing but doesn't have the complexity of using the Designer.

---

**Important**

Bear in mind that Webflow Editor will help you update content on the website, including text and images, but not the structure or layout of the page itself. For the latter, the Designer is still the best way to make those changes.

---

While Webflow Editor's features are too extensive for us to cover here, we'll go over some important basics that should help you get start using it and give you a good appreciation for it.

Let's start by learned how to access the Editor and configuring page settings.

## Using the Editor to configure page settings

Execute the following steps to configure the page settings:

1. Open the **Libraries of the World** project in the **Designer** view.
2. Click on the Webflow menu at the top left of the screen and select **Editor**, as shown in the following screenshot:

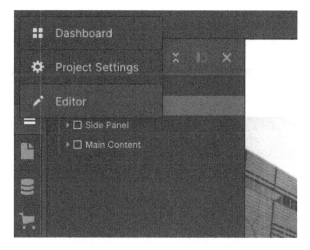

Figure 14.1 – Accessing the Editor

> **Tip**
>
> An easy way for clients or collaborators to access the Editor is to add `/?edit`
> to the end of the website's URL. So, for example, for the **Libraries of the**
> **World** project, the Editor can be accessed by typing the following URL into the
> browser: `https://librariesoftheworld.webflow.io/?edit`.
> Anyone who needs to access the Editor frequently can be advised to bookmark
> this URL.

3. Once the Editor has been accessed, it will look like you're viewing the live site, but
   with one key difference: the Editor's menu will be displayed along the bottom of the
   page, as shown in the following screenshot:

Figure 14.2 – The Editor's menu along the bottom of the page

4.  Click on the **Pages** menu item. You'll be presented with a convenient list of all the pages that make up the website you're editing, as shown in the following screenshot:

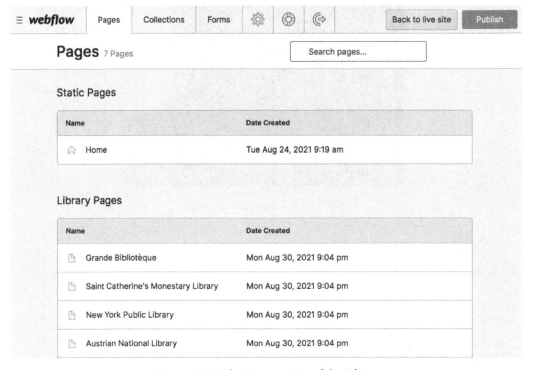

Figure 14.3 – The Pages section of the Editor

5.  Here, you can either click on the pages to navigate to them or, as you hover over each row, you can access the page's settings by clicking the **Settings** button. In this case, hover over the **Home page** row and click its **Settings** button.

6.  You should now see a full list of page settings, including settings for SEO and Open Graph, among others, as shown in the following screenshot:

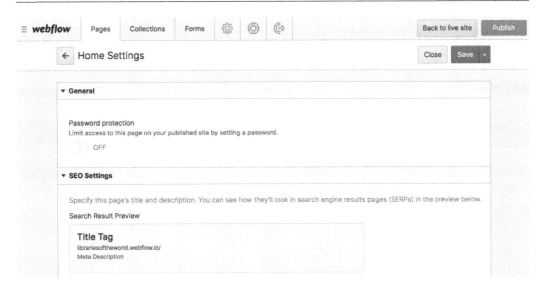

Figure 14.4 – Accessing the page's settings through the Editor

This should look familiar; we set up similar page settings in *Chapter 12, Managing CMS Projects,* for the Libraries Template page. The only difference is that this time, we're doing it in the Editor, whereas before we used the Designer.

For now, to speed up the configuration process, you can use the following settings:

**Title Tag**: `Libraries of the World`

**Meta Description**: `Discover awesome libraries around the world`

**Open Graph Title**: *Same as SEO Title Tag*

**Open Graph Description**: *Same as SEO Meta Description*

7.  Hit **Save**. You should now see some text, letting you know that you have made changes that are yet to be published, as shown in the following screenshot. Go ahead and hit the **Publish** button to push the changes onto the live site:

Figure 14.5 – Publishing saved changes

> **Tip**
>
> As a quick exercise, go ahead and check the settings of one of the library pages. So long as you have followed the instructions in *Chapter 12, Managing CMS Projects,* when we had initially configured the settings for the Libraries Template page, you should see them configured properly here too.

Editing Collection items works similarly. Go ahead and click the **Collections** menu item next. Then, click on the **Libraries** Collection to view all the libraries we've listed. You can click any of the pages to update the records by changing any of the field values or uploading any new images you like.

However, unlike the Designer, you cannot add any new fields or delete existing ones. Remember, with the Editor, you can only edit the content on the site, not change the structure of it.

While using the Editor to update content this way is simple and efficient for clients and collaborators, we may want to know what the content looks like contextually on the website.

Luckily, as one of Webflow's coolest features, the Editor allows us to change content within the context of the actual page. Let's see how.

## Editing a live page

Let's say we wanted to update some of the content on the library pages. Let's look at a few ways we can do this:

1.  With the **Webflow Editor** menu available, select the **Pages** menu item. From the list of pages that appears, select, say, the **Grand Biblioteque** page. You should see the live version of the corresponding library page, as shown in the following screenshot:

Back to Home Page

### Grande Bibliotèque

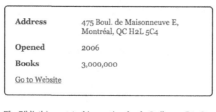

The Bibliothèque et Archives nationales du Québec or BAnQ is a Quebec government agency which manages the province's legal deposit system, national archives, and national library.

### More images

Figure 14.6 – Viewing a page from the Editor

The key thing to keep in mind is that some of the content on this page, such as the name of the library and its details, are being pulled from the CMS (that is, it is dynamic) and some were entered directly onto the page through the Designer (that is, it is static).

2. Hover over the **More images** heading, which is a static piece of content. You'll notice that Webflow Editor now allows you to select the text and change it inline, directly on the page. You can edit the text by either clicking directly on the text itself or by clicking on the pencil icon that appears. Change it to say **More images from this library**, as shown in the following screenshot:

Figure 14.7 – Changing static text content

3. You can also reveal further formatting features by selecting some text. Try, for example, highlighting the entire text heading and then changing it to italics, as shown in the following screenshot:

Figure 14.8 – Adding formatting to text

Because this change was made to a page that is using the Collection Template page, you should notice that this change gets propagated across all the other libraries too. Neat!

4.    Now, let's say we wanted to update a dynamic piece of content. On the **Grand Biblioteque** page still, for example, let's say we wanted to update the **Description** field a little. As you hover over it, you'll notice that Webflow is reminding us that this content is being pulled from the CMS, as shown in the following screenshot. Any changes that are made here will affect any other page that is referencing the same data:

Figure 14.9 – Editing dynamic content

Go ahead and add a new sentence to the end of this description paragraph. For example, you could type It is located in the heart of Montreal.

5.    Next, let's update the page's main showcase image. You can do this either by clicking directly on the image or by clicking on the image icon that appears when you hover over it. This will open a file selector, where you can choose any other image to use. Feel free to do so now.

6.    Assuming you've made at least one change, you should see a count of the changes that are ready to be published, as shown in the following screenshot. Go ahead and hit **Publish**:

Figure 14.10 – Publishing the changes

Now, before we check the live site, you may be wondering whether the changes we made to the dynamic content on the page updated the Library Item in the Libraries Collection. And that would be a good question!

We can easily verify this.

From the **Editor** menu, click on the **Collection** menu item, select **Libraries Collection** and then click **Grand Biblioteque**. If you have changed **Showcase Image**, you should see it updated here. Furthermore, you should see the changes you had made in the **Description** field as well.

As such, we can safely conclude that any changes you make to the content on a page directly with the Editor update the CMS as well. This is great news for clients and collaborators who want an easy way to update content without having to learn the complexities of the Designer.

With that, we've covered the essentials of Webflow Editor and how it can speed up and simplify the workflows that keep our website updated.

# Summary

In this chapter, we took an introductory dive into the key areas of Webflow Editor, a powerful tool that allows project creators and collaborators to quickly and efficiently manage content on a website. We took the opportunity to update some page settings and even make changes inline on the website.

Throughout this book, we've learned about various practical principles, workflows, and features of Webflow that have helped us build responsive, interactive, and dynamic websites, all without code. This journey, admittedly, was and will likely continue to be multi-layered, at times complex, and perhaps even frustrating.

But ultimately, I hope this journey has been exciting, rewarding, and empowering.

Whether you actively partake in the No-Code movement or not, or if you're at all invested in web development, Webflow can stand to play a crucial role in positioning you for future success.

Even if that's too lofty of a goal, rest assured that you now have the requisite skills to make your creative aspirations come to life.

I can't wait to see what you build.

Packt.com

Subscribe to our online digital library for full access to over 7,000 books and videos, as well as industry leading tools to help you plan your personal development and advance your career. For more information, please visit our website.

## Why subscribe?

- Spend less time learning and more time coding with practical eBooks and Videos from over 4,000 industry professionals

- Improve your learning with Skill Plans built especially for you

- Get a free eBook or video every month

- Fully searchable for easy access to vital information

- Copy and paste, print, and bookmark content

Did you know that Packt offers eBook versions of every book published, with PDF and ePub files available? You can upgrade to the eBook version at packt.com and as a print book customer, you are entitled to a discount on the eBook copy. Get in touch with us at customercare@packtpub.com for more details.

At www.packt.com, you can also read a collection of free technical articles, sign up for a range of free newsletters, and receive exclusive discounts and offers on Packt books and eBooks.

# Other Books You May Enjoy

If you enjoyed this book, you may be interested in these other books by Packt:

**WordPress 5 Cookbook**

Rakhitha Nimesh Ratnayake

ISBN: 978-1-83898-650-6

- Install and customize WordPress themes and plugins for building websites
- Develop modern web designs without the need to write any code
- Explore the new Gutenberg content editor introduced in WordPress 5 (Bebo)
- Use the existing WordPress plugins to add custom features and monetize your website
- Improve user interaction and accessibility for your website with simple tricks
- Discover powerful techniques for maintaining and securing your websites
- Extend built-in WordPress features for advanced website management

**WordPress Development Quick Start Guide**

Rakhitha Nimesh Ratnayake

ISBN: 978-1-78934-287-1

- Explore the role of themes, plugins, and built-in features in development
- Adapt to built-in modules and built-in database structures
- Write code for WordPress's hook-based architecture
- Build, customize, and integrate WordPress plugins
- Extend themes with custom design templates
- Capture and process data with built-in features and custom forms
- Improve usability with AJAX and third-party components
- Manage non-functional aspects, such as security, performance, and migration

# Packt is searching for authors like you

If you're interested in becoming an author for Packt, please visit `authors.packtpub.com` and apply today. We have worked with thousands of developers and tech professionals, just like you, to help them share their insight with the global tech community. You can make a general application, apply for a specific hot topic that we are recruiting an author for, or submit your own idea.

# Share Your Thoughts

Now you've finished *Webflow by Example*, we'd love to hear your thoughts! Scan the QR code below to go straight to the Amazon review page for this book and share your feedback or leave a review on the site that you purchased it from.

https://www.amazon.in/review/create-review/
error?asin=%3C1801075395%3E

Your review is important to us and the tech community and will help us make sure we're delivering excellent quality content.

# Index

Made in the USA
Middletown, DE
31 January 2022

59775084R00199